Cultural Change from a Business Anthropology Perspective

Cultural Change from a Business Anthropology Perspective

Maryann McCabe and Elizabeth K. Briody

LEXINGTON BOOKS
Lanham • Boulder • New York • London

Published by Lexington Books
An imprint of The Rowman & Littlefield Publishing Group, Inc.
4501 Forbes Boulevard, Suite 200, Lanham, Maryland 20706
www.rowman.com

Unit A, Whitacre Mews, 26-34 Stannary Street, London SE11 4AB

British Library Cataloguing in Publication Information Available

Library of Congress Cataloging-in-Publication Data Available

ISBN 978-1-4985-4451-1 (cloth : alk. paper)
ISBN 978-1-4985-4452-8 (electronic)

♾ ™ The paper used in this publication meets the minimum requirements of American National Standard for Information Sciences—Permanence of Paper for Printed Library Materials, ANSI/NISO Z39.48-1992.

Printed in the United States of America

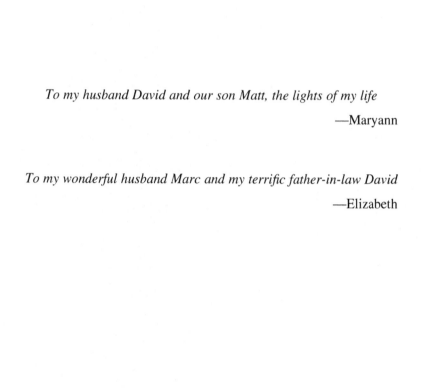

To my husband David and our son Matt, the lights of my life

—Maryann

To my wonderful husband Marc and my terrific father-in-law David

—Elizabeth

Contents

Introduction

Cultural Change in Global Consumer Societies

Maryann McCabe

Perhaps Alvin Toffler (1970) was prescient when he described a world in which everything is accelerating.[1] Since his depiction of such a world over 40 years ago in the influential book *Future Shock*, cultural change seems to occur even more rapidly with every passing day. How quickly, for example, home entertainment has transformed from major networks to cable channels to streaming content, and in the process reoriented our television-watching practices. No longer constrained by industry dictates of when and where content is available, we can watch television shows and movies on-demand, binge watch series such as *House of Cards* and *Foyle's War* and stream them all on any number of mobile devices in almost every country in the world. Entertainment as a social activity has become decidedly individual; a common ground has become decidedly fragmented. Toffler's depiction of a world full of acceleration raises, anew, questions about what catalyzes cultural change and how humans experience it.

This book addresses cultural change through the lens of business anthropology. Business anthropologists work at the interfaces of production and consumption where they conduct ethnographic research on organizational activities, products and services, and customers and clients. Such ethnographic research provides opportunity to observe currents of people, things and ideas and to study cultural change from the standpoint of interactivity between consumers and companies, corporate and nonprofit, as they respond to consumer practices and concerns. Research in the business world is becoming increasingly human-centered and dependent on understanding the consumer point of view. When business anthropologists engage in ethnographic research, they are well positioned to explore disruptive and shifting movements of products and services and to examine arcs of power in their transmission and narratives about their use in global consumer societies.

The contributing authors to this book present case studies in markets around the globe including the United States, India, China, Cambodia and Nigeria, which shed light on emerging trends and changes in the practices of people grappling with the worlds they inhabit.

The concept of cultural change, a perennial issue in anthropology, has received little attention in recent decades (Ervin 2015). Yet, with change in the world continuing at speed, our conceptual tools need to capture the flows and directions of the contemporary social order. Previous anthropological ideas about cultural change such as diffusion, acculturation and evolution (including Toffler's evolutionary notions) provide insightful views on mechanisms that instigate cultural change. However, these grand theories are metanarratives of impersonal forces. One of our goals is to query how things come together with human intention and effort. The book takes a new approach to theorizing cultural change by using assemblage theory, which focuses on the concept of agency, a process of human perception and action. Assemblage theory posits a relationship among people, objects, practices, discourses and institutions as they align, disperse and coalesce in different arrangements (Arnould and Thompson 2015, Collier and Ong 2005, Latour 2005). This theoretical perspective is oriented to identifying alignments and trajectories of cultural change.

The introductory chapter discusses assemblage theory and how it applies to our perspective on cultural change. It also describes the interfaces in which business anthropologists work, provides a definition of cultural change and highlights the case studies in terms of processes of cultural change and emerging patterns in specific areas of social life. These areas include mobile devices and smart technology, agriculture, water and beverage consumption, education, business management and distribution systems, welfare and poverty reduction, architectural design and space exploration. The concluding chapter analyzes similarities and differences across the case studies and draws lessons about cultural change using assemblage theory. Goals for the book are (1) to theorize cultural changes we are witnessing as business anthropologists, (2) to advance agency as a catalyst of change complementing previous theoretical perspectives that focus on other factors such as technology and the environment, and (3) to apply and further develop assemblage theory to explain cultural change.

THEORETICAL APPROACHES TO CULTURAL CHANGE

Anthropological Ideas

There are many theories of causation in anthropological thought on cultural change. In a recent review of anthropological explanations of cultural transformation, Ervin (2015) observes that the various theories are differentiated by whether emphasis is placed on external or internal factors in shaping change. Key to the differentiation is agency. Ervin writes,

> "To what extent do the theories favor *determinants of change*, especially external ones, such as innovated or introduced technologies, access or restrictions to sources of energy, environmental changes, opportunities for access to new resources or exchanges, and so forth?" (2015, 6)

Or, he continues,

> to what extent are the theories paying attention to the capacities of individuals and networks of people to shape their circumstances through innovation and invention, by influencing others in transaction, making use of innovated technologies, beliefs, or novel institutional practice to bring about some degree of *intentional change*? Is there *exercise of agency* as opposed to determination or restriction? (2015, 6–7)

Falling into the first camp are the grand theories of cultural change such as diffusion, acculturation and political ecology, which are metanarratives about mechanisms of change. Assemblage theory belongs to the second camp. Its concern with agency of persons, objects or ideas (including "intention") is consonant with the competitive world of business, which is oriented to innovation and change that is planned and purposeful. The approach to cultural change in this book accentuates agency and the human intention and effort of people trying to achieve personal, social and organizational goals.

Assemblage Theory

Assemblage theory is a product of theoretical developments in the post-structural era when social science began to accommodate human choice, intention and action in explaining behavior. Although society is organized by structural elements such as age, gender, social class, ethnicity and citizenship and the hierarchical relationships that they may entail, agency also plays a role in human behavior. Assemblage theory builds on the agency-related frameworks of actor-network theory (Latour 2005), practice theory (Bourdieu 1977) and power and governance studies (Foucault 1980). The notion of assemblage derives from the philosophical work of Deleuze and Guattari (1987) and DeLanda (2006). It has been utilized as a theoretical tool in recent studies of consumption (Malefyt and McCabe 2016, Parmentier and Fischer 2015, Epp, Schau and Price 2014, Canniford and Shankar 2013).

The basic premise of assemblage theory is that configurations of social forms that we may recognize as cultural patterns are not stable and fixed but fluid and temporary. The component parts of assemblages, including people, things, practices, discourses, and the organizations and institutions to which people belong or which have an impact on them, are heterogeneous. Assemblages of heterogeneous parts are prone to eventual disruption so that when displacement occurs, we can observe new assemblages coming together in present time and space. As DeLanda (2006) writes, assemblages are agentic systems of diverse components that interact with one another in ways that can either stabilize or destabilize an assemblage's identity (2006, 12). For example, a study of fine chocolate indicates a trajectory of change toward fair trade products due to a shift in consumer perception of chocolate in terms not only of the sensory enjoyment of consumption but also the social justice of production (McCabe 2015). An assemblage including chocolate products, package aesthetics, food discourses preoccupied with pedigree, consumer concern with production, the media which created awareness of alleged child labor in cocoa bean production, the US government which negotiated a Cocoa Protocol with major chocolate manufacturers to end such labor, industry which began to market ethically sourced chocolate, and the Fairtrade Labor Organization International which certifies fair trade chocolate provoked change in consumer practices. Consumer interest in fair trade chocolate has been rising at a greater rate than the rest of the chocolate market. It is the confluence of actors and actions in this assemblage that accounts for cultural change.

Assemblage theory addresses phenomena that articulate cultural shifts associated with globalization (Collier and Ong 2005). As Collier and Ong indicate, it is well suited to understanding how global forms interact with other elements occupying a common field of "contingent, uneasy, unstable interrelationships," (2005, 12) where the objective is to "frame 'the present' in terms of specific trajectories of change" (2005, 15). While looking at the ethnographic present involves taking history into consideration, the purpose of assemblage theory is to identify trends emerging in the present and to explain how fluid and heterogeneous components of an assemblage combine and hold together. This book uses assemblage theory to gain insight into current trajectories of cultural change in society gleaned through ethnographic research in production and consumption.

Assemblage theory draws upon, yet goes beyond globalization studies, by delving into the heterogeneity of cultural groups and their practices with the ongoing movement of people, objects, ideas and capital in the world. Underlying globalization studies is an assumption of West versus non-West that is evident in such concepts as glocalization, hybridity and creolization (Erickson and Murphy 2013). The dichotomy of local and global assumes a bounded notion of culture in which culture is conceived as a bounded system of collectively shared meanings, values, norms, ideals and conventions (Arnould and Thompson 2015). However, the notion of assemblage or heterogeneous network advances a more unbounded, fragmented and fluid idea of culture that allows for and anticipates inconsistency, contradiction and conflict. One of the attractions of the term assemblage, Allen (2011) argues, is that it offers the possibility of grasping how "heterogeneous elements can hold together without actually forming a coherent whole" (2011, 154).

Central to understanding social life in terms of assemblages then is discerning relatedness and how component parts converge and relate to each other. For instance, one study on consumer behavior shows how a community of surfers develops practices to deal with disruptions to the surfer assemblage (Canniford and Shankar 2013). A disruption occurred when local government built a seawall and promenade that altered a surfing locale with perfect waves. The surfers began to fight development threatening to surfing locales, organize beach cleanups and contest industries that pollute beaches. These new activities reinforced the surfer narrative of nature and allowed surfers to continue performing their romantic experience of nature. Another study demonstrates how a popular TV reality show brand disassembles when consumers reject new components of the entertainment assemblage (Parmentier and Fischer 2015). One of the new components was inclusion of petite models, which conflicted with the show's high fashion narrative involving tall models. The rejection of new components led to steady decline in viewership. The case studies in this book explore a broad range of issues in everyday life and work in order to identify how assemblages come together and disperse in time and place. Based on the case studies, we draw implications concerning the stabilization and destabilization of assemblages.

Cultural Change and Agency

To describe change in assemblages, Deleuze and Guattari (1987) employ the metaphor of a rhizome. Botanically, a rhizome is the stem of a plant that can send out roots and shoots in multiple directions. The rhizome metaphor captures continuous and unpredictable movement. It is anything but structure. As they write, "A rhizome has no beginning or end; it is always in the middle, between things, interbeing, *intermezzo*" (1987, 25). Figure I.1 shows an image of ginger growing as a rhizome.

One of the factors moving the rhizome of social life in new directions is agency. As "the sociocultural mediated capacity to act" (Ahearn 2011, 112), agency reflects human capacities to sense, feel, think and act. It therefore implies ability to accept or resist products and services and to change practices. For example, in a study of family response to geographic dispersion due to divorce, employment commuting and military service, families reconfigure

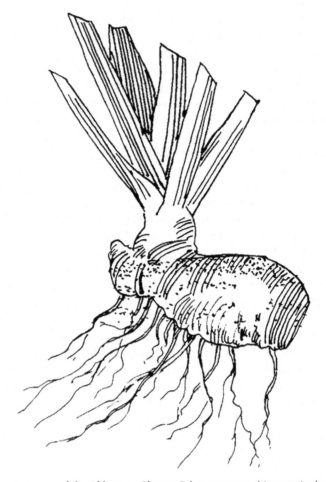

Figure I.1   An Image of the Rhizome, Ginger. Other common rhizomes include asparagus, iris and bamboo.

consumption practices through technology to maintain and strengthen family bonds (Epp, Schau and Price 2014). The authors use assemblage theory to examine changing practices such as using Skype to simulate copresence during dinner and texting while co-viewing TV from different locations. The study shows "how practice components can be decoupled and reassembled in new ways across time and space" (2014, 94). In the study, human agency is featured as a factor in cultural change.

In assemblage theory, agency is distributed among component parts of the assemblage. Anthropologists are accustomed to thinking about agency in terms of individuals and collectivities such as families, consumption communities and work groups within companies as well as in relation to organizations and institutions. However, there is debate over attributing agency to material objects (Hodder 2012). In this book, it is assumed that things such as consumer products and services possess agency at least insofar as people give meaning to things through their use of them. In popular culture, we tend to think of cultural change in terms of technology and technological things. For instance, senior citizens remember life before airplanes, young people cannot imagine life without digital devices, and we all struggle to imagine life with the driverless car of the future. Our point in this book is that while entities such as technology, energy resources and the environment are necessary to consider as factors in change, it is also important to focus on what is happening on the ground—to include agency and to examine the related nodes of activity that arise from human perception and action. Assemblage theory provides a means of incorporating all these factors as agents or actants in theorizing change by observing how people and organizations interact with things and give meaning to them. Authors in the book explore how agents who assemble over products and services in the field of production and consumption influence cultural change.

Given the spread of agency within assemblages, relatedness among component parts involves linkages to power relations. People who come together to form an assemblage typically have varying interests and priorities that may be incompatible. Relations of power in assemblages are more contingent than hierarchical. That is, they vary depending on time and place in comparison to being more permanently structured as found in government or bureaucratic organizations. As Arnould and Thompson (2015) write, assemblages "are rhizomatic structures that are infused by power relations that intersect and traverse each other rather than being imposed by top-down hierarchical orders" (2015, 8). Case studies in this book explore the tangle of people, their relationships and interactions, and the sources of power and social capital that bring assemblages into existence and keep them together for a period of time or that break them apart.

In placing emphasis on agency as a theoretical provocateur in cultural change, the book aims to contribute to further development of assemblage theory. Allen (2011) and Marcus and Saka (2006) point out that the notion of assemblage risks "thin description" without better conceptualization of how things hold together. We suggest that exploration of relatedness can enhance the conceptual resource of assemblage and increase its potential for growing into a theoretical perspective with wide significance. Our intent is to elucidate lines of articulation among parts of assemblages and identify the forces that lead to assembly or disassembly. At the same time, we intend to open the discussion on cultural change to agency as a factor complementing other factors documented by previous scholars. We hope that using the concept of

agency within a framework of assemblages will add explanatory power to
theories of cultural change.

METHODOLOGICAL IMPLICATION

Scales of Observation

There is a methodological implication for enlisting assemblage theory in
ethnographic research and analysis of cultural change. How do we trace links
among actors, map component parts and identify their relatedness? In other
words, how do we pursue a holistic approach? Desjeux (2016, 2014, 1987)
proposes a "scales of observation" method based on the practical question of
gathering information to guide research and explanation. As he writes, the
scales of observation method

> may be associated with the metaphor of the navigator who, in the 16th century,
> arrives in front of a coast, but does not know precisely where he is. The captain
> has a compass which shows him the north, a probe which allows him to identify
> shallow waters and a sextant in order to situate himself using the sun. He will
> start by describing what he sees, and then by successive approximations, after
> several journeys, but only then, will be able to draw a map. (1987, 5)

Updating from 16th century navigation to 21st century social science,
Desjeux continues,

> For qualitative socioanthropologists the basic tools are most often semi-directive
> interviews, *in situ* observation, group activities, photos and film, and today the
> internet. When we begin an investigation, particularly when the phenomenon
> in question is one which is emerging whether it is in our culture or in another
> culture, we never know exactly where we are or where we are going. (1987, 5)

With the scales of observation method, data collection and analysis may proceed from individuals, households and communities to larger organizations
and institutions and social affiliations by using macro-, meso- and microlevels of observation. To illustrate these levels, I use an example from food
systems research recently conducted by anthropology students in my classes
at the University of Rochester.

- At macro-levels of observation are the correlations between behavior and
  belonging to cultural groups, such as groups defined by age, gender and
  social class. In the case of food, there are causal links between fast food
  consumption and social class in the United States. People with lower

incomes tend to purchase more fast food meals than people with higher incomes. These connections speak to structural norms shaping and constraining behavior. The norms arise from practices of giant food corporations and government policies concerning subsidies, imports and exports.

- At meso-levels of observation are collective actors who exert pressure in response to social situations and fields of action. There are at least two sets of collective actors whose impact are felt in relation to fast food consumption. Marketing communications from the industrial agricultural system applaud the benefits of producing a large supply of food at low cost for consumers, while the nation's public markets and farmers markets rally against the industrial system by offering fresh fruits and vegetables from local farmers and allowing shoppers to use federal benefits for purchasing them through the Supplemental Nutrition Assistance Program (SNAP). In given social situations like this one, collective actors develop strategies in relationship to each other with arguments, discourses and ideologies that influence the other's behavior and that of consumers.
- At the microscale of observation are individuals, their practices and the meanings they ascribe to their actions. Based on ethnographic interviews with shoppers at the Rochester Public Market who take advantage of opportunity to use their SNAP benefits for buying fresh food through what's called a token program, participants are consciously reconstructing notions of food and meals at home. They are changing their family food provisioning practices from fast food to fresh and healthier home-cooked meals. The effect of agency and choice on this changing pattern of food preparation is observed from the microscale point of view.

Desjeux points out that there may not be a continuous link from micro- to meso- to macro-levels of observation and vice versa because, as he writes, the method "shows that causality and the explanation of phenomena vary from one scale to another, depending on whether they emphasize the correlation effect, the effect of situation, or the effect of meaning" (2014, 105). How one negotiates the scales when conducting research is the matter for the researcher to decide. The researcher typically pursues connections from one set of actors to another. Desjeux (2016) writes,

> The important thing, therefore, is not to look for the best scale of observation, but to start with the scale in which one is most competent, and to regularly change scales in order to observe what is emerging elsewhere and what is not necessarily visible at the scale of our anthropological observation. (2016, 69)

In tracing the heterogeneous parts of an assemblage, ethnographic analysis typically starts with the phenomenological experience of research participants and follows the trail to other sources of influence on emerging change in practices. DeLanda (2006), similarly, recommends linking micro- and macro-levels of social reality to replace "vaguely defined general entities (like 'the market' or 'the state') with concrete assemblages" (2006, 17). Scales of observation allow ethnographic research to pursue rhizomatic threads in assemblages wherever they may lead the investigation. Based on the case studies in this book, we identify methodological consistencies in specifying different levels of analysis for understanding how key components interact to form an assemblage.

Levels of Observation and Theories of Cultural Change

The levels of observation articulated by Desjeux above provide a framework for grasping and visualizing theories of cultural change that anthropologists have proposed and where this book's focus on agency fits in the conceptualization of transformation. Figure I.2 shows how change is conceptualized at macro-, meso- and microlevels depending on the aperture of our research lens.

At the macro-level are metanarratives of impersonal forces such as evolution, diffusion and acculturation. For example, Ferraro and Briody (2017)

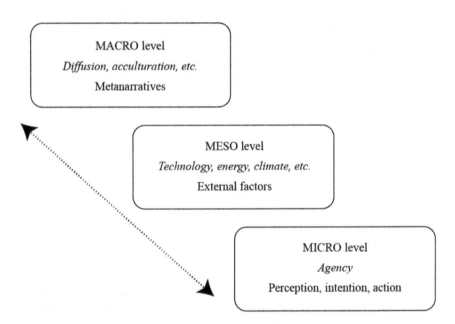

Figure I.2 Cultural Change at Different Levels of Observation. The arrow indicates how researchers may move from one level to another to explain what they encounter.

identify four mechanisms of cultural change (invention, cultural loss, diffusion and acculturation) that emerge within a given society. Anthropologists use such mechanisms to account for change at a macro-level.

At the meso-level are determinants of change such as those identified by Ervin (2015) at the beginning of this chapter, namely, technology, energy sources, environmental change and access to new resources or exchanges. These external causative factors are refracted through collective actors and the power of their discourses. For instance, proponents of worldwide adoption of mobile computing devices argue that technology has potential to offer opportunity to everyone and lessen inequality.

At the micro-level are practices of people in their everyday lives. Agency is observable at this level. Ethnographic study of people elicits their perceptions, intentions and actions as they engage with other social actors and things to create meaning. As DeLanda (2006) points out, observing assemblages at the micro-level follows the tradition of Max Weber and understanding meaningfully comprehensible social action (2006: 22). Chapters in this book rely on the micro-level of ethnography and may move among the three levels of observation in explaining instances of cultural change.

BUSINESS ANTHROPOLOGY AND INTERFACES OF PRODUCTION AND CONSUMPTION

Shift toward a Human-centered Approach in Business

Business anthropology is concerned with cultural practices in the production and consumption of products and services. Not surprisingly, the rise of business anthropology as subdiscipline and applied field of practice in the last three decades or so has occurred at the same time as business practices have become human-centered. As Beers (2016) notes,

> Competitive pressures and more empowered customers have made customer experience a critical strategic imperative for every industry and every company. The need for deep understanding about people, their experience, and how they define value has increased as businesses change to become more customer-centric. (2017, 11)

This shift in business practice toward consumer experience reflects capitalism as a constantly changing form (Thrift 2005). It is practiced differently at different times and places. As Thrift states, capitalism is "'instantiated' in particular practices" (2005, 1) and "a project that is permanently 'under construction'" (2005, 3).

One of the characteristics of contemporary capitalism, what Thrift calls "an experience economy" (2005, 7), bypasses the dichotomy of production and consumption as analytic opposites in favor of a confluence of producers and consumers working together with an active role for the consumer. The engagement of business anthropology in the economy benefited from this shift to human-centered practice in the phases of product and service development and delivery. As a result, corporate and nonprofit companies seeking to become more aware of the interests and priorities of their clients and customers have turned to ethnography. However, as Kimbell (2014) notes, far from being human-centered, ethnographic research involves the entanglement of people with many other human and nonhuman actors. The value that ethnography provides is learning at the human scale of observation, which acknowledges humans, other actants and material resources in the construction of meaning. As Kimbell writes, ethnography reveals, "how public and collective issues exist as assemblages of people, organizations, and things" and creates "new understandings of what makes up an issue and how one might engage with it" (2014, 187). Thus, the social field of production and consumption provides fertile ground for business anthropologists to study cultural change as they conduct ethnographic research on everyday practices of work and life.

Domains of Business Anthropology

There are three main domains of business anthropology (design, marketing and advertising, and organizational culture). Anthropologists work at the interfaces of production and consumption across organizations, products and services, and consumers. The work is problem-solving oriented, collaborative and often interdisciplinary:

1. Design

   When companies design or redesign products and services, a design team typically composed of designers, engineers and anthropologists conducts ethnographic research with users to understand their practices, needs and desires. "A successfully designed item," Wasson (2000) notes, "is one that is easily adopted by consumers. This may be because the product's use fits with existing behavior patterns or because it signals a new use in a clear and compelling way" (2000, 377). Design ethnography is an iterative process in which products and services are cocreated by users and researchers.

2. Marketing and advertising

   Marketing and advertising also depend on learning about consumer experience. The aim is to position a company's brand against competitors. An ethnographic team, usually consisting of company employees, members of its advertising agency and anthropologists, conducts research with consumers to understand their practices and the meanings and uses of particular products and services in the everyday lives of a target audience. Then, as Malefyt and Moeran (2003) write, a strategy is formulated that "positions the product in relation to targeted consumers and emphasizes the attributes that will appeal to them" (2003, 5). These attributes refer to symbolic representations and the embodied experience of research participants.

3. Organizational culture

Companies engage in ethnographic research for many reasons including examination of work processes and strategies, understanding and reducing tensions, identifying effective social networks, and helping restructure the organization in an effort to improve performance. Assessing organizational culture and its potential for change is the main purpose of the ethnography. As Cefkin (2012) points out, this involves "inward focus on internal operations, on how companies organize to get things done and the practices and worldviews that inform them" (2012, 103). The team conducting research is normally led by an anthropologist and includes others such as persons representing different parts of the company and stakeholder groups. While the research focuses on the structure of the organization and work practices, it also involves gaining insight on customers and their experience of the company's product or service.

When business anthropologists conduct ethnographic research at the interfaces of production and consumption, they gain access to how people perceive themselves and what they are doing in relation to others and what's happening in the world. In this sense, cultural change involves identity and the pursuits and goals that motivate and inspire people in their organizational and personal lives. Ethnography at the interfaces identifies changing subjectivities of particular sets of employees and consumers.

Acceptance of change and resistance to change is centered at the interfaces. Clashes among actors can occur. Beliefs and values, as well as practices and processes, may be quite dissimilar. Accommodation and adjustment sometimes result. Alternately, system constraints and incentives may limit acceptance or lead to strong resistance. These attitudes and behaviors play a key role in outcomes. As business plans, strategies and solutions develop, discourses and ideologies often come into conflict. The book addresses how cultural perceptions and experiences collide and are resolved in the interfaces between consumers, products and services, and organizations. Thus, the book indicates how certain discourses and ideologies gain ascendancy in market contexts and the extent to which they reflect cultural currents in society.

Business Orientation to Innovation

The three domains of business anthropology situate anthropologists within a production-consumption field alongside powerful forces or agents in the economy, namely organizations and consumers. This social field is oriented to innovation and the much less frequent occurrence of invention. Change is typically planned and purposeful as corporations and nonprofit organizations meet new challenges and take advantage of new market opportunities (Wilf 2015). Innovation is typically assumed to come from technology. For instance, a shift from landline to cellular technology is innovative because it introduced mobility and communication on the go where previous phone equipment and service was limited to place such as home or office. Cellular products gained competitive advantage over landline products. Business draws a distinction between incremental and disruptive innovation. Incremental innovation implies a series of small improvements to an existing product or service that maintains or enhances its competitive position over time, whereas disruptive innovation is conceived as a process of developing new products or services to replace existing technologies, taking root initially in simple applications at the bottom of a market and then relentlessly moving up the market, eventually displacing established competitors (Christensen 1970).

Innovation refers to new or improved products and services that consumers may accept or reject as well as to new or restructured organizational processes and work practices deemed necessary to serve customers better. It is common to consider the impact of innovation in terms of adoption or resistance. As defined by Rogers (2003), innovation is "an idea, practice or object that is perceived as new by an individual or other unit of adoption" (2003, 12). Scholars of innovation focus on adopters and rates and means of adoption (Gluesing 2012) for what matters in business is purchase. In contrast, this book considers broader processes of social and cultural change as things come together in assemblages, and people reconfigure who they are and what they are doing.

DEFINING CULTURAL CHANGE

Innovation and cultural change are concepts that deal with change although each somewhat differently. Innovation refers to change that is planned and purposeful with a goal of establishing a market or increasing market share. On the other hand, the concept of cultural change implies change in social practices and ideas from a broader perspective that results from interaction and struggle among agents in a social field. Bourdieu (1987) sets social reproduction against social change. Bourdieu's model of the habitus produces actions and dispositions to actions (competencies and generative capacities) that produce behaviors, which are repeated and passed along (1987, 13–14). People are largely unaware of such schemas because they are tacit and implicit cultural assumptions. The habitus also enables consumption wherein people appreciate and use products and services within class interests of the larger social field (Bourdieu 1993). Cultural change occurs in the larger social field of collective struggles and individual strategies, which shift depending on values assigned to them and adjust as new positions take hold and alter other positions in the field. In this way, we have tension between continuity and change. This also suggests that social transformation is not planned or purposeful.

Within specific organizations, however, planned change is a form of purposeful cultural change such as when organizations embrace the concept of culture in order to implement change in values and subsequent work practices (Ferraro and Briody 2017). Key to the notion of cultural change in society is a shift in the way people perceive themselves in relation to things, others and the world. As Paxson (2013) writes, "Anthropologists seek to understand how social change manifests not only materially—for instance, in institutional policies and standards of living—but also in less tangible ways, in how people think and feel about what they do" (2013, 12).

Most critically, then, innovative change and cultural change are analytically distinct. Cultural change is a paradigm shift in aspects of identity and meaning of things. Innovation, by contrast, is an applied practice whose goal is to bring change in the marketplace. Sometimes innovative and cultural changes are convergent, sometimes not. Following are examples to indicate how cultural change involves revision of practice with identity and meaning taking a new turn.

1. Example of cultural change in consumer life

   Many people have adopted Fitbit wristbands to monitor exercise in terms of steps taken, calories burned and heart rate motion. This focus on internal body functioning is quite different from, say, non-Fitbit wearing runners whose exercise experience has emphasized emotional exertion and exhilaration and connections with nature as encountered on the running path. Fitbit wearers conceive the self, body and exercise in biometric and machine-like ways while the runners consider the self, body and exercise in terms of emotion and affinity with nature. Fitbit use recasts the category of exercise as well as wearers' perceptions of themselves and what they are doing in a new cultural pattern. Both practices contest ideas and meanings of "health."

2. Innovation, yes, but cultural change in consumer life?

In comparison to the Fitbit example of cultural change, consider innovation that does not result necessarily in paradigm shift. For instance, Uber represents a technological innovation in ride-hailing. Uber has become a dominant player in the ride-hailing industry displacing more regulated taxi and car services. Albeit made more efficient, timely and convenient with a software interface, has the service catalyzed cultural change? Has it altered ideas about ride-hailing? About the meaning of drivers or passengers (or their relationship)? About business and its relation to labor? Does it fundamentally alter conceptualizations and experiences of transportation? It is perhaps too soon to tell. Uber may seem more like the experience of a taxi than the autonomous car of the future. While Uber has upended the marketplace by fomenting a supply-side revolution (we can all be drivers), only when innovation leads to shift in identity, category meaning or socially constructed ideas relevant to the category, does it constitute cultural change.

3. Example of cultural change in organizational life

Briody and Erickson (2017) provide an example of cultural change in the hospital setting emphasizing cultural value on collaboration. To improve patient experience by reducing wait time in the ER, a hospital implemented an innovative practice with a unit called Admission, Discharge, and Transfer (ADT). This unit, placed under ER control, achieved quicker turnaround time on diagnostic tests and faster patient discharge through roving nurses who assist discharge on all nursing floors. Central to implementation of ADT was collaboration among hospital units, which had previously perceived themselves as silos operating independently. The ADT cross-silo collaboration suggests revision of staff identity from silo-isolated to team member and a revision in the social construction of patient care. In this case, innovation catalyzed cultural change.

4. Innovation, not cultural change, in organizational life

At some point in its history, an intimate apparel firm began to offer matching sets of bras and panties (Briody and Erickson 2017). With this marketing innovation, the firm appeared to be driving and responding to customer preference. However, despite women's desire for matching sets, the company has not supplied nearly enough sets to satisfy consumer demand in recent years. Because of limited runs of matching sets, retail stores could not obtain sufficient product from the manufacturer. Blocking response to demand for matching sets was the organization of the company in silos—one silo for bras, another for panties. Upper management could not reframe ideas about lingerie and imagine cross-silo collaboration and marketing bras and panties in more coordinated ways. There was organizational resistance to the marketing innovation since managers held onto older ideas and values concerning their own products, customers and business practices. As a result, the innovation did not yield cultural change because corporate identity remained fixed in silos and the intimate apparel category framed as separate product lines.

Cultural Change in Assemblages

In this book, our definition of cultural change emanates from the consumer society in which we live. Cultural change is a cohesive pattern of change in an organizational culture or in a consumer community culture. The book conceives of cultural change broadly in order to encompass actions, values and ideologies of cultural groups in the wider society that influence formation of assemblages. For example, considering management and work practices in an organization, cultural change occurred at General Motors when the company shifted its pattern of manufacturing from the assembly line to more flexible and lean production in the latter part of the 20th century (Briody, Trotter and Meerwarth 2010). This innovation, which was influenced by Japanese models of production, revamped GM's production practices and enhanced its ability to compete in the marketplace. It also instigated cultural change by altering constructions of identity, work and car manufacture. The identity of workers was reconfigured from solo operators on the assembly line building cars by performing a task repeatedly under the supervision of a supervisor to member of a team working on a larger unit of assembly and charged with responsibility to solve problems affecting that part of the assembly process. An example related to consumer culture is the transformation in menstruation practices among women in the United States from "protection" discourse to "natural" discourse following the women's movement of the 1960s, which fostered resistance to feminine care industry communications (Malefyt and McCabe 2016). In both of these examples, the cohesive pattern of cultural change happened as a result of an assemblage of people, objects, discourse and institutions coming together in a new alignment. Business anthropologists gain insight into cultural changes like these by exploring the perceptions and behavior of people in their everyday work and life and in recognizing the relatedness of objects, ideas and people in the production of practices. The case studies in this book indicate that cultural change occurs when new or different alignments of things legitimate and normalize certain identities and practices.

DESCRIPTION OF CHAPTERS IN THE BOOK

The case studies are arranged in three sections relating to the domains of business anthropology: (1) Consumer and Design Interface, (2) Consumer and Product/Service Interface and (3) Consumer and Organization Interface. Following the case studies is the concluding chapter.

Consumer and Design Interface

Chapter 1, by Emilie Hitch, deals with introduction of modern farming equipment and practices to rural farmers in Cambodia. Hitch proposes the intriguing idea of hope as an agent of cultural change to explain a trajectory of change taking place among farmers who adopt drip irrigation equipment and develop commercial vegetable gardens in order to increase income. Investment in innovative equipment and practice provides cash and covers labor costs that allow farmers to send their children to secondary school instead of working on farms. Hope that children will attend school beyond the elementary level and enter professions other than farming fuels change in the way rural farmers practice farming. The chapter describes how an agricultural assemblage, including a human-centered design team working for an NGO, developed marketing strategies to increase adoption of the equipment among rural farmers who dream their children will have "a job with a pen."

Chapter 2 describes the shifting higher education assemblage in the United States as an increasing number of technology-mediated learning opportunities enter the educational landscape. The author, Marijke Rijsberman, discusses disruptions to higher education emerging from disconnect between traditional education and the labor market. She treats readers to an in-depth view of the complex and crowded education technology field (EdTech) such as open access university instruction. At the heart of the chapter is the analysis of ethnographic data from EdTech study participants. This analysis gives insight into work predicaments, educational options available and choices that participants make to create viable futures for themselves. Focusing on the agency of students, the chapter argues that EdTech learners will play an important role in influencing educational roads to be paved. While EdTech learners value an educational experience that leads to a traditional degree, they also call for learning opportunities connected to career knowledge and skills.

In chapter 3, Henry Delcore addresses concerns to increase educational equity through technology at a major public university serving a diverse student population with a large proportion of first-generation college students in the United States. The author describes an assemblage that came into existence through an initiative to introduce mobile devices in the teaching and learning process. The initiative sought to increase graduation rates by making student work practices more successful. During the project's seven-year history, discourses of educational equity have been marked by a persistent technocentrism where the technology (e.g., tablets, laptops, hybrids) has been prioritized over student-centered and faculty-centered ways of dealing with the digital divide. The author finds that indeterminacy, or ongoing tension of equity, technocentrism and pedagogical change, accommodates different actor perspectives and holds the assemblage together. The chapter concludes with discussion of agency and the discursive and practical changes brought by the educational technology initiative to reduce inequality in higher education.

In chapter 4, Christine Miller discusses design as a provocateur of cultural change because of design's role in reconfiguring and constructing assemblages of the future. Miller finds that design paves the way for innovation and, in turn, cultural change by giving form and substance to our imaginings. In this sense, design is future-making or world-making. The chapter explores the impact of design on the Internet of Things (IoT), the third wave of the Internet, in which ambient technology and ubiquitous computing will provide connectivity to 28 billion "things." Using such interesting examples as autonomous machine-to-machine systems, cobots or machines that work alongside human employees, and carebots which provide interactive companionship for older adults, the chapter shows how design research and practice have become human-centered with concern and empathy for users. Affirming the connection between technology and culture, Miller highlights human agency and creativity for imagining and designing alternate futures.

Consumer and Product/Service Interface

Chapter 5 focuses on cultural change in the smart devices assemblage of the United States. The authors, Jennifer Englert, Patricia Wall and Margaret Szymanski, discuss disruption triggered by introduction of the iPhone and other smart devices that has transformed people's work practices and personal lives. Based on five years of ethnographic studies among working professionals, the authors identify characteristics of interactions with new smart devices that facilitate adoption. As trajectories of change become tightly woven into everyday life, they also raise concerns about impacts on our lives and society. A key benefit of the analysis is the way the authors conceive of agency as a coevolving relationship between users and designers of digital devices. The chapter shows how cultural practices and technology continue to change in relation to each other as people make choices in using smart devices to accomplish their work and choreograph their lives, and designers innovate more effective devices for users.

Chapter 6 challenges the assumption that adoption of innovative technology such as computers and smartphones levels the playing field in society. The authors, Arundhati Bhattacharyya and Russell W. Belk, argue that power disparities in India limit access to technology for people with low incomes not only because of lack of money but also because of cultural beliefs and values. Based on ethnographic research in Kolkata and New Delhi, the authors provide insightful examples of how persons in positions of power like landlords and employers constrain poor persons from learning and using technology that could improve their lives. In comparison to the idea that consumer adoption and resistance of new technology reflects choice, this chapter offers an alternative view that highlights the role of hierarchy in limiting adoption of technological change by poor persons. The chapter concludes that agency, while spread among component parts of an assemblage, is distributed unequally due to power and economic differences.

In chapter 7, Dominique Desjeux and Ma Jingjing examine drink practices in China to identify consumer targets for introducing a new nonalcoholic beverage. The authors pursue an anthropological approach to diffusion of innovation that insists on understanding how innovations enter existing social systems. Based on ethnographic research in Chinese cities, the chapter provides a fascinating view of cultural change occurring in beverage consumption practices with recent arrival of commercial drinks disrupting traditional patterns. The authors analyze the meanings given to drink choices and show how the beverage market is structured by social factors such as generation, life cycle and gender as well as symbolic values of hot and cold associated with health, balance and the circulation of energy in the body. The analysis reveals agency as a catalyst of change, especially in negotiations between parents and children where relations of power are complicated by transgression of parental authority and new norms of taste in choosing beverages.

In chapter 8, Ejiro Onomake examines cultural change in the brokerage assemblage that constitutes a key part of Nigerian-Chinese business relationships. There is a shift from Nigerian entrepreneurs acting as individual brokers to a growing number of organizations serving as brokers. The chapter highlights the agency of Nigerian brokers and explains why they choose to associate with an organization rather than operate independently. The author conducted ethnographic research in Nigeria and brings to life the emergence of broker organizations through the case of a security firm owner who purchased safety equipment from a company in China. The chapter provides insight into entrepreneurship culture in Nigeria with an historical view of brokerage practices from precolonial to colonial and contemporary times that illuminates the shifting Nigerian brokerage assemblage. Broker organizations play a significant role in fostering economic ties and partnership relations between Nigerian business people and their Chinese counterparts.

Consumer and Organization Interface

In chapter 9, Kevin M. Newton addresses poverty alleviation in the United States. The chapter provides an engaging history of the nonprofit industry, changing discourses on causes of poverty and approaches for intervention, and points out the power of institutions to affect the lives of poor persons. The history shows how the nonprofit assemblage has shifted from a neoliberal focus on individual responsibility to a more holistic approach that includes systemic barriers to upward mobility. Set within this shift is a compelling case study of a nonprofit technology company that uses smartphone technology and behavioral economics principles to enhance the efforts of other nonprofits working toward poverty reduction. The author describes how a mobile application oriented to increasing college acceptance and scholarship awards was tested with high school students living in low-income areas. A program evaluation conducted with the student users indicates the agency of local organizations to embrace innovative interventions responsive to client needs.

Chapter 10 discusses the role of applied anthropologists working as employees within organizations in creating organizational-culture change. The authors, Shane Paul, Angela Ramer and Jo Aiken discuss the importance of reflexivity for negotiating the dual identity of insider/outsider (i.e., employee and anthropologist doing ethnography) in contrast to the traditional anthropologist conducting fieldwork and the business anthropologist acting as consultant, both of whom are outsiders trying to understand the inside. Each author presents a fascinating case study as change agent in the work practices of his or her respective organization. Case studies involve initiating a safety culture in an industrial organization, creating a professional development program in an architectural firm, and introducing human-centered design to a technology-oriented process for designing spacecraft at NASA (National Aeronautical and Space Agency). The chapter concludes with comparison of similarities and differences across the case studies, which highlights assemblages of people, ideas and things facilitating change.

In the Conclusion, Elizabeth K. Briody provides an insightful analysis of how the case studies in this book use assemblage theory and its hallmark concept of agency to explain cultural change. As she points out, the contributing authors specify key features of assemblages and unpack tensions that arise as a myriad of agentic forces collide, align and compete. Tensions may remain unresolved, thus retaining ambiguity about the present and future, or may find resolution through accommodation of new practices within existing cultural spheres. The chapter deals with a critical question in assemblage theory, namely, how the fluid and heterogeneous components of assemblages hold together. Briody defines phases in the life course of assemblages and suggests processes of holding together through different or similar interests, complementary or opposing discourses, power disparities, and shared beliefs and mutual benefits. The chapter concludes with implications for future use of assemblage theory and interdisciplinary work as business anthropologists continue to embrace application and practice in addressing organizational and community problems.

As coeditors, Elizabeth Briody and I thank our contributing authors for their fine ethnographic work in their areas of expertise. Each case study shows how agency shifts assemblages in a trajectory of change. Taken together the case studies provide evidence that cultural change is neither deterministic nor accidental but historically situated in time and place.

NOTE

1. Many thanks to Rita M. Denny for the helpful comments on an earlier draft of this chapter, to Timothy deWaal Malefyt for his scholarly advice, and to Susan J. Tontarski for skillfully rendering the figures in the chapter.

REFERENCES

Ahearn, Laura M. 2001. 'Language and agency.' *Annual Review of Anthropology* 30: 109–37.
Allen, John. 2011. Powerful assemblages? *Area* 43(2): 154–157.
Arnould, Eric J. and Craig J. Thompson. 2015. Introduction: Consumer culture theory: Ten years gone (and beyond). In *Research in consumer behavior, Volume 17*, Anastasia Thyroff, Jeff B. Murray and Russell W. Belk, eds. 1–21. Bingley UK: Emerald Group Publishing.
Beers, Robin. 2017. Humanizing organizations: Researchers as knowledge brokers and change agents. In *Collaborative ethnography in business environments*, Maryann McCabe, ed. 11–25. London: Routledge.
Bourdieu, Pierre. 1977. *Outline of a theory of practice*. Cambridge. Cambridge University Press.
———. 1993. *The Field of Cultural Production*. New York: Columbia University Press.
Briody, Elizabeth K. and Ken C. Erickson. 2017. Success despite the silos: System-wide innovation and collaboration. In *Collaborative ethnography in business environments*, Maryann McCabe, ed. 26–59. London: Routledge.
Briody, Elizabeth K., Robert T. Trotter II, and Tracy L. Meerwarth. 2010. *Transforming culture: Creating and sustaining effective organizations*. New York: Palgrave Macmillan.
Canniford, Robin and Avi Shankar. 2013. Purifying practices: How consumers assemble romantic experiences of nature. *Journal of Consumer Research* 39(5): 1051–1069.
Cefkin, Melissa. 2012. Close encounters: Anthropologists in the corporate arena. *Journal of Business Anthropology* 1(1): 91–117.
Christensen, Clayton M. 1997. *The innovator's dilemma*. New York: Harper Business.

Collier, Stephen J. and Aihwa Ong. 2005. Global assemblages, anthropological problems. In *Global assemblages: Technology, politics, and ethics as anthropological problems,* Aihwa Ong and Stephen J. Collier, eds. 3–21. Oxford: Blackwell.

DeLanda, Manuel. 2006. *A new philosophy of society: Assemblage theory and social complexity.* London: Continuum.

Deleuze, Gilles and Felix Guattari. 1987. *A thousand plateaus: Capitalism and schizophrenia.* Trans. Brian Massumi. Minneapolis: University of Minnesota Press.

Desjeux, Dominique. 2016. The itinerary approach of a business anthropologist: between mobility, diversity and networks *Journal of Business Anthropology* 5(1); 64–76.

———. 2014. Professional anthropology and training in France. In *Handbook of anthropology in business,* Rita Denny and Patricia Sunderland, eds. 100–115. Walnut Creek, CA: Left Coast Press.

———. 1987. *Scales of observation or the discovery of the discontinuity of observation between the macrosocial and the microsocial scales.* Unpublished manuscript. Translated from the French by D. Desjeux, 14/09/2016, 1–12.

Epp, Amber M., Hope Jensen Schau and Linda L. Price. 2014. The role of brands and mediating technologies in assembling long-distance family practices. *Journal of Marketing* 78 (3): 81–101.

Erickson, Paul A. and Liam D. Murphy. 2013. *A history of anthropological theory,* 4th ed. Toronto: University of Toronto Press.

Ervin, Alexander M. 2015. *Cultural transformations and globalization: Theory, development, and social change.* Boulder: Paradigm.

Ferraro, Gary P. and Elizabeth K. Briody. 2017. *The cultural dimension of global business,* 8th ed. Routledge: London.

Foucault, Michel. 1980. *Power/knowledge: Selected interviews and other writings 1972–1977.* Colin Gordon, ed. New York: Vintage Books.

Gluesing, Julia C. 2012. Diffusion of innovations. In *Leadership in science and technology: A reference handbook,* William Sims Bainbridge, ed. 123–131. Thousand Oaks CA: Sage.

Hodder, Ian. 2012. *Entangled: An archaeology of the relationships between humans and things.* West Sussex UK: Wiley-Blackwell.

Kimbell, Lucy. 2014. Design ethnography, public policy, & public services: Rendering collective issues doable & at human scale. In *Handbook of anthropology in business,* Rita Denny and Patricia Sunderland, eds. 186–201. Walnut Creek, CA: Left Coast Press.

Latour, Bruno. 2005. *Reassembling the social: An introduction to actor-network theory.* Oxford: Oxford University Press.

Malefyt, Timothy de Waal and Maryann McCabe. 2016. Women's bodies, menstruation and marketing "protection:" Interpreting a paradox of gendered discourses in consumer practices and advertising campaigns. *Consumption Markets & Culture* 19(6): 555–575.

Malefyt, Timothy de Waal and Brian Moeran, eds. 2003. *Advertising cultures.* Oxford: Berg.

Marcus, George E. and Erkan Saka. 2006. Assemblage. *Theory, Culture & Society* 23: 101–109.

McCabe, Maryann. 2015. Fine chocolate, resistance, and political morality in the marketplace. *Journal of Business Anthropology* 4(1): 54–81.

Parmentier, Marie-Agnes and Eileen Fischer. 2015. Things fall apart: The dynamics of brand audience dissipation. *Journal of Consumer Research* 41(5): 1228–1251.

Paxson, Heather. 2013. *The life of cheese: Crafting food and value in America*. Berkeley: University of California.

Rogers, Everett M. 2003. *Diffusion of innovations*. New York: Free Press.

Thrift, Nigel. 2005. *Knowing capitalism*. London: Sage.

Toffler, Alvin. 1970. *Future Shock*. New York: Random House.

Wasson, Christina. 2000. Ethnography in the field of design. *Human Organization* 59(4): 377–388.

Wilf, Eitan. 2015. Routinized business innovation: An undertheorized engine of cultural evolution. *American Anthropologist* 117(4): 679–692.

Part I

CONSUMER AND DESIGN INTERFACE

Chapter 1

I Hope When She Grows Up, She Will Have a Job with a Pen

Drip Irrigation and Hope in Cambodia

Emilie Hitch

On a tour of a vegetable farm in Northern Cambodia, the owner of the land walked us from vegetable patch to vegetable patch, pointing again and again to what he described as "modern practices."[1] The things we saw, however, were not "modern" to us: diesel engines sitting in the mud at the bank of a creek, gravity tanks made from basic plastic bins and PVC piping running down to rows of cabbages, and garden hoses with, essentially, showerheads attached to them laying between simple stakes and trellises hosting tall-climbing beans and squash. Gathering around the small shack where he kept his tools, fertilizers, pesticides, and seeds, we showed the farmer and his daughter some drawings of other types of farm equipment like small tractors and irrigation systems ... and the pride was evident in his voice as he said that yes, he would be able to afford these things soon. He then, voice full of pride, explained to us how changes to his farm already meant his daughter was able to go to secondary school instead of helping with farm labor. "I hope when she grows up, she will have a job with a pen," he said, eyes shining in imagination of that possible future.

Over the previous months, our Human-Centered Design (HCD) Team[2] of marketers, product, service and graphic designers, and ethnographers had grown accustomed to hearing about plans for the next rainy season, the next harvest ... but we were also beginning to hear about and understand how hopes for possible futures were different. The mental image this farmer painted was of an imagined time much further in the future than of plans for the next months, and much less certain.

The next day, in another village, sitting cross-legged on the cement floor of a farmhouse, we learned about "old ways" of laboring in the fields from the woman who lived there; from where we sat, we could see them in practice. A line of laborers bending down to harvest rice in the next field, and her son, walking along rows of vegetables with a watering can in each hand, stood in stark contrast to what we had seen the day before just a kilometer away. This farmer narrated her daily routine of making lunch for the laborers and for her son (who does not go to school during the growing season) and of selling seeds to her neighbors for an agricultural company. She hoped to purchase things she had seen at a "demo farm" nearby—a gravity tank on a platform and hoses to transport the water to her crops. Maybe then, she hoped, her son could go to school.

In Cambodia, where almost 80% of families live in rural areas, and only 36% of all rural households who own more than one hectare of land are able to produce more than they need to feed their family, the introduction of "modern" farming products and practices can disrupt established economies of labor (World Bank, 2016). Purchasing equipment, such as for drip irrigation, and using it to raise a profitable vegetable garden often leads to a situation where farmers can afford both the cash and labor costs of sending their children to secondary school. In Cambodia, 83% of eligible males and 85% of eligible females attended primary school during the years spanning 2008–2012 (UNICEF 2012). However, during that time, only 46% of males and 45% of females attended secondary school (UNICEF 2012). Introduction and adoption of agricultural equipment and subsequent change of farming practice had, and has, the potential to make an impact on the education level of the entire country.

Researchers have documented the orientations to community, trust, and the past among the rural poor (Zucker 2007) due to years of violence at the hands of the Khmer Rouge—often their own community members. Decades of poverty followed (Boua et al. 1982, Chandler 1991, Benedict 1985, 2007, 2008; Ung 2000). I chose to examine their orientation to the future instead, and I argue that hopes are influential in catalyzing cultural change.

For both HCD practitioners and rural farmers, hopes are embodied in objects and ideas in the present. Acting as visions of potential and possible futures, these hopes become embodied in, and realized through, the purchase and adoption of consumer goods that change the way rural farmers in Cambodia practice farming. The resulting change is one where the identity of the farmer shifts from subsistence to commercial. The category of farming is reframed to one where labor means using equipment instead of the work of hands and bodies. I focus on the hopes—concepts of possible futures—embodied in tangible objects, the purchase of these objects, and the adoption of new farming practices, that together might propel specific trajectories of change (Collier & Ong, 2005) toward possible futures.

LITERATURE REVIEW AND THEORETICAL APPROACH

What is hope? Vincent Crapanzano's work is concerned with hope as a category of "both experience and analysis" as he unpacks the differences between hope and desire (2003, 4). Crapanzano explains the difference between desire and hope through the agent of fulfillment: "one acts on desire—even if that act is not to act on desire because one has judged it impossible, hope depends on some other agency—a god, fate, a chance, an other—for its fulfillment" (2003, 6). As a category of experience, hope is a catalyst of change with limits when it comes to individual agency. In Crapanzano's analysis of "some other agency," "evaluation rests on the characterization—the moral characterization—of that agency." In other words, the morally acceptable agents of hope change over time.

Miyazaki speaks to a concept of morality, examining the "appropriation of the language of hope," and argues that hope is not an object or category, but a method of knowledge formation. Hope is an effort to "preserve the prospective momentum of the present" (2004, 120). This method "immediately triggers a series of ethical concerns regarding its content and consequences" (Miyazaki, 2004, 1). In his work, he examines "moments of hope" which occur in Fijian gift-giving and demonstrate the "limits of human agency" (2004, 12), "the spokesman for the gift-givers remains motionless ... until a spokesman for the gift-receivers takes it from him. In this moment of hope, the gift-givers place in abeyance their own agency, or capacity to create effects in the world" (Miyazaki 2004, 7).

Miyazaki's work on "moments" also brings up questions about the phenomenology and nature of time—specifically the chronological time of life histories and of cultural change. Miyazaki suggests that, "as soon as hope is approached as the end point of a process, the newness or freshness of the prospective moment that defines that moment as hopeful is lost" (2004, 8). Much more can be gained from the idea of hope by positing that hope is a midpoint. It lies between the past and the future. Thus, hopes are visions of possible futures that we live with in the present.

The idea of hope as a midpoint also is connected to models of cultural learning, particularly, the cultural learning of children. Toren (1993) argues for a model of cultural learning as a micro-historical process that informs how children make sense of social relations over time. By focusing on this micro-historical process of changing identities of farmers and their children, we can see how "our understandings of ourselves and the world are founded in our relations with one another" (Toren, 1993, 461). In the process, we examine our own social histories—how we come to know. Similarly, David Berliner (2005) makes an argument for "youth as a crucial site for understanding issues of religious memory and cultural transmission" (2005, 576). His work explores how Bulongic youth in West Africa remember a past that they have never experienced: they can articulate a pre-Islamic religious heritage that existed before their birth. He argues that "memory" is just a term for the transmission of culture, as "cultural representations, experiences, emotions, values, attitudes, and practices that are passed down from older generations to younger ones who inherit and actively negotiate them" (2005, 577).

Jennifer Cole argues that "memory ... exists intersubjectively, stretched across individuals and the wider social and cultural environment that they inhabit" (2001, 29) while Berliner points out that the "concept of memory as 'past in the present' is as old as anthropology itself; from Edward Tylor's 'survivals' to Pierre Bourdieu's 'habitus'" (2005, 577). In other words, habitus is a mechanism of collective history that aids successful cultural transmission and cultural change. From the moment of birth, individuals are surrounded by "habitus," systems of inculcated dispositions or internal historical relations, "schemata for perception, appreciation, and action," existing in those around them (Bourdieu 1972, 85; Wacquant 1992, 16). Witnessing the practices of others, gaining knowledge of cultural heritage, and one's own experiences of the way things are in that habitus, create a consciousness of the ways to do things for the individual—a consciousness of culture.

In this chapter, I examine the morally acceptable agents of cultural change in the Cambodian agricultural assemblage (see Figure 1.1). The assemblage shows two possible futures for Cambodian farmers. The assemblage on the right does not represent a commonly hoped-for future. The old farming practices continue and the farmers' children are unable to attend school beyond the elementary level.

However, the assemblage on the left represents a future hoped-for by some farmers and their families. Hope becomes embedded in a particular object or new behavior intended to catalyze cultural change toward that future. In the case I describe, parents have hope that their children grow up to "have a job with a pen." Thus, hope motivates people to "shape their circumstances through innovation ... and making use of innovated technologies, beliefs, or novel institutional practice" (Ervin 2015, 6–7). Farmers act to shape a possible future by purchasing these objects and changing their practices. In this case, rural Cambodian farmers rely on drip irrigation products (DRIP) to extend the limits of agency and create a particular, hoped-for future. Through that transaction, they are "preserving the prospective momentum of the present ... in anticipation of what has not-yet become" (Miyazaki 2004, 120). With the farmers' reliance on some other agent to realize possible futures for themselves and their children, the designers, marketers, salespeople, farming practices, and products themselves become embodiments and agents of hope. Thus, the questions my work aims to explore are the following:

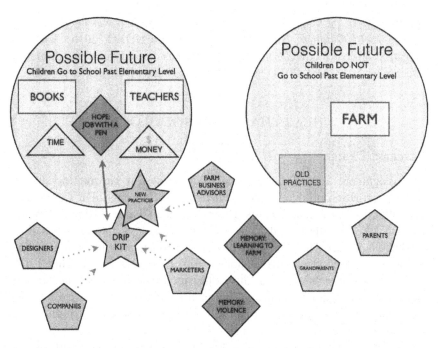

Figure 1.1 Possible Futures with and without the Drip Kit.

- What are morally acceptable agents of cultural change?
- Where are the limits of these agents when it comes to cultural change?
- How do these agents of hope change over time?

BACKGROUND

Ethnographic research informing this paper was carried out during a project at the iLab in the Cambodian country office of International Development Enterprises (iDE Cambodia). iDE Cambodia is one of the many country offices within iDE—a multinational nongovernmental organization. The iLab houses a team comprised of anthropologists, designers, business analysts, and strategists employed by iDE to design and carry out Human-Centered Design processes for both outside clients and internal teams at iDE throughout its network of country offices.

The iLab's three-phase process framework is described as Hear, Create, and Deliver. This framework aligns with a general depiction of Design Thinking initially championed by IDEO (Brown, 2009) to correspond to the name of the method itself (Human-Centered Design) and subsequently customized specifically for the social sector (IDEO, 2009). A toolkit was later published as *The Field Guide to Human-Centered Design* (IDEO, 2015). The drip irrigation project for iDE Cambodia's iLab was carried out over six months (December 2013–May 2014) using the Hear, Create, Deliver framework.

HEAR PHASE: METHODOLOGY

Research Design

The assignment for the iLab's project was to design a marketing strategy for drip irrigation products (DRIP) currently sold through iDE Cambodia's agricultural input business (Lors Thmey) by their Farm Business Advisors (FBAs). iDE and the Canadian International Development Agency (CIDA) funded the project. The goal of the project was to design a marketing strategy to increase adoption of DRIP among targeted farmers for the client, iDE. The expectation was that the kits would increase profits for the farmers, salespeople, and parent company. The plan for the research design included three phases: Hear, Create, and Deliver. Table 1.1 describes each phase and its methodology.

The HCD methodology for this iLab project was designed purposely to articulate the voice of the farmers in explaining their needs. As actors in the assemblage, HCD Team members were acutely aware of their role in propelling certain trajectories of change toward particular possible futures. To mitigate this potential social power of interventions through innovation and marketing, the fieldwork data was collected and analyzed to make explicit these needs in the "voice of the farmer." Expert interviews, knowledge of the business model, and a historical perspective on social forces at work in the social structure were essential components of the project. The fieldwork was designed step-by-step, taking into consideration the political-, social-, and kinship-related enablers and barriers which underpinned the social foundation of the farmers' worldviews. The team's objective for the analysis was not to tell the client how to sell the product from the point of view of Western designers, but to demonstrate how the product might meet the needs of farmers as agents and coagents in shaping their own circumstances through agricultural change. For the HCD Team, understanding the cultural and historical context and empathizing with the role of the farmer in the assemblage were crucial to the project's success.

The HCD Team conducted field visits in two provinces (Siem Reap and Oddar Meanchey) at two different times (December 2013 and February 2014). The goals during the Hear Phase were to gather data through in-depth interviews with farmers during farm visits, field visits with sales

Table 1.1   Research Design

	Description—IDEO Design Toolkit	Methodology
Hear Phase	Prepare for and conduct research, collect stories and inspiration. Observe and understand people's needs and desires.	Conduct field visits to two field sites
Create Phase	Translate field research into insights, themes, frameworks, prototypes, opportunities, solutions that are technically feasible.	Analyze and synthesize data, develop HCD Insights, HCD Frameworks, and Design Principles
Deliver Phase	Realize solutions with financial viability and sustainability in mind to help launch tangible solutions.	Present final marketing strategy

representatives, and meetings with key employees of Lors Thmey. For each of the field visits, the HCD Team broke into three groups composed of a lead ethnographer/designer, a secondary ethnographer/designer, and a native Cambodian hired to interpret.

Two field visits occurred, each located in a different geographical region of the country (see Table 1.2). According to the research plan, each region was selected for its different characteristics such as quality of soil, size of farmer land plots, level of flooding, and ease of access to the market. The first field visit was to Siem Reap where DRIP had been offered both via subsidy (i.e., USAID's Harvest Program) and through consumer sales. Demographics of farmers in this area matched criteria. Adopters and non-adopters were selected for research. The focus of this field visit was exploration. The second field visit was to Oddar Meanchey. In this province, commercial agronomists had sold a significant number of DRIP—showcasing high success rates were possible to attain. The focus of this field visit was to build on the learning from the first field visit by conducting in-depth interviews on key topics.

Table 1.2   Selection Criteria by Field Site

	Field Visit 1—Siem Reap	Field Visit 2—Oddar Meanchey
Farmer Selection Criteria	Broad sampling across the villages	Focused sampling on specific criteria identified in Field Visit 1 (see below)
Village Selection Criteria	**MINIMAL** influence from NGOs	**NO** influence from NGOs
	Minimal influence of Harvest Program	No change from Visit 1
	Farmers commercially minded	No change from Visit 1
	Adopters and non-adopters of DRIP	No change from Visit 1

The team identified other selection criteria for the farmers and for the villages. For example, it employed broad sampling of farmers in Siem Reap and focused sampling in Oddar Meanchey. The villages in Siem Reap had only minimal influence from nongovernmental organizations (NGOs), while the villages in Oddar Meanchey were not influenced by NGOs. In both field visits, the farmers fit the characteristics of commercially minded individuals and included both adopters and non-adopters.

Expert Interviews and Field Visits

The two research teams traveled to each of the field visit sites together. They stayed in a location central to all the selected villages for that field visit. Each morning, the project leader for the research teams contacted the chiefs of the nearby villages. (The chiefs had agreed beforehand to (1) host the research teams in their villages, and (2) help them identify which farmers met the criteria to participate in the study.) Then the teams traveled to their respective research sites.

The team met first with the village chief. The purpose was to ask respectfully for permission to conduct research in the village, learn from the chief about the general character and success (or failure) of the farms in the area, and confirm the request for help in identifying farmers in the village who had qualified for the study. Once the chiefs confirmed the farmer sample, the teams contacted each farmer and agreed on a time that day for a visit.

The team prepared a research guide with items to observe and questions to ask in Siem Reap. Its scope included farming and an anthropologically inspired frame of agricultural knowledge such as growing vegetables, farming, and agricultural equipment and techniques, as well as business, investment knowledge and habits, family values, education, and political influence. By contrast, in Oddar Meanchey, the team used the guide as well as an activity about equipment and the customer journey (where a customer first encounters the product and the steps it may take them to purchase). A card activity consisted of sorting cards with drawings of agricultural equipment (covering all stages of agricultural development) into a sequential purchase pattern. Questions emphasized purchase triggers and barriers and other elements of rationale for the order of cards.

Experts

The fieldwork began with expert interviews with seven senior level members of the client company to learn about the sales process, their goals for the project, their perceptions of the product, how the product worked, their perceptions of the customer, and (for the geographically based managers) the particularities of the area in which they work. The HCD Team met with the seven people for the expert interviews:

- Former Agriculture Program Director (Phnom Penh)
- Deputy Director, Agriculture (Phnom Penh)
- National Sales Manager, Agriculture (Phnom Penh)
- Branch Manager (Kampot Province)
- Branch Manager (Oddar Meanchey)
- Salesman (Oddar Meanchey)
- Salesman (Siem Reap)

Farmers

The farmer research sample was identified through desk research from previous studies and the initial expert interviews with the client. A profile helped to recruit participants:

> Our target is entrepreneurial vegetable farmers. These farmers are commercially minded and they grow vegetables for business rather than for subsistence. They are "wealthier" poor households; they have enough rice to subsist and have diversified basic income sources, allowing the flexibility to consider investing in a vegetable business. These farmers think about Return on Investment (ROI) specifically pertaining to optimizing their limited labor. This audience already has access to ample water, and has invested in basic agricultural inputs including seeds, fertilizers, and possibly some productivity-enhancing mechanization.

Farmers who are commercially minded have the following characteristics:

- Grow vegetables for business rather than for subsistence
- Are open to taking smart risks in farming
- Aspire to make "big" incomes via farming
- Are curious about commissions and how to get a return on investment, among other strategies
- Represent the "wealthier" poor.

The team used the phrase "commercially minded" to account for local context and to incorporate learning from the HCD Team's previous projects with rural farmers.

As Table 1.3 shows, during the first field visit, the teams met with 14 farmers (including two Farm Business Advisors), three village chiefs, and one

Table 1.3 Number and Type of Interviewees by Field Visit

Type of Interview	Number of Interviews— Field Visit 1	Number of Interviews— Field Visit 2
Farmer; Adopters	6	6
Farmer; Non-Adopters	6	3
Farmer; Farm Business Advisor	2	2
Branch Manager	1	3
Village Chief	3	2
Totals for Each Field Visit	18	16

branch manager for the client. These individuals were located in three different villages. In the second field visit (also shown in Table 1.3), the teams met with a total of 11 farmers (including two Farm Business Advisors), two village chiefs, and three branch managers. These farmers also were in three different villages. For both field visits, interviews lasted between one to three hours. Interviews with farmers often included an in-depth tour of their farm and observations of current farming and irrigation practices when possible.

Data Analysis

Data from the expert interviews and field visits was analyzed and synthesized into HCD Insights and HCD Frameworks by a larger Project Team including the HCD Team as well as other members of the iLab. The HCD Team's primary analytical framework was drawn from Design Thinking and focused the formulation of each HCD Insight and HCD Framework into a process of customer need-finding (Brown 2009, IDEO 2009). We applied the HCD Insights and HCD Frameworks to the development of HCD Design Principles to guide the creation of a marketing strategy for DRIP.

The iLab and the HCD Team defined three specific work products. The first was known as HCD Insights. They captured the motivation, needs, or mindsets of human users. HCD Insights represented the *why* behind observed behaviors. They were what users felt and desired but may not have said explicitly. The second work product was an HCD Framework, a visualization of interconnected user insights that provided an "aha!" bigger than the sum of its parts. The third product was a set of HCD Design Principles. These principles identified the most important user needs, and turned them into a clear direction. They became the foundation for a marketing strategy that responded to users' needs.

Upon completion of the interviews, the HCD Team analyzed the data using a specific process developed by the iLab. This process essentially consisted of three phases:

- Storytelling (recounting each of the interviews to the larger team)
- Data recording (listeners writing relevant information from the interviews onto post-it notes, color coded by interview)
- Data organization (sorting the post-it into key themes and patterns).

HCD Insights were developed by crafting one-sentence statements to encompass the data (e.g., observations, quotations) represented in each key theme or pattern. The HCD Insight statement is followed by a descriptive paragraph furnishing the data points that support the statement. In some cases, HCD Insights overlap or correspond to each other in such a way that they are better explained visually. In those cases, we created a HCD Framework. Together, these statements and visuals were sorted into categories, resulting in an HCD Design Principle for each one.

CREATE PHASE: FINDINGS

Findings are organized as HCD Design Principles that were produced as a deliverable for the project, supported by the HCD Insights from which they were created. These findings for the client project emerged from the fieldwork as farmers' needs. Each Design Principle is written as a needs statement, with the supporting HCD Insights (in italics) and descriptions following each HCD Design Principle. HCD Frameworks were created as a deliverable as well; they are meant to give structure and guidance to the client team as it continues to manage sales of the DRIP.

HCD Frameworks

Analysis and synthesis of the findings led to two overarching HCD Frameworks for the study. The first framework represents a new segmentation model for farmers loosely based on Rogers (2003) diffusion of innovations theory. The framework was developed through observations of the differences between two types of farmers. Those farmers labeled "Early Adopters" bought into the idea of success, that is, they *saw and believed from others' experiences,* which led to immediate purchase. Those farmers labeled "Late Adopters" are those farmers who *needed tangible proof from personal experience.* They made incremental purchases and experienced a return on investment with every purchase.

The second framework is a core needs statement with supporting definition from the farmers' perspective. The farmers indicated the importance of "experiencing success." For them, success involved the following elements: (1) no crop failure, (2) being able to access and pay back good debt,

(3) regular and fast cash earnings, (4) crops absorbed by market demand, and (5) increased profitability on the entire farm.

HCD Design Principles with Supporting HCD Insights

See Success from DRIP (Visible Success)

Confidence in an idea comes from seeing others in the village experience success. Farmers have to see others' successful outcomes to believe in a product or technique. Many mentioned, "I saw my neighbor had a good harvest, and then I decided to purchase the DRIP." For some more pro-risk farmers, seeing an example of success instills such faith in the success of the drip, that it triggers an immediate desire to buy.

Seeing even one instance of failure in the village can eliminate confidence in a product. Farmers watch each farm using DRIP in the village. Others' failure becomes "proof" that the DRIP does not work well. One tangible example of failure will spread quickly among farmers in the area, killing purchase interest.

Success is measured both by investments and visible improvements to assets. Farmers explained success as both the things they want to purchase for the farm as well as visible improvements in financial status. Indicators of success included investments in expensive farm tools as well as motorbikes/ motorcycles (commonly referred to as "motos"), trucks, and home upgrades such as solar panels.

Experience Success Without Risk (Tangible Success)

For some farmers, trying is believing. The HCD Team observed some farmers who need to "try first" to believe. Changing their farming approach drastically seems risky, acting as a barrier for adopting DRIP. When a successful crop harvest brings in a quick cash return, it can fuel the desire to reinvest and expand growing capacity.

New Techniques are an accelerator for Early Adopters. Early Adopters are excited about adopting new techniques, as these techniques are perceived to be the ticket to "success."

DRIP is a good investment because the money is paid back quickly. Farmers explained that it was important to be able to pay back the cost of the equipment quickly. When farmers talk about the cost of a DRIP, they state the return on investment in cycles of vegetables. The payback period is considered short because it only takes a few cycles to pay for it.

The first successful DRIP purchase can open a farmer's mind to investing further in new techniques. The HCD Team observed that when farmers tried DRIP even on just a small plot of land, they began to understand the function of each component (e.g., nets, plastic), and how these components worked together to optimize their farm productivity. Farmers who had used the DRIP over many cycles (1) learned how to install and maintain it (e.g., fixing components, cleaning valves, clearing blocked tubes), and (2) changed their opinion of the equipment, calling the maintenance tasks "simple" and the DRIP "easy" to use.

Confidently Sell Various Crops (Sales Success)

Farmers fear the market will not absorb the increased crop. Many farmers associate DRIP exclusively with the first crop demonstrated. Many were unaware that the equipment could be used for a wider portfolio of crops—and some thought only less desirable crops, such as "Thai cucumbers," could be grown with DRIP. They expressed three concerns: (1) they would grow crops too difficult to sell, (2) they would flood the local markets and would not be able to sell all of their produce, and (3) they would not be able to get a good price even for their current product. These perceptions reduced the perceived ROI on the investment, diminishing purchase interest.

Commercially minded farmers understand supply and demand economics and the role that market access plays in them. Farmers who have access to multiple markets are more aware of how correctly targeting the right markets at the right times, with the right crops, could positively affect their profit margins.

Earn Consistent Cash for Reinvestment (Profitable Success)

Diversifying into short-term crops generates regular cash from ongoing harvests. Farmers knew that short-term crops (e.g., vegetables) give higher, more continuous financial return than long-term crops (e.g., rice, cassava). Short-term crops require more labor with more cycles of planting and harvesting. Therefore, farmers consider how to optimize their limited land. Adding vegetable crops allows farmers to move from one annual harvest to continuous harvests—giving farmers important ongoing cash. This cash plays two important functions: (1) it relieves stress around financial budgeting, and (2) it can be reinvested into expansion of the vegetable garden—as long as the crops do not fail.

DRIP is seen as the enabler for adding more short-term crops. "New farming techniques," including DRIP, are viewed by farmers as the mechanism for shifting to short-term crops easily.

DRIP consumes less diesel/gas than a semiautomatic shower. For farmers who are already using a semiautomatic irrigation method, the "jump" to using DRIP is smaller—in both cost and method of irrigation.

Mitigate Fears and Risk of Failure (Worry-Free Success)

Long-term crops provide an important base income—but vegetables are more profitable. Rice and cassava can only be harvested once a year, but they provide the confidence and stability of a secure income foundation. A transition into new, more profitable crops is carefully done, balancing potentially risky new practices with the secure income foundation of old techniques.

Perceived high financial risks are barriers to purchase. Farmers perceived that DRIP involves many high costs upfront, and additional money for maintenance and upkeep along the way. Preparatory tasks also require a lot of labor (e.g., preparing the land), which can cost money if there are not enough family members to do the work. Purchasing components one-by-one allowed farmers to "try" the new techniques in smaller risk increments.

Farmers' fear of crop failure from unknown diseases is a barrier to trying something new.

Farmers' fear of debt becomes a barrier to purchase. Farmers perceive that DRIP will need to be paid with a large, upfront payment and they do not often have this cash on hand. Without a guarantee that the new equipment will work, a high price point seems too risky.

Purchase a Hopeful Outcome (Story of Success)

Creating a Complete Set of products plus services is effective in some areas. Oddar Meanchey was selected as the second field visit site because DRIP already had a high level of adoption in the area. The salespeople in this province bundled all the components of DRIP together into what they called a "Complete Set." In the Complete Set, farmers bought both "new techniques," because they obtained (or received) training, knowledge, and service (e.g., installation, use of DRIP, some help with disease) as well as DRIP.

Early Adopters buy into the idea of the Complete Set as the ticket to big, immediate success. The sale of DRIP as a set versus individual components affects perceptions regarding ongoing costs in the long-term. When DRIP is seen as a combination of different components, each future purchase of plastic and fertilizer is a new decision for the farmers. These purchases add "ongoing costs" that are perceived as painful. When purchasing as "a Complete Set" however, the product is seen as a bigger "investment" offering the much larger benefit of "success." As a result, the view on ongoing costs is different. Farmers do not mind replacing plastic when it is part of maintaining a larger ticket item with a larger perceived benefit in the future.

Invest in a Tangible Catalyst for Commercial Success (Product Success)

Commercially minded farmers look for investments in their farms that allow them to upgrade their portfolios of income generation over time. Farmers

believe that new investments should move them up an investment ladder—
that is, to provide a quicker or larger income alternative than existing sources
in the portfolio. Income from DRIP can help farmers to move up the investment ladder toward a better income portfolio.

DRIP saves time and energy that can be reinvested. Farmers value the time
they save for a few reasons. First, they can invest it in other farm activities
that increase their income, such as tending to their cows or preparing crop
beds on more of their land. Second, there are personal benefits in saving
physical effort and creating disposable time. Third, when labor needs are low,
children can go to school.

DELIVER PHASE: FINAL DELIVERABLE TO CLIENT

Based on the creation of the segmentation framework and the Design
Principles, the HCD Team created three core elements of the final deliverable: a marketing strategy, a new customer journey, and a repositioning of the
product as a Complete Set.

Marketing Strategy

The marketing strategy arose from the suite of HCD Insights and HCD
Frameworks, led by one particular conclusion from the research:

> Farmers that purchase DRIP do so because they buy into the promise of achiev-
> ing "success." The definition of "success" extends beyond a simple crop output
> to include the improvement of one's farm and livelihood for the long-term. To
> experience the "success" delivered by the DRIP, farmers should gain immediate
> cash profit from the sale of a harvest, and see a clear link between DRIP and
> future potential livelihood improvements.

The HCD Team built a marketing strategy focused on creating experiences for farmers to "see and believe" and to "try and believe." The strategy included designing a "trial-like" purchase experience to help farmers
build trust in the product, overcome aversion to risk, develop an investment
mindset, and overcome capital barriers. The marketing strategy needed to, in
effect, help farmers to experience the product before buying it, to give them
the opportunity to taste success before spending money.

The HCD Team also created marketing ideas and illustrative examples to
support the marketing strategy. These examples included ideas such as a Success Guarantee (failure aversion), Local Farmer Testimonial Content (stories
of success), Free Trials on Community Garden "Mini Plots" (successful trial),
a new role for the client called "Market Facilitation and Transport Coordinator"

(sales success), and a suite of support services to be offered by the sales representative; among them were crop selection advice (sales success), disease identification (failure aversion), and market consultation (profit success).

Customer Journey

A customer journey was created that incorporated the marketing strategy, frameworks, illustrative ideas, and where the sales people might encounter barriers in helping non-adopter farmers "Experience Success." The customer journey provided the sales team with a step-by-step visualization of their customers' experience through the sales process, interactions with the sales team, and use of the product leading up to repeat purchase(s). Visual examples were provided with tools and/or marketing tactics to use in overcoming barriers in each of the phases: Interest, Purchase, Experience, and Repurchase. For the Early Adopters, "seeing is believing"—meaning they reach the first purchase without having to have a "small taste of success" through a trial like the Late Adopters. From the point of Purchase, through Experience to Repurchase, all farmers follow the same journey. The customer journey was created to give high-level information about all farmers from all villages to the sales team on how to think about dissolving potential hurdles they may encounter in making a sale of DRIP and converting non-adopters into adopters.

Repositioning the Product in The Marketplace

The recommendation was made that the "Complete Set" (i.e., "new techniques" through training, knowledge, and service, as well as DRIP) include not just "equipment + services," but also the combination of four elements crucial to success for both Early and Late Adopters. In the new marketing strategy, messaging for the Complete Set was to incorporate four key elements: "Product + Service + Knowledge + Market Access."

With the new positioning as a Complete Set, DRIP could also be merchandized with a holistic "success" plan. This plan included messaging and marketing tools that showcased success (ongoing costs become investments, labor intensive steps of short-cycle crops could be eliminated), and packaging that demonstrated the kinds of profits possible through quantifying and connecting the sales of vegetables to the cost of future tangible investments (ten cucumber harvests equals money to purchase a cow or upgrade your house). In this way, the sales team would sell success as a key benefit—supporting each farmer with service elements—and directly tying the "Complete Set" to the imagined future in the farmer's mind. The intention of the new positioning was to *make an explicit connection between the purchase of a tangible product and the hopes, or imagined possible future, of the farmer.*

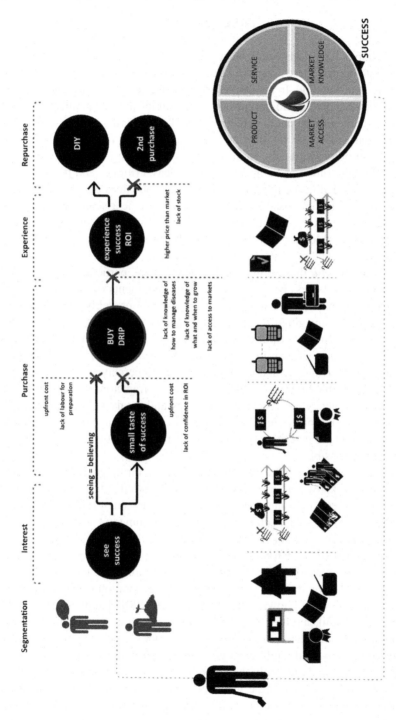

Figure 1.2   Customer Journey.

DISCUSSION

Human hopes have limits and must rely on other agents to bring possible futures into being. These agents of hope must be acceptable within the culture and context of the time. In a recent book of design anthropology case studies, the authors explore "ethnographies of the possible" and how anthropologists might study the future spaces in the minds and considerations of their subjects and "the basis of which we imagine and create possible futures" (Smith et al. 2016, 4). In other words, the future is not in the future—it is in the present. They define the future as "a multiplicity of ideas, critiques and potentialities that are embedded in the narratives, objects and practices of our daily lives" (Smith et al. 2016, 1). Possible futures are actors in the assemblage. They are "not stable and fixed but fluid and temporary. The component parts ... are heterogeneous" (McCabe, this book). Simply stated, we live *with* the future, not just *for* the future.

While living *with* these futures in the assemblage, particular objects (e.g., embodiments of hopes) become catalysts for and agents of cultural change. The purchase and use of particular things are actions deliberately taken to move toward an imagined future in a manner of someone's own choosing. If agency is a "sociocultural mediated capacity to act" (Ahern 2011) and "capacity to create effects in the world" (Miyazaki 2004), then I suggest that humans have agency and use their capacity to perceive and act upon the world, and possible futures, according to a desired trajectory of change. When limits of this agency are reached, extensions and catalysts are activated. In this case, farm equipment and "modern practices" challenge traditional ways of farming, and are emerging as morally acceptable "innovations" which are financially accessible.

Before drip irrigation and "modern practices" of farming, children in Cambodia came to know through farm labor and knowledge transfer from their parents and other family members. Today, when they attend school for a longer duration of time, the mechanisms of how they come to know shift greatly. Books, teachers, and other forms of information also shape how they make sense of the world. In the forefront of the ethnographers and designers' minds and discussions, then, became the idea of how a simple transaction of the sale of DRIP could have an impact on how an entire generation of children experiences education and knowledge formation differently than their parents. In effect, the hopeful purchase of DRIP can set a trajectory of change toward the possible future where children encounter books, teachers and secondary school education—and might even grow up to "have a job with a pen."

Thus, we can study not only the anthropology of future-making, what is in "possible futures," but also the mechanisms by which people "act upon the world" to bring them into being. Understanding how hopes and never-empty futures (Mazé 2016) become tangible agents of future-choosing—as drip irrigation equipment—illuminates one way that people intentionally make decisions in the present to explicitly change the course of their lives toward a desired possible future. In this case, parents' hopes for the possible futures of their children become embodied in drip irrigation products. A full realization of the cultural change taking place in the lives of farmers who are adopting new ways of farming will occur when the lives of their children change in aggregate.

The role of "innovation" in cultural change is crucial as it relates to both the recipients (customers) and the brokers (designers). Miyazaki (2005) stresses that one of his aims was to "investigate how certain economic concepts and neoliberal ideas served as sources of hope, that is, reorientation of knowledge" (2005, 5). Hage (2003) has argued that the generation of hope relies heavily on individuals' perceptions of their government and leadership. In the Cambodian context, it could be argued that leadership can also arrive in the form of outsiders—non-Cambodians working in international development organizations. Therefore, in this case, if hope is, as Miyakai argues, "anchored in [an] understanding of culture as a creative and inventive process," than the question of how innovation and its designers act as agents of hope is a salient one (2005, 1). In this case, it is not "society" that is the mechanism of distribution of hope. There are both intangible ideas and tangible objects delivered down every dirt path to every last-mile farm in Cambodia through the learning of modern practices and the sales of agricultural products such as DRIPs and diesel engines. For the practitioners, the HCD project challenged self-reflexivity regarding the value of skills and labor in a non-Western marketplace and their own role as agents of cultural change—which may or may not be desired. When paying attention to the worldview of the farmers and giving voice to their needs, practitioners began to perceive themselves as acceptable agents. In any case, there is agency among all the component parts of the assemblage.

The concept of hope as *the future in the present* is relevant also when considering issues of identity. If history—both cognitive and embodied—plays a considerable role in the formation of the "habitus" as explained by Bourdieu (1977), then might the future carry generative weight as well? Bourdieu's theory explains how dispositions are generated by past experiences. Dispositions are manipulated by both experiences of the past and hopes for experiences of the future. If memory forms a connection between an individuals' self-awareness in the past and present—might hope forge this same kind of connection between one's self-awareness in the present and the future? Cambodian farmers believe their hopes will be fulfilled when their children receive a secondary school–level education. Their hopes for a possible future create a disposition toward investment in farm equipment, and real changes in farming practices. If memory is an actor in the process of the transmission of culture as the past in the present (Berliner 2005), then hope is an actor in the process as well as the future in the present.

CONCLUSION

Seeing hope as an agent for change allows us to pay attention to the "capacities of individuals and networks of people to shape their circumstances through innovation and invention, by influencing others in transaction, making use of innovated technologies, beliefs, or novel institutional practice to bring about some degree of intentional change" (Ervin 2015, 6–7). It also brings up questions about the origins and distribution of hope itself.

Hage (2003) argues that "Societies are mechanisms for the distribution of hope," and the capacity of a society to distribute hope varies according to levels of particular concepts of "worrying" and "caring" among its citizens (2003, 3). In his framework, a "caring society is essentially an embracing society that generates hope among its citizens and induces them to care for it. The defensive society ... suffers from a scarcity of hope and creates citizens who see threats everywhere. It generates worrying citizens and a paranoid nationalism" (2003, 3) in which people essentially hoard—and do not share—hope out of fear and worry. His ethnographic work focuses on the effects of global capitalism ("characterized by the rise of transnational capital, a transnational capitalist class, and a transnational state" [Robinson, 2014]) and neoliberalism ("market relations and market forces operate relatively freely and play the predominant role in the economy" [Kotz, 2015]) in Australia. His work provides an interesting contextual juxtaposition with post-genocide Cambodian society that is only beginning to emerge as a player in the global economy. According to this framework, global capitalism and neoliberalism have considerably weakened societies' "capacity to distribute hope" (2003, 30). Questions emerge about the distribution of hope through other societal structures and influences (e.g., innovation, intervention, investment) and to the rural poor. Will the situation arise, as he argues has occurred in Australia, where there is a "relationship between the rise of neo-liberal economic policy and the shrinking capacity of the nation-state to distribute hope?" (2003, 3)

In Cambodia, where trust of, and expectations for, the nation-state has an unstable history and a current fragility, hopes are embodied in innovation and interventions (funded by entities outside the nation-state—such as foundations and other international development organizations). Deliberate investment in irrigation equipment in the agricultural assemblage, allowing for the mechanization of farm labor, in aggregate, can fuel a trajectory of increasing the educational level of the rural population at large. In other words, how farmers act upon the world in the present depends on their access to other agents of hope—elements in the assemblage such as designers, innovative irrigation equipment, and teachers. If they desire, and gain, such access, they can bring about a possible future in which their children go to school past the elementary level and, eventually, enter professions other than farming. Thus, hope is an agent of cultural change toward a possible future in which Cambodian children grow up to "have a job with a pen."

NOTES

1. Special thanks to the team at the iLab: Nadia Campos-Soriano, Sinin Kith, Ariana Koblitz, Helen Lerums, Phearak Maksay, Kevin Mueller, Mariko Takeuchi, Tommy Liu, our translators, and the staff at iDE Cambodia and their Country Director, Michael Roberts. A debt of gratitude also to Matthew Engelke and, respectfully, Olivia Harris for their instrumental support in challenging my anthropologist mind and obsession with hope at the London School of Economics where the seeds of this chapter were planted years ago.

REFERENCES

Berliner, David. 2005. An "impossible" transmission: Youth religious memories in Guinea-Conakry. *American Ethnologist* 32(4): 576–592.

Bloch, Ernst. 1986. *The principle of hope. vol. 1*. Cambridge, MA: MIT Press.

Boua, Chanthou and Ben Kiernan. 1982. *Peasants and politics in Kampuchea, 1942–1981*. Armonk, NY: M.E. Sharpe.

Bourdieu, Pierre. 1977. *Outline of a theory of practice*. Cambridge, UK: Cambridge University Press.

Brown, Tim. 2009. *Change by design: How design thinking transforms organizations and inspires innovation*. New York, NY: HarperCollins.

Chandler, David P. 1991. *The tragedy of Cambodian history: Politics, war, and revolution since 1945*. New Haven, CT: Yale University Press.

Crapanzano, Vincent. 2003. Reflections on hope as a category of social and psychological analysis. *Cultural Anthropology* 18(1): 3–32.

Csordas, T. J. 1997. *Language, charisma, and creativity: The ritual life of a religious movement*. London: University of California Press.

Deneen, Patrick J. 1999. The politics of hope and optimism: Rorty, havel, and the democratic faith of John Dewey. *Social Research* 66(2): 577–609.

DePaul, Kim, (Ed.). 1999. *Children of Cambodia's killing fields: Memoirs by survivors*. Compiled by Dith Pran. New Haven, CT: Yale University Press.

Ervin, Alexander M. 2015 *Cultural transformations and globalization: Theory, development, and social change*. Boulder: Paradigm.

Field Guide to Human-Centered Design, IDEO. Last accessed March 20, 2017. http://www.designkit.org/resources/1

Fong, Vanessa L. 2004. *Only hope: Coming of age under China's one-child policy.* Stanford, CA: Stanford University Press.

Hage, Ghassan. 2003. *Against paranoid nationalism: The search for hope in a shrinking society.* Annandale, AU & London: Pluto Press Australia and The Merlin Press.

HCD Toolkit, IDEO. Last accessed March 20, 2017. https://hcd-connect-production.s3.amazonaws.com/toolkit/en/download/ideo_hcd_toolkit_final_cc_superlr.pdf

Kiernan, Benedict. 1985. *How Pol Pot came to power: Colonialism, nationalism, and communism in Cambodia, 1930–1975.* New Haven, CT: Yale University Press.

Kiernan, Benedict. 2008. *The Pol Pot regime: Race, power and genocide in Cambodia under the Khmer Rouge, 1975–1979.* 3rd ed. New Haven, CT: Yale University Press.

Kiernan, Benedict. 2007. *Genocide and resistance in Southeast Asia: Documentation, denial and justice in Cambodia and East Timor.* New Brunswick, NJ: Transaction Publishers.

Kotz, David M. 2015. *The rise and fall of neoliberal capitalism.* Cambridge, MA: Harvard University Press.

Mazé, Ramia. 2016. *Design and the future: Temporal politics of 'making a difference.'* In *Design anthropological futures.* Rachel Charlotte Smith, Kasper Tang Vangkilde, Mette Gislev Kjaersgaard, Ton Otto, Joachim Halse, and Thomas Binder (Eds.), 37–54. London, UK: Bloomsbury Academic.

Miyazaki, Hirokazu. 2004. *The method of hope: Anthropology, philosophy, and Fijian knowledge.* Stanford CA: Stanford University Press.

———. 2005. Introduction to the "Hope" panel. Annual Meeting of the American Anthropological Association. Washington, DC.

Robinson, William I. 2014. Global capitalism: Crisis of humanity and the specter of 21st century fascism. *World Financial Review.* Last accessed March 20, 2017. http://www.worldfinancialreview.com/?p=1799

Rogers, Everett M. 2003. *Diffusion of innovations.* 5th ed. New York, NY: Free Press (Simon & Schuster).

Smith, Rachel Charlotte, Kasper Tang Vangkilde, Mette Gislev Kjaersgaard, Ton Otto, Joachim Halse, and Thomas Binder, (Eds.). 2016. *Design anthropological futures.* London, UK: Bloomsbury Academic.

Toren, Christina. 1993. Making history: The significance of childhood cognition for a comparative anthropology of mind, *Man,* New Series, 28(3): 461–78.

Ung, Loung. 2000. *First they killed my father: A daughter of Cambodia remembers.* New York, NY: HarperCollins.

UNICEF. 2012. Last accessed March 7, 2017. https://www.unicef.org/infobycountry/cambodia_statistics.html

The World Bank. 2016. Cambodia. Last accessed February 17, 2017. http://data.worldbank.org/country/cambodia

Zucker, Eve Monique. 2007. *Memory and (re)making moral order in the aftermath of violence in a highland Khmer village in Cambodia.* Ph.D. dissertation, Department of Anthropology, The London School of Economics and Political Science.

Chapter 2

A New Playing Field

Technology Disruption in Higher Education in the United States

Marijke Rijsberman

THE CHANGING HIGHER EDUCATION LANDSCAPE

The slowly building momentum of educational technology development, or "EdTech" for short, exploded into the pundit sphere in 2011, in the wake of publicity about three highly subscribed "MOOCs" (massive open online courses) on artificial intelligence (AI). Several Stanford professors made video recordings of their lectures, added multiple-choice quizzes and assignments, and then posted everything on the Internet, with open enrollment. In short order, 160,000 people enrolled in Sebastian Thrun's course on AI, the first of these three MOOCs. The courses by Andrew Ng and Daphne Koller were launched several weeks later, with similar enrollment numbers. No one had ever contemplated the possibility that academics might be able to command an audience on that scale.

In response, technology prophets predicted the end of higher education, as we know it, at least in the United States. Instantly, MOOCs were off on the first leg of the technology "hype cycle," which is commonly associated with outlandish predictions of world transformation. The central element in these predictions concerned the "unbundling" of the learning experience: expensive degree programs offered within university walls would be replaced with a groaning board of free or very reasonably priced stand-alone courses open to all and conferring "micro-credentials." Professors teaching at any number of institutions would create the courses. Individuals would assemble them into personalized learning experiences. Selingo, for example, envisions generations of students who "will want to absorb and apply knowledge on their terms ... and decide when, where, and how they learn and what it means to have a degree" (2013, 174). This vision of unbundled education, then, involves a welcomed power shift that increases student agency, understood as "the capacity to create effects in the world" (Miyazaki 2004, 7), and transforms higher education into a more open marketplace.

As with any roller coaster ride, the MOOC thrill was soon over. Reality set in, as it became clear that enrollments were massive, but course completions were miniscule. In the high-profile collaboration of Udacity with San Jose State University to provide three for-credit courses as MOOCs, which at least one observer dubbed a debacle (Kamenetz 2013), pass rates were 30–50 percentage points lower than their face-to-face equivalents. Analyses of not-for-credit MOOCs put completion rates at 6.8% (Jordan 2015) and 4% (Perna et al. 2013). By 2014, a Gartner report listed MOOCs as one of the education technologies that were "sliding into the trough" (Lowendahl 2015). The term "MOOCs" manages to have an old-fashioned ring to it now, and the prophets have moved on to other topics, such as space travel, self-driving cars, and synthetic life forms. At the time of this writing, American universities are still standing, still offering the same bundled degrees, still espousing the same teaching principles, and still turning away applicants in large numbers.

However, the slower cycles of cultural change are beginning to reveal fault lines in the assemblage of higher education. There is a steady stream of books by writers who have studied the issues in detail. They still envision major changes to traditional practices in higher education, in large part driven by serious challenges in the traditional model, at least in the United States. These challenges include:

- Cost-shifting to individuals, with sticker-price increases far outstripping inflation year after year as a result of government disinvestment, with a shrinking share of college and university budgets underwritten by state and federal governments
- Rising student loan debt, coupled with rising student loan default rates
- Commodification of the college experience, in the wake of the introduction of college rankings in 1983, coupled with huge variance in pricing and outcomes
- Low graduation rates for all but the top-tier institutions in the higher education market
- A disconnect between skills needed on the job and skills taught in college and graduate programs
- Significant un- and underemployment of recent college grads as a result of recession and postrecession weakness in the labor market.

Similar descriptions of current challenges to higher education are offered by Selingo (2013), Mettler (2014), Carey (2015), Craig (2015), DeMillo (2015), and McGee (2015). Juszkiewicz (2015) shows a six-year graduation rate of 40% for two-year degrees at community colleges. Lynch et al. (2010)

shows low graduation rates at for-profit schools, coupled with high debt, while Kroeger et al. (2016) emphasize unemployment and underemployment of recent graduates. These changes are coupled with rising degree requirements in hiring trends in the United States. A 2013 survey found that 30% of employers started hiring college graduates for positions previously requiring a high school diploma in the previous five years, while 20% of companies had started hiring graduate degree holders for jobs previously filled by college graduates (Career Builder 2014). The trend appears to be accelerating, as the same survey in 2015 saw increases to 37% and 27%, respectively (Career Builder 2016). Ferguson (2013) suggests that companies cite some benefits from hiring higher skilled workers in terms of quality of work, productivity, and various other metrics. The effect of this shift to higher educational requirements for workers is to decrease the job-market value of the high school diploma and college degree.

Overall, higher education in the United States has changed drastically in recent decades, in large part by failing to respond to new financial realities. Schools have upped the ante on the admissions side, in a mad scramble to fill the prospective student pipeline by emphasizing on-campus attractions. But very little progress has been made to adjust to the new economics of higher education and the new realities of the labor market. As a result, where colleges and universities were once an engine of social mobility, they now reproduce class structure and tend to magnify inequality. Mettler explains the phenomenon this way: "nearly all of the those from the highest income group who start college—97 percent—gain diplomas by age twenty-four ... compared to just 23 percent of those in the bottom quartile" (2014, 25). High graduation rates at the most expensive private institutions and low graduation rates at community colleges and for-profit professional schools (disproportionately serving lower income students) are associated with differences in socioeconomic status.

Where the emphasis on general intellectual development in the curriculum may once have been appropriate, as nearly all graduates would find meaningful and well-paid employment, the disconnect between the curriculum and the skills needed in the world of work can now seem startlingly misguided, even unconscionable. Speaking from the perspective of a university administrator, McGee explains, "What we believe is essential and what the market believes is essential don't match" (2015, 66–7). He points to a steep rise in the number of people who say that college is necessary for a successful career. "More than half of all Americans today believe that a college education is necessary to succeed in the work world, up from just 31 percent in 2000. Nearly half also believe that the primary purpose of college is to teach specific skills and knowledge that can be used in the workplace" (71). What the Internet has made possible, this shift in expectations makes attractive:

technology-enabled, career-focused learning experiences at a much lower price. The market does indeed seem favorable for other changes to cascade from these fundamental ones.

However, the market does not go to school. Individuals are the ones who make decisions for themselves, sometimes in consultation with their families, based on individual needs and values, doing individual cost calculations, and working with specific ideas about the specific outcomes they anticipate—all with imperfect access to data. They either accept the status quo or seek out alternatives, and they are unlikely to pay much attention to expert predictions of impending change in higher education. Students will play an important role in influencing which educational roads will be paved in the future and which will be abandoned. This chapter investigates their predicaments and the choices they make to create a viable future for themselves.

DATA AND METHODS

Insights presented here into individual perspectives on technology-mediated higher education are based on two years of work (2015–2016) as a lead researcher with Coursera. The company started offering online higher education in 2012 through partnerships with top-tier universities. In all, nearly 500 people who identified themselves as having an unmet educational goal of some sort were included across approximately thirty separate qualitative product research studies, using methodologies commonly used to support the product development lifecycle. My colleagues and I conducted interviews, participatory design sessions with both individuals and groups, concept testing, and surveys. The studies focused on a wide range of topics from very general inquiries concerning needs, preferences, decision-making processes, and course selection criteria to highly specific topics related to aspects of the payment, learning, and credential experiences of online courses. Most studies consisted of 10–12 participants, who were prequalified by survey and then selected to represent a range of characteristics, needs and behaviors. Some studies were conducted in person, while others were conducted using video conference software with screen sharing. All research sessions were video recorded to aid in analysis.

The Coursera research team talks to all study participants about their career goals, what education they need to realize their goals, how they plan to get that education, and what motivates their choices. About half the study participants on whom our insights are based were existing Coursera users. The remaining participants, recruited via Craigslist and a variety of paid recruiting services, were non-Coursera users who had engaged with other kinds of learning experiences, both online and offline, tech-mediated and human-mediated. Study participants, ranging in age from 22 to 65, were drawn from all continents except Antarctica, with a large majority living in the United States, Canada, and the United Kingdom. In this chapter, I focus on the experience of US students, as they are most directly relevant to the predictions about the future of US higher education that experts make. Other geographies have their own assemblages and deserve their own separate investigations.

Analysis is rapid, and findings are immediately fed back into product iterations, which will either go into future qualitative research or feed into product experimentation or A/B testing, an experimental approach to optimize product-market fit by offering different variants to similar groups of users. Those experiments are analyzed by the company's data scientists. When the researchers identify patterns in the qualitative data that are not validated through product experimentation, they are independently quantified and validated by the data science team as well. Qualitative observations about types of users, for example, are quantified in segmentation studies by the data science team.

OVERVIEW OF THE EDTECH FIELD

EdTech is a complex, crowded, and dynamic field, and much of it directly supports traditional practices and institutions rather than putting pressure on them. A brief overview of current types of EdTech most relevant to higher education is useful for understanding student decision-making processes. I divide up the field into five different high-level categories:

- Administrative Automation—Learning management technology is the least disruptive to established educational practices. Educational institutions use it to automate administrative processes at all educational levels. Blackboard and Canvas are typical examples. Administrative automation does not fundamentally affect the nature of the education offered.
- Enrichment—Technology is often used to enrich classroom instruction within the context of traditional institutions. An example of enrichment is the much-hyped use of tablets to deliver learning experiences, often by relying on gamification to make learning more engaging. This category of EdTech is heavily embroiled in battles over the quality and politics of public education at the primary and secondary levels. I count the higher education phenomenon of "flipped classrooms" in this category also. A "flipped classroom" is a course experience in which students watch video lectures and do online assignments for their homework, freeing up class time with the professor for discussion and problem-solving practice.

- Replacement—Educational technology can be used to replace classroom instruction, in two ways. First, many traditional institutions of higher education now offer part of their curriculum online, as a cost-cutting measure, replacing live interaction in a classroom with recorded lectures and automated testing. By 2011, a third of college students were already taking at least one of their courses online (McGee 2015, 78), and the numbers are likely to have increased significantly in years since. Second, entire degree programs are offered by online delivery. For-profit schools spearheaded these online degree programs, but not-for-profit and public colleges and universities are following suit. For both forms, a formal admissions process is maintained, the curriculum is bundled, and the anticipated endpoint is still any of the traditional degrees. Another important element for the learner is that the instructor and staff still provide grading and feedback, which keeps enrollment numbers at or near the traditional scale.
- Open Access—A separate category involves access to university instruction outside of university walls, whether we think of these walls as physical or digital. MOOCs fit into this category. Courses that were only available to admitted students are now available to anyone who has access to a computer and an Internet connection. While university professors and the traditional concept of a college course are central in this category, both traditional elements of admissions and the degree are left behind. Grading and feedback are typically shifted to peers, practices that allow for huge increases in scale and are experienced as the single biggest drawback by enrollees. The most prominent providers in this category are Coursera, EdX, and MIT Opencourseware.
- Nonacademic Instruction—The final category of interest is the emergence of skill-based, career-focused learning opportunities that are completely outside the realm of colleges and universities. They include services like Codecademy, Udemy, Lynda, Kahn Academy, Treehouse, and Udacity, which offer self-paced learning experiences. These opportunities have no formal admission or traditional credentials like degrees and are delivered by nonacademics. The rising phenomenon of "boot camps" (e.g., Dev Bootcamp, to name just one) also fits in this category, although the majority of them are in-person "immersives" and not tech-mediated.

Of these five categories, the last three are most directly relevant to the shifting cultural assemblage surrounding higher education. Categories 4 and 5 are, or claim to be, competitors to traditional higher education, promising access to high-paying professions through micro-credentials rather than through traditional degrees. They are the prime examples of the unbundled learning experience that is available at the moment. While it may be tempting to label these options as the new assemblage, it is probably more important to remain

Table 2.1   Learning Experience Elements by Category

Elements	3-Replacement	4-Open Access	5-Nonacademic
Academic instruction	✔	✔	-
Traditional degree	✔	-	-
Admissions	✔	-	-
Expert grading/feedback	✔	-	-
On-campus experience	-	-	-
Face-to-face instruction	-	-	-
Cost	$$-SSS	$	$

aware of continuing change in available options, as offerings in categories 4 and 5 are still developing. As Table 2.1 shows, categories 3, 4, and 5 dispense with at least a few of the elements of the traditional experience: face-to-face instruction, the immersive on-campus experience, the admissions process, traditional degrees, and instruction by an academic (as opposed to an industry professional or a peer). The price tag can change drastically, though it does not always.

Technology-mediated alternatives to the traditional experience of college or graduate school have the effect of making these basic elements optional. This optionality empowers students to consider the value of each element and choose learning experiences with only those elements they like, at least theoretically.

FINDINGS: THE EMERGING TYPES OF EDTECH CONSUMERS

In our labs, we occasionally see a person who dropped out of college, or even out of high school, and who has been successful, having found a way to make a good living with self-taught technical skills or entrepreneurial instinct. However, the overwhelming majority, though bright, positive, and self-motivated, do not evince such a high level of agency that they feel they can easily let go of the structure and "signaling value" (the ability of a credential to convey knowledge and competence) of a degree. Indeed, almost without exception, EdTech consumers attempt to achieve a finely calibrated balance between making independent choices on their own terms and accepting standard structures created for them. In other words, EdTech categories 3, 4, and 5 are an experiment on the part of learners to determine how much agency to claim (by embracing the new open models) and how much to give up (by adhering to traditional structured forms), so they can reach their goals.

This tension between individual agency and institutional structure, or unbundled learning and traditional degrees, is best understood by types of

Table 2.2 Needs by Learner Type

Needs	Non-degree Holders	New Career Seekers	Career Adjusters	Career Advancers	Hobbyists
Degree/Credit	High	Low	Medium	Low	Low
Micro-credential	Low	High	High	Low	Low
Career-oriented content	High	High	High	High	Low
Curriculum	High	High	Medium	Low	Low
Real-world projects	Low	High	High	Low	Low
Community of peers	High	High	Medium	Low	Low
Placement services	High	High	Low	Low	Low

students, based on employment status and career goals. I distinguish between nondegree holders, new career seekers, career adjusters, career advancers, and hobbyists, as shown in Table 2.2. Different types of learners care about different aspects of the learning experience. Because these aspects map partially but not completely to the categories of EdTech inventoried in Table 2.1, most learners have a choice of (imperfect) options.

Nondegree Holders

The majority of people in our studies who do not have a four-year degree tell stories of hitting a very real wall that stands in the way of their career advancement, including government hiring practices, union rules, job openings that require degrees, and applicant pools in which those degrees are well represented. Most in this nondegree holder groups conclude that they have to get a four-year degree to open up new career opportunities. Typically, the first question they ask when exploring a MOOC platform is whether the courses carry transferable credit. Debi, who dropped out of college when she had her kids, spoke for many who have not yet earned a four-year undergraduate degree. She works in an accounting firm and she cannot advance in the company without getting an undergraduate degree. When she found out that Coursera courses do not offer transferable credit, she asked, genuinely nonplussed, "Then why bother?" This is not to say that Debi and others like her have no interest in learning something. Rather, for this group, a degree is often the point of the exercise, not the learning it represents.

It is worth noting that many nondegree holders have some credits to their name, as they may have tried a traditional degree program at some point in the past. In fact, many have made some progress at multiple institutions, as the vagaries of life may have taken them from one community college to another. In the traditional model, they lose credits every time they enroll in courses at a different school.

New Career Seekers

Many new career seekers we see in our studies have followed accepted wisdom and advice of parents and counselors, went to college, and promptly stalled out upon graduation. New graduates often do not find the kind of work one would associate with a college degree. For example, John Joseph graduated with a BA in Communications and has been working part-time in retail since then. Michael graduated with a major in Business Administration and has not been able to find a full-time job at all. Brittany finds that her major in design did not teach her the right design process or tools to qualify for the online design careers that have plentiful hiring opportunities. Ethan majored in Biology and found a job in a research lab, but it is very undemanding work. "I'm not interested in pipetting for the rest of my life," he explains, "and also, you don't make any money." He does not believe that his degree in Biology gives him any other viable options. Many in this group have had an early career experience they consider an outright failure. This unfortunate scenario disproportionately affects young people who graduated into the poor labor market conditions of the Great Recession and its very slow recovery, which hurt the youngest and least experienced job seekers the most. People of color with a college degree were especially likely to struggle in their effort to find full-time work that requires a college degree.

New career seekers are inclined to look for a fresh start specifically geared to a promising niche in the labor market. Choices which many new career seekers will consider include the option of going back to school for another traditional degree more attuned to the labor market, a structured course of study offered on a nontraditional online platform, or boot camps (in category 5) geared to jobs for which labor market demand outpaces supply. I cannot speak to the relative numbers that opt for each of these solutions, but the traditional route is undoubtedly still the most common choice, even though it is by far the most expensive. Taking online courses is the most affordable of all avenues open to new career seekers, but the absence of structure and placement services is a significant downside for new career seekers. Boot camps are often an attractive option for those interested in careers in tech, because they promise a complete makeover measured in weeks or months rather than years. Following this route, one can become a web developer, an Android developer, or an interaction designer in about three months. The typical cost ranges from $15,000 to $20,000.

The boot camp experience is bundled, emphatically so. It is extremely structured, hands-on, and project-focused, often compressed into 12-hour days, up to seven days a week. The entire model refers more to apprentice-style learning modes and completely foregoes the traditional emphasis on critical thinking skills or other skills that would fall under the rubric of intellectual development. Boot camps typically try to create opportunities for students to do real-world projects for companies as part of the curriculum. Participants learn how their new skills are used in the workplace and make connections with employers. Placement services are as much a draw to new career seekers as the learning experience itself. As Evan said, "I know you can't guarantee that I will get a job, but I need to know that X% of the people who finish, they will get a job that pays this much." Boot camps do attempt to make exactly those kinds of promises.

Career Adjusters: Course Correction

Another type of career-oriented student is the person who is looking to make a change in careers by learning a new skill area related to their educational background or work experience. Typically, they are highly educated, but their education may not align with new trends in the labor market or with their personal career satisfaction. Some are "pulled" into a new direction by discovering a new field. Most are "pushed" by disappointment in the efficacy of their prior educational achievement or the pay and opportunities in their current career. One of the study participants in this situation is Erica. She has a Bachelor's degree in Literature, a Master's in Environmental Studies, a poorly paid dead-end job with a not-for-profit in environmental advocacy, and no prospects for anything more remunerative or more promising unless she makes a step-function change of some sort. She has come to the conclusion that she would have to go to law school to be able to have the career in environmental policymaking that she had had in mind when she did her Master's in Environmental Studies. She explained that she would like a degree because "a degree creates a path." By implication, without a degree she is left to hack her own way through the jungle. Erica does not feel that the degree path is open to her, however, because she "can't take on any more debt." Erica is a poster child for the crisis in higher education. Her graduate degree has not delivered on her expectations. She took out significant student loans for her degrees but now the debt forecloses the possibility of going back for another try.

In the past two years, I have heard easily a hundred variations on this particular story. Many of these tales start with the condition of being "stuck," which typically involves a study participant who has followed the traditional educational path. However, the outcomes fell far short of the traditional promise of well-paying work associated with personal and professional growth which earns one the respect of others. Ashleigh is all-but-dissertation in Physics and tried teaching, but she is not making ends meet. Patricia is a teacher, with a BA in History and an MA in Education. She loves teaching, but she cannot pay her rent. Alison has a BS in Math, ended up in IT, and cannot stand it any longer. All of them feel "stuck," and all of them believe they need more education to get unstuck.

In a different version of this story, a somewhat older study participant finds himself or herself "stuck" after a promising beginning. That individual did pretty much the same things that our younger participants did, and the career went well, at least for a while. Then the participant arrived at an impasse—laid off or about to be laid off, with outdated skills, competing with the younger group for few, and perhaps not altogether, desirable positions, and pretty much out of options. Sometimes such participants would reach their fifties before running into the quicksand. Sandra was laid off as a hospital administrator and realized "I had let my skills go a little stale," so she could not get a new job in her old field. Annie realized that she had to have more data analysis skills to be able to secure a full-time position in Human Resources, after working as a consultant while her kids were little. Herbert has recovered from a serious health problem and then realized he has fallen behind younger colleagues in his skills. He wonders whether he could still become a data scientist.

All of these stories make for a kind of modern folk tale in which we encounter scrappy and clever—and highly educated—protagonists, difficult challenges (getting a decent job, unlocking a career worth having), magic wands (degrees), good fairies (inspiring teachers, mentors, friends in the right places), blockers and antagonists (student loan debt, cold-hearted recruiters who reject one's resume in two seconds, an increasing demand for graduate degrees), and monsters (Trump University, Corinthian Colleges, and other for-profit schools with deceptive marketing practices). The one complication that distinguishes these stories from traditional folk tales is the presence of magic wands that turn out to be duds. Some degrees, like Erica's Master's in Environmental Studies, just do not unlock the hoped-for career.

These career adjusters find themselves at a crossroads. They usually consider the following options in this order:

- Going back to school in the traditional manner
- Getting a traditional degree in a nontraditional online program (category 3)
- Adding specific skills and associated micro-credentials to their resume (category 4).

The most obvious choice for career adjusters is the traditional route leading to another traditional degree. There is an overwhelming vote of confidence in degrees—the right degrees, of course—that diverges sharply from the tech advocates' account. Degrees still work to get a career off to a good start or to enable a major change—at least for some degrees, for some careers, and for some situations. The degree is like an "open sesame" in that it can move corporate recruiters to open the first gate on their journey to the treasure. Career adjusters are usually not thinking about the value of a thoughtfully structured education, as opposed to the autodidact's more haphazard learning, when considering the magic properties of a degree. Their confidence in its efficacy derives from its signaling value on their resume, where it gives off a clear signal for which there is, at present, no substitute.

It is not that career adjusters do not value a structured education, instruction by brilliant professors, the immersive on-campus experience, or other aspects of the traditional model. Yet, a significant majority of participants I have talked to over the course of two years proceed on the assumption that a degree delivers more value with respect to getting hired than doing the work one is hired to do. Jen, who works for a fitness company, offers a case in point. She would like to move up into management, from her current individual contributor position. She has been looking at open jobs at the company, and she is confident she has the skill and grit to succeed in some of them. However, a Master's degree, which she does not have, is required to be considered for all of these positions. "There's one that doesn't even say what Master's degree you should have," she points out, "so how can it make a difference?"

Many different factors hold back career adjusters from simply getting another degree, on top of the degree or degrees they already have. Cost is a very big hurdle, but a mismatch between their current life stage and family situation, and the demands of going back to school, is another important obstacle. Career adjusters are typically also extremely aware of the opportunity costs represented by several years of lost income, as they have been earning for a significant period of time. Family obligations magnify the impact of a loss of income over multiple years. Finally, they may find it impossible or extremely unattractive to move. For example, Jason, the accountant, had come to the realization that, if he went back to school to get an MBA, he would have to give up his marriage plans, as his fiancée would not move with him.

For all those reasons, an online degree program—in category 3—becomes a realistic alternative to be considered seriously by career adjusters. Online degrees are not uniformly more affordable than traditional degree programs, but they are certainly possible for the knowledgeable degree shopper who may find a reputable online program that is more affordable than a comparable on-campus experience. Unfortunately, online degrees usually do not fare well in the estimation of prospective students. Career adjusters, like most other types of learners, tend to have a high regard for learning in a traditional setting. They value a curriculum and the face-to-face learning experience. The images in Figure 2.1 represent a range of reasons why career adjusters shy away from an online degree. The images were created by participants during an exercise to compare the relative value of online degrees and online

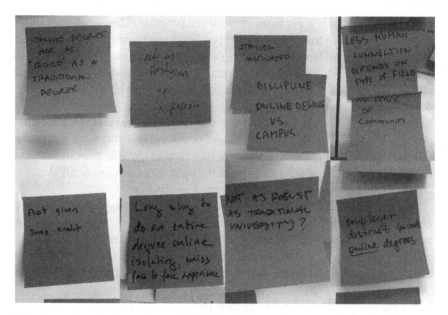

Figure 2.1 Images from a Group Participatory Design Session on the Relative Value Proposition of Online Degrees Versus Online Courses.

courses. As participants were making this comparison, they kept making an additional comparison to traditional on-campus degrees.

A university might tell prospective students that their online degree is as good as their on-campus one, but they harbor doubts. The use of the phrases "not as good," "not as prestigious," and "not as robust" is motivated by the fact that the majority of online learners believe that the traditional immersive social experience contributes to the effectiveness of the learning experience itself. For example, Margery explains, "I got my Bachelor's in an online program, with proctored exams and everything. But I know myself. It is much easier to concentrate when you're in class." Joanne said, "I function better in a classroom environment. It's more a dialogue." The sticky note referring to "no sense of community" in an online degree program refers not only to *not* having opportunities to make friends but also to having to do without the traditional social learning experience. Some of these judgments may be based on untested assumptions, but many base their opinions on personal histories of struggling to stay engaged in online courses. Career adjusters also believe that prospective employers and hiring managers share their doubts about the efficacy of online learning, as evident from the sticky note about "employer distrust" of online degrees. For this reason, virtually all research participants who consider an online degree program ask if they can list their degree on their resume without stating that it was gained in an online program. This skepticism slows down the shift from traditional on-campus programs to online equivalents.

The value of a "bundled" learning experience becomes most salient in comparison to the third option career adjusters consider: taking online courses outside of a degree program (categories 4 and 5). Discarding the degree options implies the removal of a presumably well-thought-out sequence of learning experiences created by a body of experts. This decision point is where the predictions of writers in the EdTech field are put to the test most directly. Prospective learners have a considerable hesitation about unbundling. Just taking courses without the blessing of a (supposedly) knowledgeable third party feels very risky to most individuals.

Consider the situation of Rama, who wants to be a business analyst in a consulting firm. He knows he needs additional data science skills to position himself as an attractive candidate. It is not difficult to find affordable data science courses online. But for all of the courses he can take, he asks, "Are these the right skills?" Rama's question implies two other questions:

- Are these the courses employers look for?
- How do I list these courses on my resume?

His second question goes to the heart of the challenge facing unbundled learning experiences. Bundles help a learner negotiate the transition from, "I took this class in regression analysis and that class in Bayesian statistics" to "I have broad and solid skills in statistics" or even "I am a statistician." In Rama's case, he spells out the transition in terms of certification: "I want to be able to say I am certified, like ... *You* have to say this. You have to say, 'I am a certified Business Analyst.'" The transition in Rama's explanation, from thinking about the claims he might make about himself to concluding that a respected third party should make those claims, exactly captures the challenge of unbundling for career adjusters.

Career Advancers

The fourth group of career learners is heavily represented in categories 4 and 5. Our research at Coursera suggests that this group consists primarily of knowledge workers with satisfying careers, who are looking for new, discreet skills and knowledge. An overwhelming number already has degrees. For example, nearly 90% of Coursera learners who finish courses have at least an undergraduate degree and about half of them have a graduate degree. Study participants who fit the career advancer profile but who are not Coursera users appear to be quite similar in educational background.

Career advancers typically learn something new to keep up with changes in their field. For example, a software engineer may need to learn a new programming language. A marketer may need to learn about search engine optimization. Or a learner may be thinking about a promotion to management and decide to learn people management and leadership skills. Career advancers are usually quite clear on what skills they need. In fact, they stand out by what they do not need: guidance, credit, certification, a curriculum, or a community.

Their first strategy in acquiring the new skill is likely entirely self-guided. Career advancers will often start with learning experiences that are smaller than a course—attend a talk at a conference, watch a YouTube video, read a blog post, sign up for a webinar, try a piece of software, buy (but potentially not read) a book. There are vast troves of learning resources available on the Internet and in the real world that are practical and stay one step below the level of formal education, which by comparison, offers more structure, depth, and breadth. If those how-to resources fail, career advancers may think about a course, whether online or in person. They usually look for an expert who can (1) frame the subject for them and step them through specific skills; (2) furnish opportunities to practice those skills, in a structured fashion from simple to more complex problems; (3) offer feedback on their progress; and (4) provide access to someone who can help them when they get stuck. Help does not have to come from the expert, who also does not have to be an academic. In fact, industry experts may be preferred, as having deeper knowledge of how specific skills and tools are used at work.

Career advancers emphatically do not need a traditional credential or even a micro-credential. As Kevin, a chip designer who was interested in the subject of machine learning, explained, "I don't need a certificate. If I got one, I wouldn't put it on my wall. Maybe the project, if I was really happy with the work, with what I made, I'd be more likely to put that on my wall." Many take great pride in their accomplishments and completed assignments. A high grade is certainly welcome. But the real success criterion for career advancers is success at work: speedy mastery of the new skill, a successful work project, satisfactory interactions at work, an improved performance review, or even a promotion.

There are two reasons behind career advancers' indifference to credentials, of any size. First, credentials help one get hired in the absence of relevant work experience. Career advancers already have a job, and they do have the relevant work experience should they need to get hired in the future. If they do opt to pay to get a credential, it is often more about self-motivation than about getting the credential, since the payment increases the likelihood that they will find the time to study.

Another characteristic of career advancers is the confidence they derive from their own past record of success and the high degree of self-efficacy they have acquired along the way. Their confidence enables them to be successful in online courses with minimal guidance, whether in the form of advice on what to learn or in the form of coaching in the face of challenges. They are not easily discouraged or frustrated when encountering difficult material. This learner type is in a position to exercise agency to the fullest extent. They are avid consumers of fully unbundled learning experiences. In sum, online courses in categories 4 and 5 and career advancers are a marriage made in heaven. Advancers do not need these courses to be part of something bigger, like a degree program or a smaller bundle. And they love the flexibility of learning wherever they happen to be and whenever they have some time available. What the online offerings replace for them, though, is not the core offerings of colleges and universities, but rather their extension programs, which are already unbundled.

Hobbyists

The last group of learners does not have a career goal and are strongly interested in the open access category (4). The hobbyists learn with an eye to intellectual development for its own sake, almost as a kind of high-brow entertainment. Many of them are older, and they may organize their time in retirement around educational activities, taking courses at their local university as well as online. Most hobbyists loved their own college experience and wholeheartedly subscribe to the traditional educational model. Though embracing a new delivery vehicle, the hobbyists operate within the traditional cultural assemblage, of which they are ardent fans. For them, the unbundled educational offerings are extremely appealing, especially the offerings in the liberal arts. However, they are less inclined to pay for online courses than for classroom-based courses.

DISCUSSION

By now it should be clear that many of our participants do not conform to the portrait of the typical student painted in EdTech advocates' books describing an unbundled future for education. Most evoke future students as extremely self-actuated, empowered, and knowledgeable people who will engage with education entirely on their own terms. In Selingo's words, they "will want to absorb and apply knowledge on their terms and decide when, where, and how they learn and what it means to have a degree" (2013, 174). The Thiel Fellowship program, which seeks to lure high school grads away from college and straight into the Silicon Valley startup culture, proves that some people fit this profile even at a very young age (Bowles 2015). But our data suggests that such young people are very rare exceptions. The assurance and self-confidence needed to embrace a fully unbundled learning experience is most common among career advancers, who are older and much more experienced, and among hobbyists, who do not have anything to prove and have only themselves to please. Neither career advancers nor hobbyists are likely to have pursued bundled degree programs in significant numbers before the advent of the new educational technologies. They would rather have availed themselves of such offerings as extension programs, which are also unbundled. The difference that technology disruption has brought them is greater convenience and a liberation from a specific time and place for their learning.

On the other hand, most of the people who would have pursued bundled learning experiences in the traditional model are still likely to do so. Non-degree holders, especially, are strongly focused on the same bundled experiences that have long been offered. Greater standardization supporting course credit as something approximating a universal currency would work best for these students. A universal course currency is especially important for degree seekers as they are often not ready to make a commitment to any particular institution. To the best of my knowledge, there are very few credit-bearing MOOCS and none that offers universally transferable credit. The scarcity of credit-bearing MOOCs means that, under current conditions, degree seekers have a choice between traditional on-campus programs or degree-oriented online programs in category 3 (replacement). The choice is difficult for this group because they tend to prefer the traditional face-to-face instruction of the one option and the lower cost and greater flexibility of the other.

New career seekers and career adjusters are considering and sometimes pursuing new bundles. They look for job placement services, as assurance that their investment of time and money will translate to a good-enough job. They also look for a new kind of certification to help them transition from learning to competence, from a state in which they can claim to have taken a course to a state in which they can claim to have a general competency. That transition, which implies sufficient skill to apply their new knowledge to real-world problems and to keep learning, independently, as the need arises, is implicitly assumed to be achieved by completing a curriculum. The actual efficacy of a curriculum of study is less important than its presumed efficacy in the culture at large. Stated otherwise, it is the job of bundled educational experiences to allow graduates to make certain claims about themselves that are not, at this time, granted to individuals speaking purely for themselves based on unbundled educational experiences. New career seekers and career adjusters feel they need to make precisely such claims about themselves to get a job. For this reason, providers in categories 4 and 5 are beginning to offer more structure and to re-bundle their offerings in new ways.

In fact, most providers in categories 4 and 5 are beginning to provide the basic structure of a degree program even if they do not confer any degrees.

Udacity (category 5) was the first to launch their "nanodegree" in 2014, trying to replicate the structure of the degree and providing a nod to degrees in the naming. Coursera (category 4) launched Specializations in 2014 to attempt to achieve a similar objective. EdX (category 4) started their MicroMaster's in 2016. Lynda (category 5) created Learning Paths in 2016, just before it became LinkedIn Learning. In other words, micro-credentials are growing into medium-sized credentials attached to new bundles, which are like degrees in that they are granted upon completion of a curriculum. They are unlike degrees in that they are more closely optimized to the job market, take less time to complete, cost (much) less, and lead with placement services. This model is very different from Selingo's (2013) confidence that in the near future students will declare what it means to have a degree.

Students are most confident that these new bundles will be efficacious in fields that are newly emerging or undergoing rapid change. The prime example is data science, or any of its subfields like machine learning, artificial intelligence, computational biology, quantitative finance, or business analytics. Neuroscience, genetics, and software engineering are other examples where category 4 and 5 providers of online learning may have an advantage over traditional institutions, since they are more nimble in creating new bundles. Any online curriculum in a new or very fast-moving field is likely to be most efficacious where traditional institutions are lagging. In those fields, there is less likely to be competition from job seekers who have a degree that can trump their online learning without a degree. In addition, the involvement of industry experts in the curriculum design or even delivery of the course or courses also raises the confidence that one is learning the "right skills." If Google is willing to say that the skills taught are the skills it expects its employees to have, it becomes significantly easier for new career seekers and career adjusters to make the gamble on the new options. In other words, employers play a large part in determining what bundles, if any, become a new standard.

CONCLUSIONS

The higher education assemblage is in flux with a trajectory of change toward EdTech. Technology has opened up alternatives to more traditional higher education options. However, these alternatives are still developing in response to the choices made by the different types of learners they serve. The learners themselves are exercising agency to varying degrees; they are helping to create and support not only unbundled educational options, but also bundles that are more career-oriented, shorter, and more affordable. Career advancers and hobbyists are picking and choosing courses as they see fit, and new career seekers and career adjusters are searching for new bundles.

Parts of the higher education assemblage are moving at different rates of speed. EdTech startups are moving relatively fast and appear to be responsive to the need of individuals for unbundled options and for new bundles, depending on life stage, employment status, and career goals. The new bundles must offer a tangible and reliable short-term return on a relatively modest investment, where the return is understood as improved career outcomes. Traditional institutions are changing much more slowly, if at all, to new pressures in the market. Increasing numbers of more affordable online versions of traditional degree programs are probably the clearest indication of significant changes in future offerings. How these offerings will change the institutions that support them is not yet clear.

While the future of EdTech is shaped by the agency of learners, the learners themselves are making their choices in a larger landscape of continuing government disinvestment with cost-shifting to individuals. The cost of traditional education continues to rise, while corporations continue to demand more and more education in their hiring practices. The number of options is increasing in terms of the range of educational experiences accessible to the prospective student. Nevertheless, it is too soon to tell whether the options are affordable, effective, and supportive enough for all who need higher education to succeed in the current economic landscape.

REFERENCES

Bowles, Nellie. 2015. The real teens of Silicon Valley: Inside the almost-adult lives of the industry's newest recruits. https://stories.californiasunday.com/2015-06-07/real-teenagers-silicon-valley, last retrieved May 29, 2017.

CareerBuilder. 2014. Education requirements for employment on the rise, according to CareerBuilder survey. Press Release. March 20. http://www.careerbuilder.com/share/aboutus/pressreleasesdetail.aspx?ed=12%2F31%2F2014&id=pr813&sd=3%2F20%2F2014, last retrieved April 29, 2017.

CareerBuilder. 2015. More than 1 In 4 employers are hiring employees with master's degrees for positions that had been primarily held by those with four-year degrees in the past, according to new CareerBuilder survey. Press Release. March 17. http://www.careerbuilder.com/share/aboutus/pressreleasesdetail.aspx?ed=12/31/2016&id=pr940&sd=3/17/2016 last retrieved April 29, 2017.

Carey, Kevin. 2015. *The end of college: Creating the future of learning and the university of everywhere.* New York, NY: Riverhead Books.

Craig, Ryan. 2015. *College disrupted: The great unbundling of higher education.* New York, NY: Palgrave.

Demillo, Richard A. 2015. *Revolution in higher education: How a small band of innovators will make college accessible and affordable.* Cambridge, MA: The MIT Press.

Ferguson, Matt, Lorin Hitt, and Prasanna Tambe. 2013. *The talent equation: Big data lessons for navigating the skills gap and building a competitive workforce.* New York, NY: McGraw-Hill Education.

Jordan, Katy. 2015. MOOC Completion Rates. http://www.katyjordan.com/ MOOCproject.html, last retrieved June 11, 2017.

Juszkiewicz, Jolanta. 2015. *Trends in community college enrollment and completion data, 2015.* Washington, DC: American Association of Community Colleges, March. http://www.aacc.nche.edu/Publications/Reports/Documents/CCEnrollment_2015.pdf, last retrieved June 11, 2017.

Kamenetz, Anya. 2013. What we can learn from the Udacity/San Jose MOOC debacle. in The Hechinger Report, July 26. http://digital.hechingerreport.org/content/ what-we-can-learn-from-the-udacitysan-jose-mooc-debacle_779/, last retrieved June 11, 2017.

Kroeger, Teresa, Tanyell Cooke, and Elise Gould, Elise. 2016. The class of 2016: The labor market is still far from ideal for young graduates. Economic Policy Institute, April 21. http://www.epi.org/files/pdf/103124.pdf, last retrieved June 11, 2017.

Lowendahl, Jan-Martin. 2015. *Hype cycle for education.* Stamford, CT: Gartner, Inc. July 8.

Lynch, Mamie, Jennifer Engle, and Jose L. Cruz. 2010. *Subprime opportunity: The unfulfilled promise of for-profit colleges and universities.* Washington, DC: Education Trust. November. http://edtrust.org/wp-content/uploads/2013/10/Subprime_report_1.pdf

McGee, Jon. 2015. Breakpoint: *The changing marketplace for higher education.* Baltimore, MD: Johns Hopkins University Press.

Mettler, Susan. 2014. *Degrees of inequality: How the politics of higher education sabotaged the American dream.* New York, NY: Basic Books.

Mintz, Steven. 2012. More than half of job applicants lie on their resumes: Advice for employers to spot falsified resume information. August 2. http://www.workplaceethicsadvice.com/2012/08/more-than-half-of-job-applicants-lie-on-their-resumes-advice-for-employers-to-deal-with-manipulated-resume-information-a.html, last retrieved June 11 2017.

Miyazaki, Hirokazu. 2004. *The method of hope: Anthropology, philosophy, and Fijian knowledge.* Stanford CA: Stanford University Press.

Parr, Chris. 2013. Not Staying the Course. Inside Higher Education, May 10. https:// www.insidehighered.com/news/2013/05/10/new-study-low-mooc-completion-rates, last retrieved June 11, 2017.

Perna, Laura, Alan Ruby, Robert Boruch, Nicole Wang, Janie Scull, Chad Evans, and Seher Ahmad. 2013. The lifecycle of a million MOOC users. MOOC Research Initiative Conference. December 5. http://www.gse.upenn.edu/pdf/ahead/perna_ruby_boruch_moocs_dec2013.pdf, last retrieved June 11, 2017.

Rivard, Ry. 2013. Udacity project on 'pause.' Inside Higher Education, July 18. https://www.insidehighered.com/news/2013/07/18/citing-disappointing-student-outcomes-san-jose-state-pauses-work-udacity, last retrieved June 11, 2017.

Selingo, Jeffrey J. 2013. *College (un)bound: The future of higher education and what it means for students.* Boston, MA, New Harvest.

Chapter 3

Changing Culture through Technology Adoption

Promoting Tablet Use at a Public University

Henry D. Delcore

What happens when a state educational technology project, framed in terms of "equity," collides with student work practices and the consumer market for mobile devices? In 2014, California State University, Fresno (commonly known as, Fresno State), launched a tablet initiative, called DISCOVERe, intended to alter the way faculty teach and students learn. This chapter explores the structures and practices that collided to produce the resulting assemblage and the discursive and practical changes it has wrought. Throughout, I seek to highlight the "heterogeneous, contingent, unstable, partial, and situated" (Collier and Ong 2005, 12) nature of both the assemblage and its effects on institutional discourses and practices surrounding technology and learning.

Building on a framework of assemblage and practice theory, I illustrate how the DISCOVERe assemblage draws from a wide range of social and cultural features, including state institutions and projects, market-based technology developments, claims about educational equity as a social good, and technocentric tendencies in discourse and practice. Importantly, however, no social form is realized without human praxis. Given an assemblage of heterogeneous, sometimes contradictory elements, it fell to specific agents to realize the assemblage in practical form. University administrators, faculty, and students all left their mark on the assemblage, pushing it in some (sometimes contradictory) directions.

There is some evidence that the DISCOVERe assemblage has altered student work practice by offering students courses where they have the opportunity to feel more engaged in their schoolwork. More decisively, however, DISCOVERe has made achieving technological equity—or bridging the "digital divide"—an indispensable part of the University's larger drive for educational equity. Henceforth, talk about student success and equal educational outcomes for a diverse student population will not occur without, at least, registering the question of access to and adoption of the latest educational technology.

Below, after theoretical orientation and methodology, I describe the institutional and discursive elements of the DISCOVERe assemblage. Next, I explore the agentive impact of administrators, faculty, and students, showing how each shaped the formation and direction of the assemblage over time. Then I present an ethnographic vignette, a faculty recognition luncheon, during which the various, competing discourses and agencies of the assemblage were on display. In conclusion, I return to the conceptual utility of assemblage theory in understanding cultural change.

THEORETICAL ORIENTATION

Assemblage theory provides the organizing framework for understanding DISCOVERe. Collier and Ong (2005) draw on the work of Delueze, Guattari, Latour, and others (e.g., Deleuze and Guattari 1987, Latour 1993) to articulate a compelling framework for understanding cultural change. Their version of assemblage theory emphasizes the contingent interplay of structures and practices, producing novel, if contingent, social forms: "As global forms are articulated in specific situations—or territorialized in *assemblages*—they define new material, collective, and discursive relationships" (Collier and Ong 2005, 4, emphasis in original). Collier and Ong's conception of assemblage formation closely follows Deleuze and Guattari (1987), with territorialization as the ordering of disparate elements into an emergent unity, the assemblage.

Assemblage formation, as applied here, hinges on agentive practice, which I conceptualize using Bourdieu's theory of practice (Bourdieu 1977a, 1977b, 1986, 1990; Bourdieu and Wacquant 1992). Bourdieu offers the concept of habitus, or embodied dispositions, as the link between field (structure) and practice (agency) (Bourdieu 1977b, 487). As each actor within the field of higher education at Fresno State enacts a habitus, jockeying for position, leveraging various forms of capital (Bourdieu 1986), they also accomplish the territorialization of the assemblage. Not all actors contribute to the process of territorialization equally: various forms of social, cultural, and economic capital are unequally valued, and some actors have the authority to impose themselves and their visions on others. However, Arnould and Thompson's (2015) interpretation of the role of power in assemblage theory reminds us that power relations are not necessarily hierarchical: they can also intersect and traverse, potentially perpetuating the status quo while also offering ways to contest it (see Arnould and Thompson 2015, 8–9).

METHODOLOGY

The data presented below was derived from four major studies, all conducted at Fresno State: a study of student information and communications technology (ICT) use on campus in 2012–13; a study of student tablet adoption in 2014–15; a follow-on study of student tablet use in spring, 2016; and my own ongoing engagement in meetings and private conversations around the DISCOVERe initiative from 2012 to the present, during which I was both gathering information and advocating for certain kinds of adjustments in the program.

In 2012–13, I led a study of student ICT use on campus with Fresno State anthropologist, Dr. James Mullooly, and research assistants from among students in the Department of Anthropology. The study sought to discover patterns in student ICT use to inform facilities planning on campus (see Delcore, Teniente-Matson, and Mullooly 2014). We conducted 183 hours of observation and 393 intercept interviews with undergraduate students in four specific locations on campus, focused on the relationship among work tasks, devices, and social others in and around the on-campus workspace (e.g., a table in the library). We also recruited undergraduate students to record 20 photo diaries in fall 2012, and 28 in spring 2013. Each student photo diarist recorded images of ICT-enabled schoolwork over a two-week period followed by a debriefing interview with the research team. Data processing and analysis included production of field notes from the observations and interviews, development of a coding system, notes coding, and exploration of emergent themes in student work practice using ATLAS.ti qualitative data analysis software.

In 2014–15, I helped supervise the dissertation research of Philip Neufeld, then an EdD candidate in the Doctoral Program in Educational Leadership at Fresno State. Neufeld's study (Neufeld 2015) aimed to test the universal theory of acceptance and use of technology (UTAUT; see Venkatesh et al. 2003) in the context of institutional promotion of tablet computing at Fresno State. Working closely with me, Neufeld's methods included surveys, photo diaries, and focus groups. A two-phase survey probing the relevance of the UTAUT model for tablet adoption was administered to undergraduate students in DISCOVERe courses (N=655 and N=442). Eleven student participants completed photo diaries focused on tablet use for schoolwork over a ten-day period followed by debriefing interviews. We also conducted two focus groups with students and one with teaching assistants, exploring expectations about tablet use as an aid for learning and sources of influence and support for tablet adoption (see Delcore and Neufeld 2017, and Neufeld and Delcore, in preparation). Analysis of the survey data included regression analysis to discover any relationship among the determinants in the UTAUT model with regard to behavioral intention and use behavior, and to identify the effects of the moderator categories (i.e., race/ethnicity, first-generation student, and gender). We applied a closed set of codes from the UTAUT model to the qualitative data and used an analysis platform (dedoose.com) to analyze code frequency and co-occurrence.

In spring, 2016, I conducted a series of day-long shadows with two Fresno State students, recruited from among the photo diary participants of the tablet adoption study. The students were both male upperclassmen. One was a Latino first-generation college student, the other a white continuing-generation (i.e., at least one parent with a bachelor's degree) student. The participants were chosen because socioeconomic status (SES) and ethnicity were two sources of statistically significant difference we discovered in the survey data with regard to the variables in the UTAUT model. I shadowed each student every other week during the spring 2017 semester, observing and interviewing them on their ICT-related work practices (Delcore 2018). To clarify the themes in this small data set, I closely coded the notes using a code set derived from the previous tablet adoption study.

In their work on assemblage theory, Collier and Ong (2005, 7) emphasize the importance of technological "reflexive practices," or the way institutions and actors debate the most appropriate technological means for achieving some goal. In this spirit, I recognize here my own role as an agent in the assemblage. From 2012 onward, I have been closely engaged in technology policy at Fresno State, particularly as it relates to the DISCOVERe program. For example, in 2013–15, I served on the Information and Educational Technology Coordinating Council, the top-level ICT policymaking committee on campus, chaired by the University president. As an ICT researcher on campus, I have presented my findings at numerous committee and task force meetings, and have met frequently with campus leaders to discuss how research might inform campus ICT policy and programs. In 2015, I joined the DISCOVERe program and participated in the summer institute for course redesign. I taught a DISCOVERe course in fall 2015 and fall 2016. In all of these contexts, I have continually gathered data on the discourses and agents at work while also participating in the process as a faculty member and advocate for various policy positions, often in alliance with some actors and in tension with others.

THE DISCOVERe ASSEMBLAGE

The DISCOVERe assemblage has three parts. First, a major welfare state institution, the California State University (CSU), provides the institutional context within which various discourses and practices around equity and technology collide, resulting in the DISCOVERe assemblage. The second major part of the assemblage is the *discourse on educational equity*, which calls for the CSU to provide the public good of higher education to a diverse population. Further, the CSU is expected to ensure the educational success of all students, regardless of ethnic, racial, or SES background, including efforts to help all students gain access to the technology they need to succeed. However, in the assemblage described here, the optimistic discourse of a state institution leveling the playing field for the public good was dogged by a persistent technocentrism (Papert 1990a, 1990b), in which technology itself sometimes achieved priority over more student-, faculty-, and work-centered ways of understanding the "digital divide." Equity and technocentrism existed in creative tension within the assemblage and their relationship to each other was never fully resolved. The third part of the assemblage, *student work practices*, constitutes one aspect of campus culture that DISCOVERe seeks to change. Importantly, student work practices include the devices students choose to accomplish work, as well as the consumer market for those devices.

The Public University and the Welfare State

The DISCOVERe assemblage starts from a base of a major welfare state institution: the CSU. According to "A Master Plan for Higher Education in California" (California State Department of Education 1960), the mission of the CSU is to provide undergraduate and master's degree educational access to the top one-third of California's high school graduates. At the time of its adoption in 1960, the Plan represented a model welfare state intervention in public life, as it aimed to leverage state resources for a widely accepted public good: an educated population. Serving approximately 474,200 students in 2016 (CSU 2017), the CSU is the largest university system in the United States. It is also highly diverse, including a large proportion of first-generation college students seeking higher education at a relatively affordable, state-subsidized cost.

Fresno State is the main CSU campus serving the Central San Joaquin Valley, one of the largest and most productive agricultural regions in the world. The area is also very diverse with relatively high poverty rates, both demographic factors that are reflected in Fresno State's student body. Of 24,136 students enrolled at Fresno State in fall 2015, 11,048 (46%) identified as "Hispanic" (FSOIE 2015). That same fall, 3,388 (14%) of Fresno State students identified as "Asian," most from among relatively recent Southeast Asian refugee and immigrant populations (FSOIE 2015). Finally, in fall 2015, 70.9% of over 5,000 new undergraduates enrolling at Fresno State were first-generation college students (FSOIE 2015), indicating relatively low SES. Hence, Fresno State is positioned to provide the public good of higher education to a very diverse and often socioeconomically disadvantaged population.

Equity and Technocentrism

The discourse on educational equity forms the second major part of the assemblage. This discourse positions the CSU as a major provider of public good in the form of quality, low-cost education for a diverse population, including students from low SES and minority backgrounds. The equity discourse further calls for CSU campuses to close persistent retention and graduation gaps between white and continuing-generation college students and their underrepresented minority and first-generation peers. This goal remains an urgent task for all campuses, including Fresno State. In 2010, the most recent year for which data is available, nonwhite students who were first-time freshmen (i.e., non-transfers) had a six-year graduation rate that was 14.4% lower than their white peers. The graduation rate for first-generation college students was 10.6% lower than continuing-generation students (FSOIE 2017).

Since the CSU is a teaching-focused institution, much of the equity talk revolves around the best ways to *teach* students who often arrive academically underprepared for college, strapped for resources, and from families lacking the cultural capital that is often valued in higher education (e.g., familial knowledge about how to succeed in college). In particular, the system has emphasized "student-centered learning" as crucial to serving a diverse student body. To accomplish a shift from teacher-centered teaching (e.g., lecture-based) toward student-centered learning, pedagogical innovation has been highly valued, as evidenced by the proliferation of teaching and learning centers at CSU campuses, including the Center for the Scholarly Advancement of Learning and Teaching at Fresno State. Further, as mobile technology has penetrated student life, pedagogical innovation and educational technology have become closely linked.

Administrators and faculty alike invoke the specter of the "digital divide" to describe the challenges of making the most recent educational technology and pedagogical approaches available to students who may hail from rural communities with limited Internet access, or families where the latest devices are not affordable. While the "digital divide" has been criticized as too simplistic (Selwyn 2004), the concept is still a major theme in administration efforts to promote equity.

Dr. Joseph Castro, who took office as Fresno State President in 2013, made the role of technology in educational equity an urgent campus issue when, as one of his first actions, he launched the tablet initiative known as DISCOVERe. It formally launched on January 13, 2014, with the aim of reducing the cost of course materials while transforming pedagogy through the integration of tablet computing into teaching and learning. Specifically, the program sought to facilitate student success through mastery of course content and experience with the latest in tablet technology, plus the use of low-cost digital course materials. The president, the provost (the University's vice president of Academic Affairs), and other campus leaders have repeatedly stressed equity concerns as central to the effort to ensure that all students have access to educational technology, support, and faculty with excellent pedagogical preparation. Program faculty attended an intensive one-week orientation regarding the use of technology in instruction, followed by intensive course redesign with support from instructional designers. Course redesign efforts stressed integration of mobile technology into the curriculum with an emphasis on student interaction and collaboration, both fundamental to student-centered learning.

For fall 2014, the DISCOVERe Task Force, appointed by the president to guide the program, selected one tablet model each for Windows (Lenovo ThinkPad 2), Android (ASUS MeMO Pad), and Apple iOS (iPad Air). Initially, each student who enrolled in a DISCOVERe course could receive a $500 need-based grant toward the purchase of a new tablet device. Each tablet included a one-year 4G data service so students could connect to the Internet from anywhere. The initial costs of the program were funded by an aggressive private fundraising campaign led by the president. In fall 2014, the program included 1,079 students and 32 faculty. By fall, 2015, the program included approximately 5,400 students and 132 faculty, touching about one in six Fresno State undergraduates.

The DISCOVERe initiative puts into practice the widespread contention that all students deserve equal access to the latest, best technology, together with the best pedagogy, to facilitate learning. However, the focus on pedagogy sometimes took a back seat to a focus on the technology itself. For example, President Joseph Castro was talking about the tablet initiative within days of arriving in Fresno in 2013.

"Spending $500 on a handheld computer and less on digital textbooks over a four- or five-year college career simply makes more financial sense," Castro said Monday during a meeting with The Bee's editorial board. "These are emerging to displace laptops in the not-too-distant future, so they can be used to write papers and be on the Internet," he said. (eCampus News 2013)

The president seemed to contend that the very existence of tablets as an increasingly popular device type itself justified a University tablet initiative. The contention that a technology demands our attention because it *exists* resonates with Papert's (1990a, 1990b) characterizations of technocentrism in education (on technocentrism and the broader concept of technological determinism, see also Adas 2006 and Marx 2010). According to Papert, "Technocentrism is the fallacy of referring all questions to the technology" by asking questions like, "Will technology have this or that effect? Will using computers to teach mathematics increase children's arithmetic skills?" (Papert 1990b). According to Papert, such questions deflect attention from more fundamental issues. It is not computers that "will achieve this or that result; it is how we use these things" (Papert 1990b).

Papert recognized that talk about computers in education "might be used innocently as shorthand for more complex assertions" (Papert 1990a, 23). Still, he argued:

> such turns of phrase often betray a tendency to think of "computers" ... as agents that act directly on thinking and learning; *they betray a tendency to reduce what are really the most important components of educational situations—people and cultures—to a secondary, facilitating role.* The context for human development is always a culture, never an isolated technology. In the presence of computers, cultures might change and with them people's ways of learning and thinking. But if you want to understand (or influence) the change, you have to center your attention on the culture—not on the computer. (1990a, 23, emphasis added)

We might take President Castro's remark, quoted above, as a kind of innocent shorthand; in the years to come, he and other campus leaders would articulate other, more nuanced, less technocentric reasons for pursuing DISCOVERe. But the constant slippage between the discourse on equity and pedagogical transformation, and the more technocentric "tablet initiative" talk, remained a major indeterminacy throughout the study period.

Student Work Practices

Student work practices constitute the third part of the assemblage and one aspect of campus culture that DISCOVERe seeks to change. That is, DISCOVERe seeks to engage students in more student-centered, collaborative models of learning by giving them tablets to use in classes where faculty practice a transformed pedagogy. In the encounter between project plans and student work practice, DISCOVERe has met with some success at culture change, but also considerable (though passive) resistance.

DISCOVERe was first conceived as an iPad initiative. After considerable advocacy by some campus IT leaders and faculty, it evolved in a platform-agnostic direction: students were able to choose tablets from across the spectrum of available platforms, a recognition that consumer choice and existing work practices were important features of campus culture. Still, the initiative has struggled to keep abreast of the rapidly changing consumer market for tablets *and* hybrid (2 in 1) devices, which combine the portability of a tablet with the functionality of a laptop, including a standard-sized detachable keyboard and robust computing power. In short, Fresno State has sought to transform teaching and learning on a 25,000-student campus, where time is divided into 14-week semesters, while the consumer market screams ahead with little regard for academic conventions and timelines.

AGENCY AND INDETERMINACY

Administrators, Faculty, and Staff React to a New President's Initiative

Within weeks of arriving in Fresno in late summer, 2013, President Castro announced his intent to launch a teaching and learning initiative centered on tablets. The president had the authority to start the program and hence define some of the terms of the assemblage that emerged around it. In his statements about the program, Castro has repeatedly stressed themes of equity and inclusion, as well as cost savings on textbooks as motivations for launching DISCOVERe. However, during the early days of the initiative, from fall 2013 to launch in spring 2014, faculty and staff actors also exerted influence. My analysis cannot unravel all the political moves actors made to shape DISCOVERe. Instead, I focus on the ways agents in the assemblage engaged the discourse of equity in tension with technocentrism.

The equity-technocentrism tension revolves around the question, why tablets? Tablets certainly had the attention of educational leaders in 2013. Apple launched the iPad in April 2010, and by fall 2011, about 600 school districts nationwide had one-to-one (one device for every student) iPad programs (Koebler 2011). The first university-based one-to-one programs were launched in fall 2010 (Nuez 2010, Stringer and Tobin 2012) and quickly proliferated. President Castro engaged this educational technology context by arguing that cost savings and emerging trends in online, mobile work justified a University tablet initiative.

However, among college students, tablet use remained relatively rare in 2013. According to the unpublished results of a survey conducted by Fresno State's office of Technology Services in spring 2012, over 90% of Fresno State students used laptops and nearly half used desktops for academic purposes. Among students who used laptops and desktops, about 90% rated them as important to their academic success. By contrast, only 10% reported using a tablet for academic purposes and tended to consider them relatively unimportant to their academic success. In the 2012–13 study of student ICT use that I conducted on Fresno State's campus, I found that laptops and desktops remained mainstays among Fresno State students. Observations and interviews conducted on campus in 2012–13 illustrated that students preferred laptops and desktops for crucial tasks like composing text documents and other digital artifacts (such as videos, digital art work, and electronic portfolios), with smartphones and tablets important for consumption-oriented tasks like reading, checking email, and checking in on learning management systems (see Delcore, Teniente-Matson and Mullooly 2014).

In October 2013, I presented findings from the prior year's study of ICT use on campus to about thirty administrators, IT staff, and faculty. I framed the findings in terms of the tools students choose to accomplish tasks, and explained the continued dominance of laptops and desktops, and the relative rarity of tablets, as a function of student work practice. I stressed that my findings were focused on student work at the time of the study, not the potential value of any campus intervention to alter student ICT-related work. Still, there was little in my report to affirm President Castro's intentions to launch a tablet initiative. Unsurprisingly, the senior administrators present were attentive but largely silent, though a colleague from the school of education delivered a vigorous rejoinder to my comments. Like President Castro, he was an avid user of Apple products and he argued that iPads were ideal for collaboration and could satisfy all student work requirements. He emphasized his position by describing a recent journey to an international conference. He claimed that in the airport in Singapore, "everyone was using these," while holding his iPad up for emphasis. "We should be putting these in our students' hands," he concluded.

My colleague's assertion exemplifies the decontextualization and recontextualization that occur when actors adopt global forms and adapt them to local circumstances (Collier and Ong 2005, 11). In this case, the work of recontextualization also carried technocentric implications. Was the iPad suited to student work because it answered some deficiency in student work practice or their technological requirements? Or was delivering iPads to students appropriate because the device was new and popular and our students deserved to be on the cutting edge? Holding up the iPad for emphasis, my colleague seemed to tilt toward the latter, more technocentric position. On the other hand, he was also productively using the contrast between a global, high-tech city and the relatively parochial Central Valley of California to make a point: when it comes to technology, the racially and ethnically diverse, first-generation students at Fresno State *deserve equity* with the globetrotting elite one finds in an airport in Singapore.

His intervention was not the only time in the session when someone literally brandished a device to make a point. During a related presentation, a campus IT manager who was known to advocate for a device-agnostic position argued for closer attention to the rapidly changing market for devices. He held up his Microsoft Surface, a hybrid device that had been on the market for a little over a year, and pulled the device's keyboard off to demonstrate that it looked like a laptop but could be easily transformed into a tablet. The sight of faculty and staff holding up iPads and Surfaces like banners reminds us that the materiality of devices can make them seem like ends in themselves, rather than tools to accomplish work.

Plans for the president's initiative continued throughout 2013–14. Castro identified a Task Force composed of administrators and faculty to guide the program and an implementation team from within the University's Division of Academic Affairs. Within the Task Force (of which I was not a member), a small group of faculty and IT staff successfully pressed for a platform-agnostic (i.e., not exclusively iPad) initiative, recognizing that success hinged on accommodating student work practice and the kinds of devices students acquired on the market. By the end of spring, 2014, President Castro had dubbed the program, "DISCOVERe." (Program managers and University communications shifted to using "DISCOVERe" to refer to the program. However, faculty, staff, and some administrators continue to colloquially refer to it as the "tablet initiative." Fresno State's website about DISCOVERe calls it "DISCOVERe—Fresno State Tablet Program.")

After the DISCOVERe launch in spring 2014, the equity-technocentrism tension continued, both in the way the program was presented and in the way it was received. A University publication in spring, 2014, stressed the goals of breaking down the digital divide and hence improving student success and graduation rates, both firmly a part of the equity discourse (Armbruster 2014, 22). A faculty member is quoted as saying that DISCOVERe would make the classroom "more interactive and exciting, which will enhance student learning and increase participation," registering the idea that student-centered learning promotes educational success and equity (Armbruster 2014, 22). Yet, in the same piece, a key program manager asserts, "(w)hen students have the tablets in their hands, the real creativity will come out," clearly centering the technology itself as a catalyst for student success (Armbruster 2014, 23). President Castro was quoted as saying, "Tablets are a teaching and learning tool that Fresno State will embrace to meet the needs of today's tech-savvy students—those already enrolled and future students from throughout the Valley and state who already are using tablets in K-12 schools" (Armbruster 2014, 22). The president's statement implies, technocentrially, that the spread of tablets in other educational institutions *itself* justifies DISCOVERe.

In fall 2014, 32 faculty volunteered to be in the first DISCOVERe cohort, with about 40 courses and 1,079 students. In the ensuing years, DISCOVERe leaders and supporters have stressed, in discourse and in practice, the program's roots in pedagogical transformation, student-centered learning, equal access to technology, and ultimately, educational equity. But technocentric claims have constantly seeped into the discourse on campus, shaping the way it has been received. For example, several faculty have written blog postings and open letters to the president calling for a less technocentric orientation for DISCOVERe. One colleague told me, privately, "DISCOVERe is a solution in search of a problem."

Persistence and Change in Student Work Practices

Students engaged the DISCOVERe assemblage through their registration in DISCOVERe classes, as well as their work practice choices, including device acquisition. By some measures, such as device adoption rates among students, it is unclear whether DISCOVERe is actually altering student work culture. Unpublished results from a survey of technology use among Fresno State students in spring 2015 (DISCOVERe's second semester), found that 54.2% of 649 respondents owned a tablet. That same spring, a nationwide survey of college students by the EDUCAUSE Center for Applied Research (ECAR) found that 54% owned a tablet (Dahlstrom et al. 2015, 21). Hence, in 2015, Fresno State students did not own tablets at a significantly higher rate than their peers. However, it is unknown whether, as a result of DISCO-VERe, lower SES students at Fresno State use tablets at a higher rate than lower SES students elsewhere. Unfortunately, Fresno State did not collect device ownership data in 2016 or 2017. DISCOVERe's effect on tablet adoption rates among Fresno State students, compared to their peers nationwide, awaits further study.

On the other hand, in our 2014–15 study of tablet adoption for schoolwork among Fresno State students (Neufeld 2015), we found that the DISCOVERe program, then in its first year, had succeeded in altering the culture of schoolwork for some students. For example, Jorge, a first-generation Latino student, reported that by enrolling in an English course in the DISCOVERe program, he acquired his first tablet, an iPad Air. Jorge reported positive experiences in the course and while he had expected to use his tablet only in the DISCO-VERe course, his uses quickly expanded. For example, in a science course in which the instructor lectured quickly, he learned how to download the PowerPoint slides ahead of time and view them on his tablet in class as an aid to following the lecture.

We also found evidence that DISCOVERe was having some of the program's desired effects on collaboration and student engagement. For example, Antonio, a continuing-generation Latino student, reported that he liked his DISCOVERe history course better than a "normal" history course: "It seems a little bit more fun. It seems like I'm more engaged. ... We're all just getting along, it's becoming a class." Antonio's experiences were representative of students who took a DISCOVERe course from a well-prepared instructor who effectively accomplished course redesign using mobile technology for student-centered learning. The University's office of Institutional Effectiveness has also generated unpublished data indicating that students report being significantly more engaged in their DISCOVERe courses than other, non-tablet courses, and that DISCOVERe students have slightly higher GPAs and retention rates than their peers.

At the time of the tablet adoption study, however, the market for consumer devices was changing rapidly. In early 2015, IT market research firm Gartner reported that hybrid device sales were on track to reach 21.5 million units in 2015, a 70% increase over 2014 (Gartner 2015). Hybrids were quickly appearing on campus. In the tablet adoption study in 2014–15, we found evidence that students from higher SES backgrounds were already choosing hybrids at the expense of both laptops and tablets. One student interviewee said that her hybrid (a Microsoft Surface) fulfilled all of her computing needs and that she had ceased using both her laptop and tablet. Yet hybrids were still "under the radar" of the DISCOVERe "tablet program": they were not included on the 2014–15 list of approved devices.

We also found evidence that DISCOVERe's tablet focus was failing to address the ongoing student need for laptops. Research on student technology use nationwide reveals that laptops remain the student "academic workhorse": "Almost all students own a laptop or a smartphone; virtually no students own only a tablet (Brooks 2016, 5). Brooks continues: "Laptops, presumably due to their power and flexibility, continue to be the most important device in the student arsenal of digital devices; 93% of students said that laptops are very to extremely important for their academic success"; only 41% made this statement of tablets (Brooks 2016, 13). Unfortunately, Latino and lower SES students at Fresno State struggled to maintain access to high-quality laptops. In tablet adoption interviews with lower SES students, we found that they and their families had less rich device collections than their higher SES peers. In particular, they struggled with keeping and maintaining laptops: their laptops tended to be older, have maintenance problems, and were often shared with other household members.

Sensitivity to the SES of students in the study helped us make sense of another finding: factors driving tablet adoption varied by segment of the student population (Neufeld 2015). Latino students and lower SES students had higher performance expectations for tablets; in other words, more than their peers, these students expected that their tablets would help them learn more effectively. DISCOVERe was providing some of these students with new tablets and we inferred that their poorer device collections encouraged optimism about the potential for DISCOVERe-promoted tablets to improve their schoolwork. However, they still considered laptops as essential to schoolwork. We wondered whether the University might be promoting a technocentric orientation toward technology, with an emphasis on newer, more mobile devices as categorically better, even as laptops remained central to student work practice.

Finally, higher SES students were experiencing the tablet moment at Fresno State in yet other ways. Some turned to the consumer market to acquire hybrids and lightweight laptops, like the MacBook Air. But their acquisitions led to a problem: in focus groups, higher SES students complained that they were forced to buy a new tablet, without any campus subsidy, simply because they enrolled in a DISCOVERe course to fulfill a requirement. Imani, for example, was angry because she purchased a new MacBook right before the fall 2014 semester began, but was forced to purchase a tablet because she was enrolled in a DISCOVERe course; she perceived her MacBook to be sufficient for her work and did not see the need for a new tablet. Higher SES students also had a tendency toward less sustained tablet usage over time. In a focus group with graduate assistants, we learned that they had observed higher SES students progressively choosing to work on laptops over tablets as the production of text documents and other digital artifacts ramped up during the spring 2015 semester.

Clearly, DISCOVERe, from its first year, had some of the desired effects on student work. The initiative began at a time when tablet adoption among college students was still low but rising. Students with relatively poor device collections adopted tablets via DISCOVERe and used them to increase engagement and collaboration in and out of class. However, student work practice maintains the need for laptops due to their robust ergonomic and computing features and utility for composing text documents and other digital artifacts. Inequalities among students meant that higher SES students were able to access newer, lighter laptops and they increasingly turned to those devices as assignments came due late in the semester. Some higher SES students also exploited the new market for hybrids to displace both laptops and tablets, an option not available to students in DISCOVERe's first year. Hence, the DISCOVERe program, while aiming for educational and techno-logical equity, was caught flat-footed vis-à-vis both persistent inequalities in US society and the rapidly changing consumer market for devices. Both the market for devices and consumer preferences, including student consumer preferences, continue to evolve. The 2016 ECAR survey found that, nation-wide, students' tablet ownership gains were slowing down and student use of tablets for schoolwork was in decline, from 47% in 2014 to 39% in 2016, perhaps due to a larger decline in tablet use among 18–24-year-olds (Brooks

2016, 12). It remains to be seen how DISCOVERe will respond to these larger social and market-influenced trends.

Faculty Interventions

Faculty have played a variety of roles in the DISCOVERe assemblage. Some faculty have criticized the program, mostly in private. Others have managed parts of the program, or opted to offer a DISCOVERe course (myself included). Several DISCOVERe instructors have become well known on campus as enthusiastic supporters of the program, speaking at administrator and faculty committee meetings and other fora. Finally, several faculty have conducted research and advocated for certain positions—a role I also have played. Faculty playing these roles have had various degrees of influence on DISCOVERe. Below, I highlight my role as an advocate for changes to the program, the influence of a colleague who managed parts of the program in its early stages, as well as the role of several outspoken faculty fans of DISCOVERe. Together, the interventions described below illustrate agency within an assemblage where power relations may be more characterized by intersecting and traversing structures than strict, top-down hierarchies (see Arnould and Thompson 2015).

   In late fall 2014, Philip Neufeld and I met with campus IT leaders to share preliminary findings from our tablet adoption study, and we presented those findings to the DISCOVERe Task Force in January 2015. First, however, two DISCOVERe faculty shared overwhelmingly positive reports about their DISCOVERe classes during the preceding semester. Next, Neufeld and I shared some positive findings, which showed that the intensive use of mobile technology by well-prepared faculty resulted in students feeling engaged and effective. However, we also shared our concerns that lower SES students were being encouraged to use tablets at the expense of laptops, and we presented data about student anger with being forced to acquire a new device to enroll in a DISCOVERe course. We stressed that DISCOVERe might adapt to the changing market for devices by including hybrids in the program. Our criticisms were met with little reaction; as the meeting had run over time, there was no discussion and the administrator chairing the meeting adjourned it.

   I have found that it is difficult to gauge the effectiveness of interventions like the one described above. However, I have learned that my interventions have affected the DISCOVERe assemblage in some identifiable ways. For example, IT administrators and staff have told me that they appreciate my attention to data as a basis for decision-making, and that my research findings in the 2012–13 study helped sink early plans for an iPad-only tablet initiative.

My argument for more attention to hybrids also bolstered the advocacy work of others on that issue. The fall 2015 DISCOVERe device list included the Microsoft Surface, potentially helping lower SES students acquire a hybrid device, like their higher SES peers, but at a subsidized cost.

Faculty members in administrative positions have also exerted influence. In fall 2015, I joined the DISCOVERe faculty. At the inaugural training session for the new cohort, we heard a talk from a business school colleague who recently joined the administration to help run the program. The colleague had been among the actors who pushed for a device-agnostic program. He said that he increasingly saw DISCOVERe as a "mobile technology initiative," recognizing that students brought a variety of mobile devices and were able to accomplish their work with them, even if they fell outside the formal DISCOVERe device list. At this point, the assemblage had shifted, slightly, from an emphasis on "tablets" toward an emphasis on "mobile technology." By fall 2016, the device list was gone entirely, replaced by a list of specifications that student-owned devices must meet to qualify for enrollment in a DISCOVERe course. Even these minimal specifications were not mandatory, perhaps because by fall 2016, subsidies for students to acquire new tablets were gone, replaced by a tablet-lending program to support DISCOVERe students with limited resources.

Although the new University president had conceived DISCOVERe as a "tablet program" with a preference for iPads, faculty playing a variety of roles (e.g., enthusiastic supporter, program manager, skeptical researcher) influenced its eventual practice. As a result of these contending agencies in a structure where power was more diffuse than hierarchical, the program shifted over time, from an iPad-centered concept, to a device-agnostic tablet program, to a "mobile technology initiative."

The Indeterminacy of an Assemblage on Display

In October 2016, I attended a DISCOVERe faculty recognition luncheon. The luncheon served the immediate goal of thanking faculty who had volunteered to teach DISCOVERe courses during the first two years of the program. It also served as a platform for campus administrators, faculty, and even a student to voice their support for DISCOVERe. In the process, the discursive slippage and the various agencies of the DISCOVERe assemblage were clearly on display, as various actors took the stage to describe their experiences.

The provost stressed the agency exerted by President Castro. She praised his leadership and noted that, during his first week in town, in fall 2013, he was featured on the "front page, above the fold" of the Fresno Bee "holding a tablet." Despite the technocentrism inherent in calling out this image, the rest of her remarks stressed pedagogical transformation and measurable outcomes. She claimed that the goal of DISCOVERe was "to transform the way we educate our great students and to transform their lives," and that assessment data compiled by University researchers had revealed that 92% of DISCOVERe students said they felt "more engaged," had higher retention and GPAs, and were on track for graduation.

President Castro, after greeting and thanking the crowd, described his initial idea for DISCOVERe as "a hunch" built on the drive for equity: "I grew up in the Valley so I know that many of our students are on the wrong side of the technology divide." He recalled wondering, how do we connect with those students and "help them succeed?"

The remarks by the provost and the president exhibited the same tensions among technocentrism, equity, and pedagogical change that run throughout DISCOVERe. The image of the president on the front page of the newspaper holding a tablet evokes a technocentric focus on the device itself. But Papert's previously cited caution about the use of shorthand applies, since the provost also stressed the opportunity for pedagogical transformation via tablet use, as well as positive outcomes data. The president, likewise, evoked the digital divide, a discourse that is both technocentric *and* equity-oriented. Above all, however, he stressed that we must help students succeed, an assertion that referenced the equity concerns on a campus with a diverse, heavily first-generation student body.

Neither the provost nor the president sought to resolve competing justifications for DISCOVERe. Indeed, a resolution would be both unlikely and pointless, because the assemblage around DISCOVERe is composed of these exact indeterminacies. Further, to understand the assemblage is to keep the agency of educational leaders in focus: neither the provost nor the president benefits from cutting off any potential discursive resource in the drive to justify the program and prove its value. Herein lies the central discursive ambiguity of the DISCOVERe assemblage: the tension among values like equity, measureable outcomes like student success and graduation rates, and an abiding faith that the latest technology is good for its own sake (technocentrism). To keep it all in play is to retain discursive and practical latitude.

The president invited a Latina student from Fresno to address the crowd. She began by thanking the professors present for making their courses more interactive and student-centered. She described how she benefited from the collaborative group work in her DISCOVERe course, as well as easy access to course materials like PowerPoint lectures and readings. Referring to her DISCOVERe course, she said, "It kept me engaged," affirming the outcomes-oriented approach of the provost.

Finally, a faculty member who had been involved with the program from its early stages took the microphone. Her comments were discursively complex. She described how some faculty colleagues have been skeptical about DISCOVERe from the start. She related how early on in the initiative, she told a senior colleague, "K-12 are adopting tablets; we need to be ready for those students." However, her colleague questioned her reasoning, and she admitted that, until recently, she did not have an adequate response. "It is not about the device," she continued, in a nod to the pitfalls of technocentrism. Now, she said that she can show faculty that "tablet pedagogy" can save you time by making you more efficient, giving you more time to do research, for example. She also noted that she was in the first DISCOVERe cohort, and the focus was on, "What can we do for our students?" Her main answer was that tablets foster a more student-centered pedagogy because tablet classes were not structured around lectures. Instead, every student in class has access to the tools and information provided via the device, with the instructor as facilitator.

My colleague's speech told a "to-technocentrism-and-back" narrative. Early on, she admits that she stressed the need to simply keep up with students' expectations about technology based on their prior schooling. In effect, Fresno State must be involved with tablets because public schools are involved with tablets, a rationale that is perhaps the very definition of technocentrism. Over time, however, she came to develop justifications based on faculty self-interest and the student-centered learning component of the equity discourse.

Importantly, the speakers with their contending claims and discursive tendencies were *not confused*. The constant slippage among technocentrism, equity, pedagogical transformation, and evidence of altered student outcomes indexes the fact that the DISCOVERe assemblage is indeed a complex, contingent thing composed of all these discourses and rhetorical tendencies, plus the actors who put them into practice.

The DISCOVERe assemblage (see Figure 3.1) is rooted in the political economy of the United States, including dimensions of social inequality, as well as the technology industry and the consumer market for information and communication technology. More immediately, the assemblage is located in the institutional space of California's public higher education system. The social and institutional base, and the shape of the assemblage itself, is represented by uneven lines and an imperfect circle, as these social entities are nonlinear and constantly evolving. The arrows represent major discursive and practical aspects of the assemblage. Some, like the discourse on educational equity, change slightly, refracted by the discursive and practical work of the agents in the assemblage. The circles represent major nodes of agency, where various actors exert influence on work practice, the discourse on equity, and the nature of the assemblage itself.

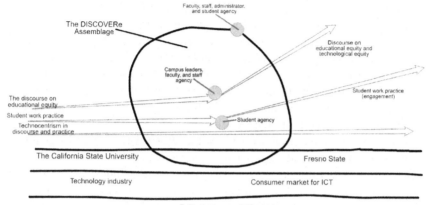

Figure 3.1 The DISCOVERe Assemblage.

CONCLUSIONS

Little about the DISCOVERe assemblage was predetermined. In 2013, President Castro was positioned as a new educational leader in a time of great excitement around tablets as an educational technology. Playing off the excitement around iPads, in particular, and the proliferation of one-to-one programs at other institutions, he launched DISCOVERe. But from there, the many structures, agencies, and discourses of the University became relevant. The program started as an iPad initiative, then evolved in a platform-agnostic direction, due to the actions of faculty and IT staff with knowledge of student work practice and a healthy respect for the power of the market to shape student-owned technology. DISCOVERe now stands as a mobile technology initiative, with no prescriptive device list, though it retains the moniker, "tablet program." Throughout the debates about what the University *should* do, the discourse of educational equity remained central—to the president's pronouncements justifying the program, and to the University public relations machine behind him. Yet, the US cultural emphasis on the fastest and latest technology was always at play, sometimes in support of DISCOVERe, sometimes against it, and always intertwined with other values, such as my colleague's plea to put the latest technology in our students' hands.

How has DISCOVERe altered student work practice? We know that some students, like Jorge and Antonio, have used DISCOVERe to become first-time tablet owners; they have found new, unexpected uses for their tablets, and reported feeling more engaged by the redesigned courses. On the other hand, SES inequalities among students remain entrenched, with higher SES students maintaining advantaged access to the latest devices and the choice to turn to newer laptops and hybrids when their work requires it. Some lower SES students optimistically acquired tablets with DISCOVERe help in the first few years of the program, but the depth of DISCOVERe's effect on device ownership remains unclear. We can assume that lower SES students still struggle to maintain access to high-quality devices, such as laptops, which they deem central to their work.

The more decisive change wrought by the DISCOVERe assemblage relates to the way the University approaches questions of educational equity. The University is now fully invested in delivering not just student-centered learning, but also pedagogical transformation through the intensive use of mobile devices in teaching and learning. In this way, the DISCOVERe assemblage has territorialized global and national tendencies to value access to the latest technology as the key to bridging the "digital divide" and giving all students a shot at both educational and social success. Henceforth, University actors who wish to speak and act on the issue of educational equity will have to contend with the linked discourse on technological equity, whether or not they support the University's efforts to change culture.

The DISCOVERe assemblage persists, for now, as the initiative enters its seventh semester in fall 2017. Assemblage theory helps highlight the way the heterogeneous parts of such an assemblage come together in a fluid, unstable, and contested way. Agents, from the president to students, took up the discursive and material resources around them to pursue the values and projects they found important in the moment, pressing claims from unequal yet continually negotiated positions. Ironically, the discursive indeterminacy (equity or technocentrism?) and shifting materiality (iPad, tablet, hybrid, or "mobile technology"?) at the heart of the assemblage enabled diverse actors to stay in the field and the assemblage itself to persist. Assemblage theory helps us see the temporary, contingent, indeterminate nature of an assemblage like the one described here. Indeed, we must recognize that the DISCOVERe assemblage is one pedagogical shift, one budget crisis, one leadership change, one market or device-use trend away from unraveling or transforming into something new.

REFERENCES

Adas, Michael. 2006. *Dominance by Design: Technological Imperatives and America's Civilizing Mission.* Cambridge, MA: Harvard University Press.
Armbruster, Shirley Melikian. 2014. "Fresno State's Tablet Program." *Fresno State Magazine*, Spring 2014:22–23. Accessed May 8, 2017. http://www.fresnostate.edu/

advancement/ucomm/documents/magazine/archive-full-pdfs/fsmagspring14-full. pdf.

Arnould, Eric J., and Craig J. Thompson. 2015. "Introduction: Consumer Culture Theory: Ten Years Gone (and Beyond)." In *Research in Consumer Behavior, Volume 17*, edited by Anastasia Thyroff, Jeff B. Murray and Russell W. Belk, 1–21. Bingley UK: Emerald Group Publishing.

Bohn, Sarah, and Caroline Danielson. 2017. "Poverty in California." San Francisco: Public Policy Institute of California. Accessed April 20, 2017. http://www.ppic. org/main/publication_show.asp?i=261.

Bourdieu, Pierre. 1977a [1972]. *Outline of a Theory of Practice.* Translated by Richard Nice. New York: Cambridge University Press.

———. 1977b. "Cultural Reproduction and Social Reproduction." In *Power and Ideology in Education*, edited by Jerome Karabel and A.H. Halsey, 487–511. New York: Oxford University Press.

———. 1986. "The Forms of Capital." In *Handbook of Theory and Research for the Sociology of Education*, edited by John G. Richardson, 241–258. New York: Greenwood.

———. 1990 [1980]. *The Logic of Practice.* Translated by Richard Nice. Cambridge: Polity Press.

Bourdieu, Pierre, and Loic Wacquant. 1992. *An Invitation to Reflexive Sociology.* Chicago: The University of Chicago Press.

Brooks, D. Christopher. 2016. "ECAR Study of Undergraduate Students and Information Technology, 2016." Research report. Louisville, CO: EDUCAUSE Center for Analysis and Research. Accessed May 10, 2017. https://library.educause.edu/~/ media/files/library/2016/10/ers1605.pdf.

California State University (CSU). 2017. "Facts About the CSU." Accessed March 23, 2017. http://www.calstate.edu/csufacts/2016Facts/.

California State Department of Education. 1960. "A Master Plan for Higher Education in California, 1960–1975." Accessed March 23, 2017. http://www.ucop.edu/ acadinit/mastplan/MasterPlan1960.pdf.

Collier, Stephen J., and Aihwa Ong. 2005. "Global Assemblages and Anthropological Problems." In *Global Assemblages: Technology, Politics, and Ethics as Anthropological Problems*, edited by Aihwa Ong and Stephen J. Collier, 3–21. London: Blackwell.

Dahlstrom, Eden, Christopher D. Brooks, Susan Grajek, and Jamie Reeves. 2015. "ECAR Study of Undergraduate Students and Information Technology, 2015." Research report. Louisville, CO: EDUCAUSE Center for Analysis and Research. Accessed May 10, 2017. https://library.educause.edu/~/media/files/library/2015/8/ers1510ss .pdf?la=en.

Delcore, Henry D., and Philip Neufeld. 2017. "Student Technology Rollouts in Higher Education: Lessons From DISCOVERe." *Journal of Research on Technology in Education* 49:43–54. Accessed March 23, 2017. doi:10.1080/15391523.2017.1293575.

Delcore, Henry D., Cynthia Teniente-Matson, and James Mullooly. 2014. "The Continuum of Student IT Use in Campus Spaces: A Qualitative Study." *EDUCAUSE Review Online*, July/August. Accessed March 27, 2017. http://er.educause.

edu/articles/2014/8/the-continuum-of-student-it-use-in-campus-spaces-a-qualitative-study.

Delcore, Henry D. 2018. The Lifescapes of Public University Students: Extending Work Practice to Macro and Micro Levels. *Human Organization* 7(1).

Deleuze, Gilles, and Felix Guattari. 1987 [1980]. *A Thousand Plateaus: Capitalism and Schizophrenia.* Translated by Brian Massumi. Minneapolis: University of Minnesota Press.

eCampus News. 2013. "Fresno State's Joseph Castro Touts Tablets Over Textbooks." *eCampus News*, September 3. Accessed March 3, 2017. http://www.ecampusnews. com/around-the-web/2013-fresno-states-joseph-castro-touts-tablets-over-text-books/.

Fresno State, Office of Institutional Effectiveness (FSOIE). 2015. "New Undergraduate Cohort Demographics from Fall 2011 to Fall 2015." Accessed May 6, 2016. https://tableau.fresnostate.edu/views/Enrollment/DemographicsNewUGRD? perce nt3AisGuestRedirectFromVizportal=y& percent3Aembed=y.

———. 2017. "6-Year Graduation of Full-Time, First-Time Freshman Cohorts: Entry Cohorts from Fall 2003 to Fall 2010." Accessed March 23, 2017. https:// tableau.fresnostate.edu/views/RetentionGraduation/AcademicGap?:isGuestRedire ctFromVizportal=y&:embed=y.

Gartner. 2015. "Gartner Says Worldwide Hybrid Device Shipments on Pace to Reach 21.5 Million Units in 2015, Up 70 Percent from 2014." Accessed April 20, 2017. http://www.gartner.com/newsroom/id/3077817.

Koebler, Jason. 2011. "More High Schools Implement iPad Programs." *US News and World Report*, September 7. Accessed May 10, 2017. https://www. usnews.com/education/blogs/high-school-notes/2011/09/07/more-high-schools-implement-ipad-programs.

Latour, Bruno. 1993 [1991]. *We Have Never Been Modern.* Translated by Catherine Porter. Cambridge, MA: Harvard University Press.

Marx, Leo. 2010. "Technology: The Emergence of a Hazardous Concept." *Technology and Culture* 51:561–577.

Neufeld, Philip. 2015. "Understanding Variations in Acceptance and Use of Tablet Technology by Students at a Public Four-Year University." Ed.D. diss., California State University, Fresno.

Neufeld, Philip, and Henry D. Delcore. In preparation. "Towards a Critical Techno-Pedagogy: Situatedness and Variations in Student Adoption of Technology Practices."

Nuez, Ramon. 2011. "An iPad for Every Seton Hill University Student." *Huffington Post*, May 25. http://www.huffingtonpost.com/ramon-nuez/an-ipad-for-every-seton-h_b_526277.html. Accessed May 10, 2017.

Papert, Seymour. 1990a. "Computer Criticism Versus Technocentric Thinking." MIT Media Lab Epistemology and Learning Memo No. 1. Accessed May 11, 2017. http://learning.media.mit.edu/publications_papert.html.

———. 1990b. "A Critique of Technocentrism in Thinking About the School of the Future." MIT Media Lab Epistemology and Learning Memo No. 2. Accessed May 11, 2017. http://learning.media.mit.edu/publications_papert.html.

Selwyn, Neil. 2004. "Reconsidering Political and Popular Understandings of the Digital Divide." *New Media &* Society 6:341–362.

Smith, Merritt Roe, and Leo Marx, eds. 1994. *Does Technology Drive History?: The Dilemma of Technological Determinism.* Cambridge, MA: The MIT Press.

Stringer, Jenn, and Brian Tobin. 2012. "Launching a University Tablet Initiative: Recommendations from Stanford University's iPad Implementation." EDU-CAUSE Learning Initiative Brief. April 2012. Accessed May 10, 2017. https:// library.educause.edu/~/media/files/library/2012/4/elib1202-pdf.pdf

Venkatesh, V., M. Morris, G. Davis, and F. Davis. 2003. "User Acceptance of Information Technology: Toward a Unified View." *MIS Quarterly* 27:425–478.

Chapter 4

Enchanted Objects, Social Robots, and the Internet of Things

Exploring the Role of Design in Innovation and Cultural Change

Christine Miller

> Designers work the scene of technological emergence: they hack the present to create the conditions of the future.
>
> —Anne Balsamo (2011, 6)

How does design harness the power of imagination in paving the way for innovation and, in turn, cultural change that impact relations among human and nonhuman actors in social and commercial communities? What is the role of design in reconfiguring and constructing the assemblages of the future? How are we preparing—and being prepared—for the onslaught of change that will result from the "third wave" of the Internet, popularly referred to as the Internet of Things (IoT)? Let's begin framing these questions with a story.

Fantasy writer Anne Bishop (2015) describes a world populated by humans and non-humans—the terra indigene, the earth natives or "Others" who inhabited the wild spaces. In the creation story, the two groups were kept separated by physical distance until the human populations began to venture from their settlements and found that the world they thought was their own was actually shared with other creatures. Bishop writes, "The Others looked at the humans and did not see conquerors. They saw a new kind of meat." Wars were fought for territory. The first two waves of human colonization were rebuffed. However, human civilization continued to advance until, in the third wave, humans were able to negotiate with the terra indigene for settlements that allowed them to establish a foothold in the new world. But all did not go smoothly.

The humans cut down trees to make room for their settlements. They did not respect the land as the "Others" did. Different values shaped their respective cultures. Human societies did not function like the societies of the

*terra indigene. Tensions arose and at times ignited into bloody encounters,
as they did with the discovery of the enslavement by some humans of other
human females, the cassandra sangue, who were able to foresee the future.
These young women were kept in compounds where they were isolated from
other humans and from each other, periodically being tapped—bled—for
their visions, which were then sold to clients. In terra indigene society, where
the primary directive was to take care of the pack and protect the young, it
was wrong for one being to enslave another.*

*Meg, a 24-year old female and one of the main characters in the story, has
escaped from one of these compounds. Life in the compound has all she has
ever known. She did not have a name, but was known instead as cs759. She
did not have friends, personal belongings or interests. She had no knowledge
of the world except what she was "taught" through notebooks containing
images of things that would allow her to describe the images she saw in her
visions. Within this tightly controlled environment her only pleasure was the
erotic sensations that accompanied the visions. Consequently, her unlikely
escape thrust her into a world that she knew only from pictures rather than
through experience. Lost in a new world of foreign sights, sounds and sensations, she was taken into the care of the "Others" and was settled into a new
life in a community inhabited by terra indigene and a few humans. While this
new life was far preferable to what she left behind, adapting to the change
was overwhelming. Something as seemingly simple as getting a haircut or
having a coworker move a stack of CDs would leave her at best feeling des-
perate and often catatonic.*

By now you might be feeling empathy with Meg. How is she to cope?
Her struggle to keep up with the pace of change may feel somehow familiar
and disturbing. It is not unlike what those of us who live in the industrialized
world, and those who live on its periphery, experience as we confront the
dynamic reconfiguration of assemblages resulting from technological innovations and the accelerating pace of change in contemporary society.

IMAGINARIES OF THE FUTURE: DESIGN AND
THE THIRD WAVE OF THE INTERNET

". . . worlds are as much made as found"

—Nelson Goodman. (1978, 22)

Like Meg we are confronted with coping and adapting to the disruptions
resulting from an increasingly technology-driven world inhabited by driverless vehicles, social robots, and "cobots" or collaborative machines (e.g., the
industrial robot "Sawyer" that works alongside human employees), and data

collection networks that make transparent once private details of everyday life. Drawing on examples from product development, thought experiments, parody, film, and popular culture, the aim of this chapter is to suggest how design, in its broad applications, paves the way for innovation, the diffusion of new products, services, ideas, business models or processes. Together, innovation and diffusion give rise to cultural change by giving form and substance to our imaginings, specifically in the realm of technology and its implications for possible futures. The chapter explores the concept of design-as-future-making, using the "third wave" of the Internet, or the Internet of Things, as a case in point.

Jankowski et al. (2014) described the IoT as the third wave in a series of technological leaps. They explained that the first wave of the Internet introduced the fixed Internet connecting approximately one billion users. The second wave brought the mobile Internet connecting another two billion users. It is estimated that by 2020, the emergence of ambient technology and ubiquitous computing will provide connectivity to 28 billion "things" during the third Internet wave. Many of these "things" will take on jobs that are now filled by the human beings, from manufacturing and retail to law, banking, and medicine. Technically, the Internet of Things or IoT has been defined as:

> A dynamic global network infrastructure with self-configuring capabilities based on standard and interoperable communication protocols where physical and virtual "things" have identities, physical attributes, and virtual personalities and use intelligent interfaces, and are seamlessly integrated into the information network, often communicate data associated with users and their environments. (Bahga and Madisetti 2014, 22)

The IoT is made possible by ambient devices and ubiquitous computing that "allows for the transmission of sensing and signaling information, the process and storage of information, and the delivery of new services" (Rose 2014, 194–95). Although IoT technologies are diverse and still immature (Pelino et al. 2016), the concept of autonomous machine-to-machine (M2M) systems that require far less, if any, human intervention has rapidly taken hold in the business environment. In tandem, design-driven innovation has been widely adopted within big corporations. Responding to over a decade of corporate acquisitions, Olof Schybergson, CEO of design firm Fjord (recently acquired by Accenture) noted that

> Design is so central and at the forefront of the most interesting work in digital that simply hiring it in when you need it, if you need it, is not really a good long-term game anymore ... *Investing in it and making it part of you is something that's sustainable and trustworthy and believable to your clients* [italics added]. (Hurst, 2013)

How does embracing design equate to corporations being trustworthy and believable? The aura of authenticity is related to recent developments in the evolution of design that encourage empathy for "users" and promote human-centered over object- and thing-centric design. For many future-watchers, authors, and scholars, the combined power of design and corporate business conjure visions of a dystopian future in which rampant technological innovation is driven by globalization, free-market capitalism and neoliberal ideologies. The growing power and potency of design have drawn criticism. Lucy Suchman (2011) critiqued design as future-making, calling out designer Bruce Mau's concept of "Massive Design" which he claimed "is not about the world of design" but about "the design of the world" (2011, 5). She notes the hubris in a claim by a Silicon Valley technologist that "the future arrives sooner here" and in the "attendant mandate to enact the future that others will subsequently live" (2011, 2). Citing Barry (2001), Suchman notes that a mark of a technological society is that it "privileges change and then figures change as technological innovation" (2001, 201). She continues

> Innovation, in turn, is embedded in the broader cultural imaginary that posits a world that is always lagging, always in need of being brought up to date through the intercessions of those trained to shape it: a world, in sum, in need of design. (2011, 4–5)

The presence of design has grown exponentially in contemporary societies that embrace technological innovation. Suchman's critique of design was shaped by her experience of living in Silicon Valley and by working in the technology sector where driving/designing technological innovation is the *modus operandi*. The designers and technological innovators she refers to see a world that needs updating, *a world that is lagging and in need of fixing*. Suchman suggests that professional technology designers, by virtue of training and position, envision themselves as those to do the fixing. They create the futures "that others will subsequently live" (2011, 2).

Suchman's critique influenced by her work in Silicon Valley and by a reaction to instances of design hubris does not account for current trends in design research and practice that reflect the shift from object-centered to human-centered design. Technology-based change is a significant portion of what is produced through contemporary design practice. However, as design has become increasingly user- and customer-focused (like business), design for technological innovation without consideration of human factors is being relegated to the past. Over time, the scope of human factors has expanded beyond consideration of ergonomics and cognition to include user experience (UX) and human-computer interaction (HCI), for example. As the field has evolved from its industrial beginnings, designers rarely work in isolation, but instead are team players at the front end of innovation in medicine, education, law, business, government, and other fields where technological innovation alone is not capable of addressing the complex issues societies are facing.

This exploration is focused on design as an evolving practice and on its capacity to influence cultural imaginaries, the patterned sets of symbols, ideas, meanings, values, and institutions that envision possible alternative present or future worlds, specifically in relation to what has been conceptualized as the third wave of the Internet. It is also concerned with design's capacity to shape and reconfigure assemblages. In the ongoing evolution of design, collaboration with anthropologists and other social scientists and the adaptation of ethnography as a key component of design research helped facilitate the shift from object-centered to human-centeredness. The role of anthropology in design-as-future-making, or what Gatt and Ingold refer to as "anthropology-by-means-of-design" (2011, 50), is explored through the lens of the evolving transdisciplinary field of design anthropology.

DESIGN AS AN EVOLVING PRACTICE

Design has long been in the business of shaping functionality and form. However, as the field of professional design has matured, designers have become increasingly aware of being engaged in future-making, the transformation of existing conditions, relations and practices, and world-making. Design scholar Susan Yelavich notes that design "not only demonstrates that world-making is possible, but is also the very essence of what design does. Design acts otherwise" (2014, 17). Along with this awareness is a growing sense among designers of their responsibility about why, how, what, and for whom they design, as well as the consequences engendered by their designs.

At the front end of the broad cultural imaginary, designers, artists, filmmakers, and others in the creative industries, craft prototypes illustrate scenarios of "what might be." They introduce visions of possible futures that inspire, provoke, and embody innovation and cultural change. Without a sense of responsibility and an ethical stance, the potency of design raises concerns and even alarm. Recognizing their responsibility for the artifacts they create, a cadre of design thought leaders has emerged to contribute their perspectives to a critical trajectory in the field of design studies (Teixeira and Zimmerman 2016). According to Yelavich,

They assert design's role in developing active capabilities to negotiate our material, natural, political and social entanglements. They ask us to be aware of how we choose to live in the world and what it might be. They remind us that design's greatest possibility, its primary responsibility, is the reduction of suffering and the maximization of potential. (2014, 17)

Yelavich (2014) describes the central values that have emerged in design practice as "the virtue of dialog across fields, the significance of social collaboration, and the importance of craft in shaping the future." She notes

Craft is understood expansively to mean a fundamentally social way of working with people through the medium and intelligence of materiality. With the arrival of smart materials that fuse artificial intelligence with the native intelligence of metals, fibers, and synthetics via sensors, microprocessors, and photovoltaics, materiality also includes composites of pixels and bytes and the floes of electrical current. The line between the ephemeral and the solid, between the natural and the artificial, has long since disappeared. (2014, 20)

DESIGN-AS-FUTURE-MAKING

Design creates the conditions for cultural change by giving form and substance to our imaginings. From the perspective of design as future-making, we have entered "a new moment within design studies in which design is fully conceived as a practice that continuously reimagines its own possibilities" (Appadurai, 2014, 9); it is a driver and shaper of social and cultural change. Design today is explicitly linked to innovation and communication of "the new," and thus, to participation in the reconfiguration of existing assemblages: emergent wholes made up of heterogeneous components, often existing as networks that bridge local and global actors. Innovations that disrupt the practice routines that dominate all aspects of human life require existing assemblages to adapt "as new relations and capacities among components emerge" (Epp, Schau, and Price 2014). Design has emerged as a powerful social, cultural, political, and economic force that gives form and substance to abstract ideas, suggesting how assemblages might be reconfigured or created to adapt to new technologies and global dynamics. By crafting prototypes and scenarios of "what might be," designers introduce visions of possible futures that embody innovations that entail transformative social and cultural change. Design creates a sense of "real-ness" that allows us to glimpse possible futures by engaging us in exploring yet unrealized worlds. Through a variety of media, these explorations depict, suggest, and pave the way to landscapes of potential cultural and social change.

From festival to parody to product design, the examples that follow explore a sample of the ways in which design serves to give form and substance to *what might be.*

Cultural Imaginaries

"... worlds are as much made as found."

—Nelson Goodman (1978, 22)

Although the role of design in future-making has been criticized, its power to harness the collective imagination is undeniable. The critiques of design in future-making put forward by scholars from a variety of fields (Margolin, 2002, 2005, 1989; Papernak, 1984; Suchman, 2008, 2011) are only mentioned here in this chapter. Instead, the intention is to examine examples from popular culture and the commercial market space of how design, in its broadest definition, gives form and substance to cultural imaginaries, patterned sets of symbols, ideas, meanings, values, and institutions that reflect possible future scenarios.

American philosopher Henry Nelson Goodman (1978) alluded to the construction of assemblages in describing the process of world-making, writing that

> Much but by no means all world-making consists of taking apart and putting together, often conjointly: on the one hand, of dividing wholes into parts and partitioning kinds into sub-species, analyzing complexes into component features, drawing distinctions; on the other hand, of composing wholes and kinds out of parts and members of subclasses, combining features into complexes, and making connections. Such composition or decomposition is normally effected or assisted or consolidated by the application of labels: names, predicates, gestures, pictures, etc. Thus for example, temporally diverse events are brought together under a proper name or identified as making up "an object" or "a person"; or snow is sundered into several materials under terms of Eskimo vocabulary. (Goodman 1978, 7–8)

The event known as "Wasteland Weekend" (2014), a multiday post apocalyptic festival held in a desert location outside of Bakersfield, California (Merlan, 2016), fits Nelson's description of the process of world-making. As an example of world-making, the Wasteland provides a forum and stage for the cultural imagination of thousands of participants who gather to give expression to visions of a world that combine elements of *Mad Max*, *Waterworld,* and other films, video games, and social media that fall within the postapocalyptic genre. This genre is a cultural, social, and commercial phenomenon that is supported by the creative industries which include most aspects of design. To see how design brings to life this particular postapocalyptic vision of the world see *Wired* magazine's coverage in "Wasteland: This Mad Max Festival Makes Burning Man Look Tame" (Merlan 2016).

Wasteland Weekend is a member of Postapocalyptic (2016), a web-based gateway to content and entities that comprise an apocalyptic and postapocalyptic assemblage. By crafting physical and virtual worlds, various forms of design create a portal to possible futures. In the case of the Wasteland and related venues, humans imagining a postapocalyptic world recreate society in the aftermath of a technological society gone awry. Contemporary humans can immerse themselves in worlds that simultaneously create "imaginary" yet physically "real" future worlds using a form of performance art known as costume play or *cosplay,* allowing them to assume fictional identities and engage with other cosplayers in the production of a new and novel subculture.

Venues such as WasteWorld provide a glimpse into one of many cultural imaginaries that are brought to life by design. All aspects of the event—the assemblage that includes venue site, costumes, vehicles, arenas, vendors, and commercial marketplace—are carefully designed to create a cohesive depiction of a postapocalyptic culture, society and worldview. Participants are transported into a scenario that links the present trajectory of technological advances to a possible future endgame. Earth's technological civilization has collapsed as a result of an apocalyptic event, either a man-made event such as war or a natural disaster brought on by accelerated climactic change. These scenarios, described in science fiction and other genres, portray worlds that have been ravaged by an apocalyptic event where only scattered remnants of technology and civilized society have survived. E.M. Forster's *The Machine Stops* (1909/2016), a classic example of an apocalyptic endgame scenario, describes a world in which humans are not able to survive on the surface of the earth and have become dependent on an omnipotent Global Machine to meet all their needs. The Machine eventually fails and all the humans who are dependent on it perish.

How is the present state of technology, society, and culture envisioned in possible future, whether these visions are postapocalyptic or utopian? Design plays a prominent role in giving form and substance to present and near-future technologies. The future is now, particularly, in the commercial and industrial realm.

Things, Thing-Ness, and Agency

Actor-network theory (ANT) is a useful complement to assemblage thinking. Arguing that nonhumans have the capacity for agency, the mediated capacity to act in heterogeneous networks, science and technology scholars Bruno Latour, Michael Callon, and John Law developed ANT in the early 1980s as a way to examine the processes of innovation and knowledge-creation in science and technology. Drawing on works from science and technology studies (STS), large scale technological systems, and semiotics, ANT has been characterized as a "material-semiotic" approach to analyze heterogeneous

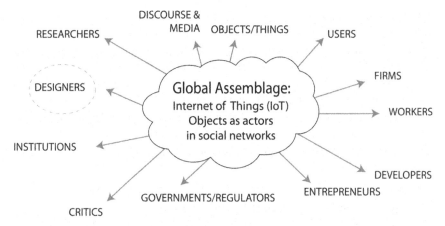

Figure 4.1 Assemblage Thinking Focuses on Agency and the Dynamic Relationship between and Among People, Institutions, Objects, Discourses and Practices.

relations between things (material) and concepts (semiotics). ANT helps to explain how material-semiotic networks emerge as dynamic assemblages in which heterogeneous actors (i.e., humans, nonhuman things, and concepts) are involved in creating meaning. The relations among actors must be continuously reinforced through performing practices that keep the network intact. Because relations between actors may be contentious and contested, maintenance of network is an ongoing social process. As depicted in Figure 4.1, designers play a significant role in ANT networks that comprise the dynamic assemblage of the IoT by giving form and substance to our imaginings. They suggest how *what is* might be transformed into *what might be,* thereby creating the conditions for social and cultural change.

Design's role in the process of maintaining and creating actor networks is not new. Historically, the role of design has been to suggest and articulate the form and substance of things and environments. Today design's role has expanded to include articulating relations among heterogeneous actors. Contemporary designers explore questions such as "How might a particular network be maintained, morphing into something new by adding new components and capabilities? How might the actor network materialize? What relations might be possible between agents? What might it look like and how might it feel, both tangibly and intangibly?"

Enchanted Objects

David Rose, MIT Media Lab scientist, describes his concept of enchanted objects as "objects that will respond to our needs, come to know us, and learn to think ahead on our behalf." They are animated by the ambient technology of the IoT. Enchanted objects are "ordinary things made extraordinary." They are unlike contemporary technological innovations such as the smartphone that Rose (2014) describes as "a confusing and feature-crammed techno-version of the Swiss Army knife … a jealous companion that turns us into blue-faced zombies." He concedes that although the smartphone is convenient and useful for some tasks "it is a dead end as the human-computer interface" because "it has little respect for humanity." "What enchants the objects of fantasy and folklore, by contrast, is their ability to fulfill human drives with emotional engagement and élan" (Rose 2014, 7).

Design in parody and thought experiments

Parody and thought experiments have been used to imagine what relations might be like between human and nonhuman actors and to explore the dilemmas and possibilities that emerge from their interactions. Interaction designer Simone Rebaudengo (2012) created one such future scenario in a video, *The Story of Brad the Toaster* that portrays what human-object relations might become as "things" acquire the capacity for increased agency through the IoT and M2M communication. *The Story of Brad the Toaster* provides a glimpse of what it might be like in a world of enchanted objects.

Brad is a toaster that is one of a new breed of products designed to maximize the use of scarce resources and minimize the accumulation of cast off appliances that end up in landfills. Recognizing these constraints, appliances like Brad are designed to be "hosted" rather than purchased. Brad is an

Figure 4.2 **"Addicted Products: The Story of Brad the Toaster" Vimeo, May 1, 2012 by Simone Rebaudengo.** Courtesy of Simone Rebaudengo.

active agent in the IoT assemblage. He is integrated into multiple networks: an external network connects him to shops where he might order additional supplies, a peer network in which he communicates with other toasters, and a local network where he is able to communicate with another appliance, for example, the refrigerator, and his human host. Through the narration, Rebaudengo tells the story of how Brad comes to be hosted by Charles, how he settles into his new home, and how over time he become increasingly stressed by not being used as often as the other toasters to which he is connected. Eventually Brad decides Charles is not deserving of his services. He contacts the home office and requests to be relocated to a new host. Brad's departure leaves Charles, his former host, feeling "gutted."

As the third wave of the Internet, IoT is opening possibilities for "things" like Brad to assume agency in dynamic actor networks. For example, the emerging IoT is actualizing new relations between human and nonhuman actors in the complex networks like factory floors and domestic and commercial environments.

Robots, Cobots, and Carebots

Robotics has been prevalent in areas that include manufacturing and medicine (e.g., robotic-assisted surgery). Most robotic applications were designed as machines to perform a limited repertoire of tasks and to have little resemblance to the human actors that deploy them. For example, surgical robots like the da Vinci Robot surgical system look very similar to early industrial robots. Interestingly, they exhibit none of the humanoid characteristics or agency of social robots, and as yet are not designed to "collaborate" with human actors.

More recent advances in robotic systems, for example, "collaborative machines" or cobots and social robot caregivers (carebots), have expanded the role of robots to act collaboratively with human partners. In these applications, machine actors not only take on a more humanoid appearance, but also exhibit basic social skills and are able to respond "emotionally" to the humans with whom they interact (Manyika et al. 2017, 11).

Cobots

Industrial robots have been used in factory settings since the early 1950s. Distinctly machine-like in appearance, "Early industrial robots had limited 'intelligence', autonomy and operational degrees of freedom. They were mostly designed to perform one or two sets of repetitive tasks in a highly controlled environment" (A. Robinson 2014). The design and engineering of early industrial robots was primarily concerned with their functionality in factory environments.

These early industrial robots were at home on assembly lines, blending in with other machines while somewhat inconspicuously replacing the need for human labor. Unlike cobots, the latest evolution in robot automation, there was no pretense about appearing humanoid. Figure 4.3 below shows cobots and humans working together. Cobots, while retaining the machine characteristics of their ancestors, now sport a "face" and eyes that are cast down and attentive to the task being performed. The design of cobots reflects the shift from very expensive, fixed position robotic machines with a limited task repertoire to more affordable, agile, reprogrammable nonhuman partners capable of performing multiple tasks alongside human employees. The introduction of cobots marks a distinct turn to the social role of nonhuman actors on the factory floor, begging the question of how this trend will impact cultural change, particularly in the area of human labor and employment. Projections for the sale of collaborative robots in manufacturing and assembly, consumer services, and other areas over the next few years suggest major growth in the robotics industry (Tobe 2016).

Collaborative robots are broadening their presence in manufacturing, but also increasingly in consumer and service environments. According to The Robot Report (Tobe 2016), an online website that monitors and tracks industry news and events, the forecast for robot sales is expected to be close to 136,000 units up from 2,344 units in 2014. By 2020 consumer-related sales of robots is expected to reach nearly 78,000 units, more than the 57,433 units projected for manufacturing in the same period.

Figure 4.3   Smart and Collaborative: Robots for the Real World. The sleek design of "Sawyer", which has more in common with an iPhone than a conventional industrial machine, represents the current evolution of factory automation. Courtesy of Rethink Robotics, Inc.

Social Robots

The application of robotics in the social realm is gaining increasing attention. For example, Dutch film maker Sander Burger's 2015 documentary *Ik ben Alice* ("Alice Cares") portrays Alice, a prototype care-droid developed by the US firm Hanson Robotics. Alice's doll-like characteristics are paired with the size and face of an eight-year old girl and an adult female voice. She is designed to serve as an interactive companion for lonely elders. The role of design is implied in a review in the *Hollywood Reporter* that describes how in the film:

> Burger shows Alice "visiting" the apartments of three octogenarian Dutch ladies, the contraption overcoming their hosts' initial wariness and quickly forming chatty bonds. This prototype "care-droid" represents the technology at a relatively early stage, with Alice unable to move anything apart from her head, eyes (which incorporate tiny cameras) and mouth. Her body is made much more obviously robotic in appearance than the face, to minimize the chances of her interlocutors mistaking her for an actual human. Such design-touches are discussed by Alice's programmer in meetings with social-workers, which Burger and his editor Manuel Rombley intersperse between the domestic exchanges that provide the bulk of the running-time. (Young 2015)

Burger's documentary explores how robot technology might be able to assist senior citizens in the western world (Burger 2015). The film depicts a social experiment in which Alice, a carebot, is developed in order to meet future demands for care of elderly citizens that are lonely or suffering from dementia. The *Hollywood Reporter* review (Young 2015) describes the film as suggesting "the benign side of artificial intelligence."

> Burger shows Alice "visiting" the apartments of three octogenarian Dutch ladies, the contraption overcoming their hosts' initial wariness and quickly forming chatty bonds. This prototype "care-droid" represents the technology at a relatively early stage, with Alice unable to move anything apart from her head, eyes (which incorporate tiny cameras) and mouth. Her body is made much more obviously robotic in appearance than the face, to minimize the chances of her interlocutors mistaking her for an actual human. Such design-touches are discussed by Alice's programmer in meetings with social-workers, which Burger and his editor Manuel Rombley intersperses between the domestic exchanges that provide the bulk of the running-time.

Social robots are already being deployed in business and commercial environments. "Pepper," a humanoid robot developed by Omar Abdelwahed, a designer for the Japanese technology company, SoftBank, is four feet tall and weighs 62 pounds. Already on the job in Japanese Pizza Huts and a Belgian hospital, Pepper was in residence for several weeks at B8ta, a futuristic tech store in Palo Alto, California. After meeting Pepper at B8ta, the author of an article in PC magazine reported:

> Upon first glance, Pepper doesn't seem like much. Not only is she diminutive, but she has just a head, arms, and torso; there's little more than a plastic bulge where her legs should be, making her look a bit like a mermaid without a fin. That's intentional, SoftBank Vice President Steve Carlin explained. "Pepper understands how to create an empathetic bond" with humans, he said, something that isn't possible if she were human-sized, since she'd appear scary to children and threatening to adults. (Brant 2016)

Although they share some common characteristics, robots that have distinctly social roles differ in appearance from their industrial kin. Like Alice and Pepper, they are more human-looking and are designed to encourage the humans they engage with to develop humanlike relationships with them. Many robots that are designed to serve in a social capacity play on the human response to *neoteny*, or cuteness, that mimics childlike features such as large, unblinking eyes and big heads (Rose 2014, 37), characteristics that are core elements of toy design. Rose argues:

> Human beings attach to objects and imbue them with lifelike personalities. It doesn't take much for us to start thinking of and interacting with an object as if it were human. Give a device a blinking LED, a hiplike curve, a smile-shaped grill, and we start to impute personality to it. It seems trustworthy, mercurial, arrogant, friendly. When a machine can move around, our expectations for intelligence and personality are further sparked. "Throw in a face," as Sherry Turkle, the MIT sociologist, says, "and we're goners." (2014, 37)

As a real world example of how this theory can be seen in product design, Rose points to "hundreds of blogs" that report people's attachment to their Roomba vacuum cleaners: "the smilelike curve on its top, combined with its dumb but deliberate determination—bumping into one thing after another but never daunted—and the way it spins and emits a continuous mechanical purr that make a Roomba too cute and charming to resist" (2014, 38).

Citing recent research on human-robot interaction, Rose (2014) notes that the principle of reciprocity, which states that how we behave toward others influences how they will behave toward us, not only underlies human-to-human conduct, but also applies in human-object relations. According to Rose, the human tendency to form attachments to objects that are perceived to suggest even a glimmer of personality is significant. As robots become more humanlike, we arrive at a point of ontological conflict or "category confusion" (Rose 2014, 41). The more robots look and behave like humans, the more uncomfortable with them we become. Rose acknowledges Masahiro Mori as coining the term "uncanny valley," explaining that

> His insight is that as a machine gets closer and closer to humanness, the likeness becomes so good that any imperfection becomes unacceptable, even creepy. We have no problem with an industrial robot, or a C-3PO, because they are clearly not flesh and blood. They don't threaten or confuse our own sense of self. Frankenstein, on the other hand, approaches a human facsimile. He is mostly constructed of human parts. He walks, talks, and seems sentient. Thus, his non-human components—the bolt in the neck, stiches in the forehead, the lurching walk—make him disturbing. Mori concluded that it was foolhardy to create robots that attempt to exactly mimic humans. (2014, 40–41)

This section has provided examples of how advanced robotics has been deployed in various settings such as in factories, homes, and surgery rooms. Rather than a one-size-fits-all solution, each type of robot is designed to fulfill a role in a dynamic assemblage of human and nonhuman actors. Technological innovation in the domain of M2M communication, ubiquitous computing, and ambient devices is steadily but subtly replacing the need for human participation. Citing recent projections on employment for males ages 25–54 former US treasury secretary Lawrence Summers stated in recent blog post that "Job destruction caused by technology is not a futuristic concern. It is something we have been living with for two generations." Although women make up 50.8% of the US population (HRSA 2012), the impact of job destruction on women's employment is not addressed in this blog post.

Mirroring multiple viewpoints, the proliferation of automation, robotic agents, and related third wave of the Internet (IoT) have sparked a range of responses from unfettered praise, promotion, and acceptance to caution, suspicion, and fear. One thing for certain is that the current wave of technological innovation, now referred to as "The Fourth Industrial Revolution" (Schwab, 2016), will continue to generate massive and ongoing cultural change.

DESIGN + ANTHROPOLOGY AND SOCIAL TRANSFORMATION

New technologies have always generated unintended consequences that are difficult to anticipate before and even as they are occurring. Balsamo (2011) argues that this "persistent blind spot is symptomatic of an impoverished understanding of the relationship between technology and culture." Citing Slack and Wise (2005, 6) she notes, "the dominant perspective—what they referred to as the 'received view of the relationship between culture and technology' is that culture and technology are separate domains of human life."

> This received view is well represented in common understandings about technology that, for example, see it as the main "engine of progress," and that propagate beliefs in technological determinism, along with the myth that people have little or no control over technology writ large. Holding tight to the received view significantly impacts the imagined process of technological innovation. Like blinders on racehorses, it literally limits the vision of the track ahead. (2011, 4)

The consequences of a limited vision include not only a narrowed range of possibilities for new technologies, but also preset the explanation for technological failure as resulting from unforeseen conditions and forces. The dominant perspective that separates the technological from the cultural obscures the likely causes of technological failure while simultaneously limiting "the imaginative space of innovation in the first place" (Balsamo 2011, 4).

Design anthropology, defined as an emerging transdisciplinary field that embodies elements of design and anthropology, provides a counter perspective that eschews technological determination, positing instead that technology and culture are inextricably linked. As a transdisciplinary field that includes practitioners from diverse disciplines, design anthropology embodies an emerging set of principles that characterize its interventionist, transformative approach. These principles include:

- Commitments to collaborative process
- Commitment to transcending disciplinary boundaries
- Participatory design to include a wide range of stakeholders
- Ongoing methodological experimentation
- Prototyping and testing
- Rigorous critique
- Design for social impact (Miller 2016)

Design anthropological projects are characterized by rigorous critique and iterations that take into account both intended and unintended consequences of proposed designed artifacts. The explicit aim, to achieve transdisciplinary collaboration, challenges team members to think beyond disciplinary boundaries, to articulate and to demonstrate their individual contributions. This necessitates subordinating individual disciplinary biases and focusing instead on the dynamics of the whole system and how other disciplinary perspectives can contribute and add value.

Based on the work of Rabinow, Marcus, et al. (2008), Ingold (2011, 2013), Otto and Smith (2013), and others, Anastassakis and Szaniecki (2016) have argued:

design anthropology has the potential to create a new paradigm for knowledge production not only in anthropology, but also in design, opening up a third space with its own research and training practices. Promoting correspondence and collaboration among designers, anthropologists, and other citizens implies that all of us are co-creators of significant practices that can transform the present while creating alternatives for the future. (2016, 124)

Design anthropologists seek to move anthropology "beyond the mere description and analysis of contexts" proposing instead "a restoration of the 'designerly' dimension in anthropological practice" (Gatt & Ingold, 2013). According to Gatt and Ingold, a characteristic of design anthropology, or "anthropology-by-means-of-design," is the "deliberate interweaving of research and artifact production during fieldwork" (2013, 150). According to Anastassakis and Szaniecki, conceptualizing design in the broad sense opens the way for dynamic improvisation in everyday life "and therefore an anthropology constituted by means of design becomes inherently experimental. From this position, the key to the combination of design and anthropology lies in the concept of correspondence" (2016, 124). Correspondence is not describing or representing the world, but responding and collaborating with it. As Anastassakis and Szaniecki wrote:

Thus, while anthropology by means of ethnography is a descriptive practice, anthropology by means of design is a practice of correspondence, which however, should not be limited to predicting as traditional designers do. To shift from predicting to correspondence, emphasis must go from the form itself to the process of conformation. In this perspective, design creativity does not lie in the novelty of the prefigured solutions, but in the ability of inhabitants of the world to respond to the changing circumstances of life. (2016, 124–25)

The design anthropological perspective stands in sharp contrast to the dominant understanding of innovation in business and the popular press in which innovation is nearly synonymous with technology and where the value of innovation is based exclusively on economic costs and returns (Balsamo 2014, 3). Rejecting the notion of technological determinism, the design anthropological perspective asserts the connection between culture and technology and acknowledges the persistence of human agency and creativity in imagining and designing alternative futures.

"Encountering the possible"

In presenting a series of examples from a series of design anthropological "experiments," Binder (2016) notes that moments of discovery cannot be planned or controlled, but instead "grow from the design anthropological encounter as an experience of simultaneously becoming knowledgeable and taking possession of agency to enter emerging landscapes (Teiler et al. 2011)" (2016, 278). The experience does not require stepping out of the everyday flow of acting in the world, nor does it set the intention of arriving at a goal. Instead, Binder uses Schechner's notion of *actuals*, "the outcomes of staged encounters in which the subjunctive 'what if' touches upon the real" (2016, 278).

This approach to "encountering the possible" is mirrored in an iterative process of design that begins by thoroughly researching "what is" relative to a problem or area of concern. It then moves to explore the realm of "what if" by creatively brainstorming possibilities. How might we transform "what is" into something different or conceive it in a completely new way? In the final stages, possibilities become "concepts" that are prototyped, tested in the world, and examined in light of existing constraints and underlying assumptions to determine "what works." Rather than focusing on innovation writ large, the iterative design process encounters the possible through a series of collective improvisations that do not privilege technology over the social and cultural. Referring to the design anthropological encounter "as an experience of simultaneously becoming knowledgeable and taking possession of agency to then emerging landscapes," Binder explains:

> In the design laboratory, it is this actualization of the movement of the present that is both exposed and held back as an experience of difference. It is not action as either a cause or an effect of networks, but a moment of *becoming* which, paradoxically, is at the same time both imagined and real. (2016, 278)

The design anthropological perspective and approach can be described as a "zone of experimentation" where people are able to collectively imagine, prototype, and test concepts: "The design proposal becomes a thing around which to gather, a thing that is not detached from what it invokes" (Binder 2016, 279).

Transforming the dominant paradigm

The mindful combination of elements from design and anthropology has opened a space for collective experimentation with possibilities and imagining alternative futures. Recent developments demonstrate how the design anthropological approach can be applied to break free the gravitational pull of the "received view" of the relationship between technology and culture that perceives them as separate. How might design anthropological thinking and doing be deployed at a scale to transform the existing paradigm that privileges technological innovation, technological determinism, and economic value over other forms of capital?

Developments in design and anthropological theory and practice hold promise for challenging the dominant perspective of innovation as a "thing" or object, focusing instead on the new and "unique arrangements" that are made possible by a novel idea or invention. Balsamo posits:

> Where the term "invention" applies to a novel idea or thing, innovation implies the creation of unique arrangements that provides the basis for a reorganization of the way things *will be* in the future: in this sense, all innovations rearrange culture. (Balsamo 2011, 3)

Rather than waiting until cultural change is finally recognized, we can deploy design anthropological theory and practice to anticipate *in advance* the consequences of technological innovation before it is too late to correct the costly errors that result from social and cultural ignorance.

CONCLUSIONS AND DISCUSSION: IMAGINING AND DESIGNING FUTURE WORLDS

> There is always inherent, in the best research work, a sense of play, of something driving the choices made in thinking through multiple possibilities and taking some responsibility for what it *ought* to be, not just what it will be.
>
> —(Robinson 2010, 10)

This chapter has presented examples of how design has paved the way for cultural change by harnessing the power of imagination to introduce visions of possible futures. Design plays an important role in reconfiguring assemblages through the design of new artifacts. Many of these examples already exist in the present, presaged by images once perceived as the stuff of science fiction and fantasy. The sense of play that Robinson (2010) alludes to is a necessary element in an iterative design anthropological process: play allows for creating zones of experimentation in which multiple possibilities can be imagined, prototyped, tested, critiqued, and refined. Design anthropological practice and theory can be applied to help think through alternatives, allowing us to anticipate *in advance* the consequences of possible futures and the impact that they are likely to have on existing practices, assemblages, and reconfigurations of actor networks and social relationships.

The emergence of the Internet of Things (IoT) has been cited as an example to demonstrate the dynamic nature of the assemblage known as the Internet. Over time, the Internet has evolved through three stages or waves as new technologies have been invented and are either accepted as innovations and adapted to by other components of the assemblage or rejected. The influence of specific components has changed. For example, the role of government regulation has consistently lagged in responding to innovations even though the development of the Internet was initially funded by DARPA (the Defense Advanced Research Projects Agency), a US government R&D agency. Likewise, design and designers have gained agency as design has shifted from an object-centered to human-centered focus that is situated in a holistic, systems perspective. Beyond engineering, designers have been called upon to address complex "wicked" (Buchanan 1992, Rittel and Webber 1973) problems at the front end of innovation in many fields, including medicine and health care, law, transportation, education, and the integration of advanced technology. Through all three waves of the evolution of the Internet, the media has moved from traditional print- and audio/visual-based mediums (i.e., newspapers, magazines, radio and television) to web-based social media platforms. In the meantime, firms have scrambled to adapt to the increasing pace of change not only in technology, but also in the relations and practices brought about by subsequent waves of the Internet's evolution due to consequences of wider societal and cultural changes.

Figure 4.4 depicts how the Internet assemblage has evolved over the three waves. Development of Wave 1, the fixed Internet, was led by computer science researchers, who were located in government or institutional R&D labs. Entrepreneurs willing to take risks drove development of the information technology market. Workers were introduced to computing and "the Net" in the workplace. The price of personal computing was a barrier to widespread adoption, with computers and Internet access too expensive for most

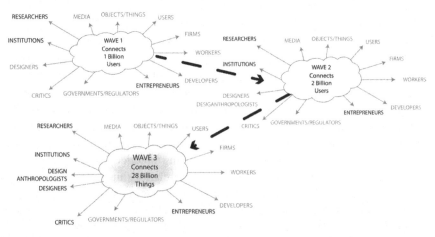

Figure 4.4   Three Waves of the Internet Depict the Dynamic Nature of Assemblages.

households. Critics raised physiological and mental health concerns and a looming "digital divide." Web design emerged as a professional occupation.

Wave 2 introduced mobility. Development continued to be led by entrepreneurs; however, a growing number of firms realized the potential of mobile technology particularly the smart phone. Increased bandwidth and cheaper computers drove home computing and online shopping. Web-based audio and video sharing platforms began to emerge. Productivity gains increased with widespread factory and office automation. Increased discourse about "net neutrality" sparked debates about keeping the Internet free and open. Gaming and social media took off, further increasing the demand for professional designers and prompting new fields such as interaction (IxD) and user experience (UX) design. Growing sophistication of online education prompted institutions to develop MOOCs (massive open online courses) and increase STEM (science, technology, engineering, and mathematics) programs. Big Data arrived.

Wave 3, the IoT, represents networks of connected human and nonhuman actors (e.g., objects or things) driven by the profusion of connected devices and Big Data generated by sensors and social media. The Internet backbone, the primary data routes linking large strategically interconnected computer networks, and central routers, were not designed to carry the immense amounts of traffic that is being generated by the IoT. Objects acquire agency within social networks through M2M communication, in many cases replacing the need for human participation (e.g., in factory, retail, hospitality). The impact of automation on workers fuels job loss and threats to identity. Most new technology and business model innovation emerge from entrepreneurial networks. Because of their scale, firms play an important role in driving technological innovation out to social groups. Designers play an important role in bridging online and off line life. They dominate fields such as information design and the design of services, interactions, experiences, products, and processes. Critics raise concerns about the impact of automation on job loss and the downsides of Big Data specifically, threats to security and privacy, and the proliferation of undocumented sources of information and "news." Governments continue to play regulatory catch-up. Unable to get in front of technological innovation, regulations are typically not proactive and instead are passed in response to critical situations.

In the Internet of Things (IoT) objects are acquiring agency through their connectedness within nonhuman and human networks; automation greatly reduces the need for human actors. The capacity for object/thing agency, which will continue to increase in the third wave of the Internet, is proportional to the significance of "things" in relation to other elements of the assemblage that make up the IoT. Smart Cities, connected homes, automated vehicles, cobots, carebots, and other robotic applications are rapidly becoming a part of everyday life. The unintended consequences of the current wave of technological innovation are only beginning to be considered outside the realm of fiction writers such as Anne Bishop. We can relate to her character, Meg, as she tries to cope with the barrage of change over which she has little control.

The transdisciplinary field of design anthropology holds a space for challenging technological determinism and relocating the nexus of innovation from major actors such as corporate interests that privilege economic value to communities that balance economic, social, and other forms of capital to create new markets, new technologies, and new ecosystems of players. As an emerging field, design anthropology faces the challenge of developing the capacity and strategies to practice in the complex spaces of innovation that are the hallmark of the contemporary.

REFERENCES

Anastassakis, Zoy and Barbara Szaniecki. 2016. "Conversation *Dispositifs*: Towards a Transdisciplinary Design." In *Design Anthropological Futures,* edited by Rachel Charlotte Smith, Kasper Tang Vangkilde, Ton Otto, Joachim Halse, and Thomas Binder, 121–138. New York: Bloomsbury.

Appadurai, Arjun. 2014. Foreword to *Design as Future-Making*, edited by Susan Yelavich and Barbara Adams, 9–11. New York: Bloomsbury.

Balsamo, Anne. 2011. *Designing Culture: The Technological Imagination at Work.* Durham, NC: Duke University Press.

Bahga, Arshdeep and Vijay Madisetti. 2014. *Internet of Things: A Hands On Approach.* Charleston, SC: Bahga and Madisetti.

Barry, Andrew. 2001. *Political Machines: Governing a Technological Society.* London: Athlone.

Binder, Thomas. 2016. "The Things We Do: Encountering the Possible." In *Design Anthropological Futures,* edited by Rachel Charlotte Smith, Kasper Tang Vangkilde, Ton Otto, Joachim Halse, and Thomas Binder, 121–138. New York: Bloomsbury.

Bishop, Anne. 2015. *A Vision in Silver: A Novel of the Others.* New York: Penguin Group.

Brant, Tom. 2016. "Meet Pepper, A Humanoid Robot That Understands Emotions." *PC Magazine*, August 12. Accessed March 12, 2017. http://www.pcmag.com/news/346955/meet-pepper-a-humanoid-robot-that-understands-emotions

Buchanan, Richard. 1992. "Wicked Problems in Design Thinking." *Design Issues* 8(2):5–21.

Burger, Sander (writer). 2015. Ik ben Alice. J. Doolaard (producer). KeyDocs, Amersterdam.

Epp, Amber M., Hope Jensen Schau, and Linda L. Price. 2014. "The Role of Brands and Mediating Technologies in Assembling Long-Distance Family Practices." *Journal of Marketing* 78:81–101.

Forster, E. M. 1909/2016. *The Machine Stops*. Lexington, KY: CreateSpace Independent Publishing Platform.

Gatt, Caroline and Tim Ingold. 2013. "From Description to Correspondence." In *Design Anthopology: Theory and Practice*, edited by Wendy Gunn, Ton Otto, and Rachel Charlotte Smith, 139–158. New York: Bloomsbury.

Goodman, Nelson. 1978. *Ways of Worldmaking*. Cambridge, MA: Hackett Publishing Co.

Health Resources and Service Administration. 2013. "Women's Health U.S.A. 2012." Accessed March 13, 2017 https://mchb.hrsa.gov/whusa12/pc/pages/usp.html

Hurst, Nathan. 2013. "Big Corporations are Buying Design Firms in Droves." *Wired*, May 15. Accessed March 13, 2017. https://www.wired.com/2013/05/accenture-fjord/

Ingold, Tim. 2011. *Being Alive: Essays on Movement, Knowledge and Description*. London: Routledge.

Ingold, Tim. 2013. *Making: Anthropology, Archaeology, Art and Architecture*. London: Routledge.

Jankowski, Simona, James Covello, Heather Bellini, Joe Ritchie, and Daniela Costa. 2014. "IoT primer The Internet of Things: Making sense of the next mega-trend." Accessed March 13, 2017. http://www.goldmansachs.com/our-thinking/outlook/internet-of-things/iot-report.pdf

Manyika, James, Michael Chui, Medhi Miremadi, Jacque Bughin, Katy George, Paul Willmott, and Martin Dewhurst. 2017. *A Future That Works: Automation, Employment, and Productivity*. Accessed March 18, 2017. http://www.mckinsey.com/global-themes/digital-disruption/harnessing-automation-for-a-future-that-works

Margolin, Victor. 2002. *The Politics of the Artificial: Essays on Design and Design Studies*. Chicago, IL: University of Chicago Press.

Margolin, Victor. 2005. "The Liberation of Ethics." In *Ethics? Design?*, edited by Clive Dilnot, Vol. 1: 160. Archeworks: Chicago.

Margolin, Victor (editor). 1989. *Design Discourse: History Theory Criticism*. Chicago: University of Chicago Press.

Merlan, Anna. 2016. "Wasteland: The Mad Max Festival That Makes Burning Man Look Lame." *Wired*, September 29. Accessed March 13, 2017. https://www.wired.com/2016/09/wasteland-mad-max-festival-makes-burning-man-look-lame/

Miller, Christine. 2016. *"Design Anthropology: Discovery and Evidence of Emerging Pathways in Anthropology."* Paper presented at the American Anthropological Association Annual Meeting, November 16–20, 2016, Minneapolis, MN.

Otto, Ton and Rachel Charlotte Smith. 2013. "Design Anthropology: A Distinct Style of Knowing." In *Anthopology: Theory and Practice*, edited by Wendy Gunn, Ton Otto, and Rachel Charlotte Smith, 1–29. New York: Bloomsbury.

Papernak, Victor. 1984. *Design for the Real World: Human Ecology and Social Change*. Chicago: Academy Chicago Pulishers.

Pelino, Michele, Frank E. Gillett with Christopher Voce, Michell Mai, and Laura Easton. 2016. *TechRadar™: Internet Of Things, Q1 2016: Software Technologies For IoT Have Hit The Growth Phase, But Security And Standards Lag*. Accessed March 13, 2017. https://www.forrester.com/report/TechRadar+Internet+Of+Things+Q1+2016/-/E-RES121873

Post-Apocalyptic.com. 2016. Accessed March 13, 2017. http://post-apocalyptic.com

Rabinow, Paul. George Marcus, James D. Faubion and Thomas Rees. 2008. *Designs for an Anthropology of the Contemporary.* Durham, NC: Duke University Press.

Rebaudengo, S. (Writer). 2012. *Addicted products: The story of Brad the Toaster* [video]. Accessed March 13, 2017. https://vimeo.com/41363473

Rittel, Horst. W. and Melvin M. Webber. 1973. "Dilemmas in a general theory of planning." *Policy Sciences 4*, 155–169.

Robinson, Adam. 2014. The History of Robotics in Manufacturing. Accessed March 13, 2017. http://cerasis.com/2014/10/06/robotics-in-manufacturing/

Robinson, Rick E. 2010. "*After Ethnography.*" Paper presented at the User-Centered Design, Telefonica. Madrid, Spain. http://www.iota-partners.com/

Rose, David. 2014. *Enchanted Objects: Design, Human Desire, and the Internet of Things.* New York: Scribner.

Slack, Jennifer Daryl and J.MacGregor Wise. 2005. *Culture and Technology: A Primer.* New York: Peter Lang.

Schwab, Klaus. 2016. "The Fourth Industrial Revolution: what it means, how to respond." World Economic Forum—Global Agenda—Fourth Industrial Revolution website. Accessed March 13, 2017. https://www.weforum.org/agenda/2016/01/the-fourth-industrial-revolution-what-it-means-and-how-to-respond/

Suchman, Lucy. 2008. "Feminist STS and the Sciences of the Artificial." In *The Handbook of Science and Technology Studies 3rd edition,* edited by Edward J. Hackett, Olga Amsterdamska, Michael Lynch, and Judy Wajcman, 139–164. Cambridge, MA: The MIT Press.

Teiler, A., Thomas Binder, Georgio De Michelis, Pelle Ehn, Giulio Jaccuci, Per Linde, and Ina Wagner. 2011. *Design Things.* Cambridge, MA: MIT Press.

Teixeira, Carlos and John Zimmerman. 2016. *Transforming Design Matters: Steering Committee Workshop to Envision Design Research Organization for US and Canada.* Accessed March 13, 2017. https://www.id.iit.edu/news/workshop-to-envision-design-research-organization/

Tobe, Frank. 2016. Collaborative Robots are Broadening Their Marketplaces. Accessed March 13, 2017. https://www.therobotreport.com/news/collaborative-robots-are-broadening-their-market-spheres

Wasteland Weekend. 2017. Accessed March 13, 2017. http://www.wastelandweekend.com/about/

Yelavich, Susan and Barbara Adams, Editors. 2014. *Design as Future-Making.* London: Bloomsbury.

Young, Neil. 2015. "'Alice Cares' ('Ik ben Alice'): Rotterdam Review." *The Hollywood Reporter,* January 27. Accessed March 13, 2017. http://www.hollywoodreporter.com/review/alice-cares-ik-ben-alice-766744

Part II

CONSUMER AND PRODUCT/SERVICE INTERFACE

Chapter 5

The Changing Nature of Everyday Practice

Smart Devices as Disruptive Agents of Cultural Change

Jennifer Watts-Englert, Margaret H. Szymanski, and Patricia Wall

In the 1970s, Xerox[1] pioneered collaborations between anthropologists and technologists so that trends in people's everyday practice could be leveraged for innovation (Szymanski et al. 2011). The sensibility was that for technologies and solutions to be adopted and effective, they should be designed with an understanding of how people were currently accomplishing their work (Blomberg and Burrell 2012). Work practice study—the holistic, human-centered description of people's practice as they use tools and technologies in their natural environments to accomplish their activities—grounded innovation in customers' current and emerging needs. Initially, studies about work in the office (Suchman 1987, Orr 1996, Sellen and Harper 2003) and later investigations of human practice in a variety of other work environments (Szymanski and Whalen 2011) and leisure settings (Wall et al. 2010, Isaacs et al. 2012, Rangaswamy and Arora 2015) revealed trends and opportunities for human-centered technology and organizational development (Jordan and Putz 2004, Whalen and Whalen 2011, O'Neill and Martin 2013).

In this chapter, we bring to the forefront people's everyday practice amidst a landscape of smart devices (e.g., smartphones and tablets) and myriad applications. Across a series of studies spanning five years, we explore the disruptive change that iPhones and other smart devices triggered by giving users anytime access to the Internet with the swipe of a finger and creating an app economy that enables users to do almost anything they want with the phone (Kelly 2012). The ways in which people are choosing to use these technological resources, individually and collectively, are shaping cultural practice and over time, cultural change.

LITERATURE REVIEW

The smart device landscape is ideal for examining cultural change through a lens of assemblage theory focused on agency. Within this landscape, human intention and effort collide head on with tools and systems that exercise their own influence on users. As Allen (2011) argues, assemblage theory is a way of understanding how "heterogeneous elements can hold together without actually forming a coherent whole." In the smart device landscape, people are combining different elements in flexible ways where each instance of smart device practice is in itself a composed assemblage that meets a human need in the moment: at the café it provides conduit for up-to-the-minute work status; it is a digital document holder for the plane boarding pass and the retail coupon; at social outings it is a multimedia repository for sharing. The ways people are integrating smart device practices into their lives along a continuum of incremental change become "the normal way."

Our view is that people's everyday practice is an "improvisational choreography of action" (Whalen et al. 2002, Johansen et al. 2016) whereby people actively create the stage upon which their lives are lived, assembling their resources to support the types of actions and lifestyles they desire. Like Whalen and his colleagues (2002), we believe it is important for an analysis of people's practice to "take account of its contingently *produced* nature" (Whalen et al. 2002, 255) and to identify how the features of practice are brought together in the moment. As technology innovations are introduced and resources and environments change, people are the primary agents in improvising ways of acting anew. An important part of the choreography of action is arranging elements so they are effective together; this arrangement is the key to the adoption of practices that are prerequisite to cultural change.

In the smart device landscape, people and smart devices both have agency in shaping cultural practice. The situatedness of practice (Wertsch 1985, Suchman 2007) highlights how human activity is embedded in environments with ideas, objects, and conditions that both shape practice and are practice-shaped. In the smart device landscape, this situatedness results in a reflexive relationship between people's actions and the actions enabled by smart devices and their apps. For instance, the Sleep Cycle alarm clock is an app that tracks your sleep patterns and wakes you at the lightest sleep phase so you feel more rested. With this app, when asked how you slept last night, you can hold up your iPhone and show technology-based documentation of your actual sleeping activity and compare your night's rest with your friends (Isaacs et al. 2012). This app is redefining how people conceive of a night's sleep; since it can be analyzed retrospectively in the detail of its occurrence, a night's sleep is no longer bound to a post-event evaluation. As people choose to track and augment their lived experiences, personal smart devices and smart devices in collectivity are creating a distributed cognition that provides resources for capturing, reflecting upon, and sharing their actions (Hollan et al. 2000). Yet even as device functionality becomes more personalized and sophisticated, devices provide an extendable platform for users to add, modify, and remove capabilities, and thereby making them flexible enough to address needs in different scenarios and environments. This elasticity in device functionality facilitates closer adoption and subsequent cultural change.

In this chapter, we look at how everyday practice has been changing amidst the smart device landscape by examining practices over multiple points in time and in various settings of use, to understand the synergies between human and technological agency. The complexity of studying cultural practice in this domain cannot be overstated; people's expertise and use of smart devices is evolving amidst a proliferating explosion of choices and functions (Mathew 2015). We describe how we captured the impact of this technology on everyday practice across a series of studies, informing how agency contributes to an explanation of change in the smart device landscape. We also explore the resulting trajectories of change that emerge from the adoption of these devices.

Throughout our research activities, we identified the characteristics that facilitated the adoption of the smart technology we were studying. *Convenience* was one of these characteristics because the devices are small, portable, intuitive, and readily available to support a wide variety of tasks. Another reason for such tight integration into people's lives is *personal productivity*. Since these devices are always close at hand, people use them to accomplish a myriad of tasks during micro-moments throughout the day (Watts-Englert et al. 2012, Garreta Domingo 2016). A third reason why these devices are so interwoven into everyday experience is that their functionality allows them to serve as *social resources* that expand how we connect with one another in face-to-face and asynchronous scenarios. This functionality has redefined what it means to communicate, maintain relationships, and share experiences. Finally, and perhaps most importantly, the capacity for *personalization* has facilitated the creation of mutual relevance between users and their smart devices. Not only can users choose the types of functionality they want to install on their devices, but the functionality itself allows the device to provide personalized services that are tailored to a user's particular experience. For example, tracking apps allow a smart device to provide detailed information to help users understand and adjust their personal habits and practices. Also, apps that contain personal notes and to-do lists expand human capabilities by distributing cognition and personal history across a person's collection of devices. These characteristics of convenience, personal productivity, social resource, and personalization invoke trajectories of change, in which cultural practice and technology design continue to evolve in relation to each other.

DATA AND METHODS

Our findings come from a series of studies conducted over five years, 2007–2012. These studies were designed to inform product development and design, and to identify emerging trends on the cutting edge of work practice: how new technology was impacting mobility, distributed teamwork, communication, security, social media, information flow, and paper use. Specifically, these studies focused on how knowledge workers interacted with smartphones, tablets, cloud computing, and other emerging technologies to accomplish their work (Watts-Englert et al. 2017). Participants were recruited by a professional recruiter and through our team's personal contacts. In this chapter, we report on the findings from a total of 57 open-ended interviews, and 30 full days of shadowing.

Future of Work Study 2007–2008

For the first study in our series, we interviewed and observed 26 participants (Watts-Perotti et al. 2011). Twenty-four participants worked at home, and 15 participants were mobile workers, who conducted at least 50% of their work outside a bricks-and-mortar office (Watts-Perotti et al. 2010). Some participants fit into both categories—working at home at certain times and

Figure 5.1   Participant Creating Diaries of Daily Activities.

Figure 5.2 Participant Creating Collages to Illustrate Current and Ideal Work Environments.

conducting mobile work at other times. We used a combination of interviews, observations, diaries, and collages to gain a broad understanding of how work was changing (Watts-Perotti et al. 2009). The interviews occurred in locations where participants typically worked: coffee shops, home offices, and cafes. Participants prepared for the interviews by completing a diary for seven days, which allowed them to become more aware of their work practices and habits (see Figure 5.1). During the interviews, participants created a collage illustrating how their current work environment compares to their ideal work environment (see Figure 5.2). This study examined a variety of topics including where people did their work, how they coordinated and accomplished their work in various settings, how they managed information (or not), how they incorporated paper and printing into their work, and how they balanced work life and personal life (Watts-Perotti et al. 2009).

Future of Work Study 2009

In a second study, we focused specifically on mobile workers who used smart phones. We recruited 17 participants who worked outside a bricks and mortar office for at least 50% of their work hours. Many were mobile for close to 80% of their work time (Watts-Englert et al. 2012). Since smartphones were just beginning to be adopted, our goal was to understand the capacity that these devices had for influencing work practice. We recruited lead users of smartphones (Urban et al. 1988). These participants used smartphones for more than just phone calls and emails, including texting, note taking, and a variety of apps like mileage trackers, music, photos, and GPS. Participants worked in a wide range of knowledge-work jobs including sales, design, rental properties, consulting, and startups, and represented a range of ages from early 1920s to late 1950s. We conducted open-ended interviews with each participant and shadowed them for a full workday. We observed them wherever they did their work, including riding with them in their cars and shadowing their meetings and other activities throughout the day (Watts-Englert et al. 2012). Participants also created visual maps to illustrate the places where they conducted their work, and the tools they used to support work in these places.

Back to the Future of Work Study 2011

A couple of years after the second study, we went back to the field to explore how the use of smartphones had evolved since our earlier studies. We also focused on the emerging use of tablet computers (e.g., iPads), cloud computing, and social media. In this third study, we conducted 14 open-ended interviews at the location where participants conducted a majority of their work (often a coffee shop or other transient meeting or work space). Participants used the technology we wanted to study (e.g., smart phones, tablets, cloud computing, social media) in both their work and personal lives. They represented a variety of knowledge-work professions including K-12 education, event planning, ministry, property management, a print shop owner, and nonprofits. In addition to the interviews, we also observed eight of the 14 participants for a full day of work.

These studies were complemented by a year of synthesis, during which we created prototypes and concepts to facilitate conversations within the company. We conducted a fourth study in 2012, which explored how healthcare professionals used mobile devices and other new digital technology and practices to support their work. We also drew from a year-long study, in 2014, of 19 participants in Europe and the United States, exploring how people respond to modern issues of personal privacy in the digital landscape. These studies were supported by an internal advisory board, which included professionals from various business and infrastructure groups across the company. Advisory board members provided input into study questions, shadowed us in the field, provided access to interested groups, and advocated for our research throughout the company (Watts-Englert et al. 2011).

FINDINGS

Smart devices, initially smartphones and tablets, have proven to be disruptive agents of cultural change. Since the introduction of consumer-affordable cell phones in the late 1990s, mobile technology sales have continued to grow worldwide at an impressive rate (Statistica, 2016). The introduction of the Apple iPhone in 2007, a device that combined a mobile phone, MP3 player, camera, audio recording, Internet access, and the ability to add new functionality (via the App Store), revolutionized the paradigm for mobile computing and communication. This technology enabled people to be easily connected online—anywhere, anytime, providing an expandable sandbox that allowed people to use mobile capabilities in new ways. The Apple iPhone initiated a trajectory of cultural and technological evolution that transformed people's interactions and practices across work and personal contexts. In this section, we discuss the factors of convenience, personal productivity, social resources, and personalization, which facilitate close adoption of this technology into peoples' everyday lives.

Convenience

By 2008, when we embarked on what was to become a series of studies exploring the future of work, a variety of Personal Digital Assistants (PDAs) and mobile phones had already come and gone in the market. Blackberry phones were the predominant devices used by professionals in corporate business contexts. The introduction of the first-generation iPhone in 2007 changed the game, providing easy to use, touch-enabled mobile devices that were appealing in consumer and commercial business markets. Smartphones met a growing need for people who worked, at least part of time, outside a conventional office (e.g., at home offices, on the go road warriors). There was also a growing consumer demand for devices that integrated popular features such as phones, messaging, cameras, MP3 players, and Internet access. Once in the hands of users, mobile technologies transformed human practices and were, in turn, transformed by emerging practices in new and unexpected ways.

In our studies, we observed people eagerly embracing the convenience of these new mobile devices. They were compact, extremely easy to use, and had the ability to connect to people, information, and resources around the world. These devices also integrated important capabilities into one device, reducing the need to carry multiple technologies (e.g., cell phone, MP3 player, camera) and the assorted cables and charging devices necessary to keep them running. People immediately started to use these capabilities in innovative ways. For example, one participant created a bicycle holder for his iPhone so he could view and interact with it while he commuted to work. He said: "I can ... listen to the radio, track my mileage and text a colleague—all while I am riding my bike to work!" This device changed the face of his commute by enabling the accomplishment of multiple objectives on this exercise-based trip to and from work.

In another example, we observed a mobile doctor utilize his smartphone to facilitate his visits to patients in their homes. Before heading out each day, he referred to the pre-programed route and driving directions on his smartphone that he set up the day before. He made any necessary adjustments to the day's route if there were changes in the patient roster for that day. While on the road, he routinely used calls, texts, and the phone's Internet browser to keep in touch with office staff, issue orders for labs, set up referrals to specialists, check insurance coverage, update his schedule, and notify patients of any schedule adjustments for their appointment (e.g., if he were running early or late). Although he carried a laptop to connect to the electronic patient records system while he was with patients, he also used his smartphone to connect to this system when it was not convenient to set up his laptop.

These examples illustrate how people improvise and use available resources to shape their practices to meet emergent needs. Improvisation does not always work the first time. Experimentation and refinement accompany adoption of new apps and capabilities. For example, one participant said that he was constantly searching for new apps to help him further streamline the way he made use of his phone to accomplish his work tasks. At the time of our study, he had cobbled together a set of apps and tools to keep his work process digital. However, these apps did not integrate smoothly with each other. For example, he used the LiveScribe digital pen to take meeting notes, and then stored these notes in multiple locations, each of which served a different purpose. The LiveScribe app allowed him to replay the audio of the meeting, but did not allow him to share the notes, so he also stored his notes in two other locations: OneNote, which enabled him to access the notes from his computer or mobile devices, and a shared online drive, so he could share the notes with colleagues. Through experimentation, he created a workflow using apps to manage notes. He was always on the lookout for ways to make this and other tasks easier. Adopters of new technology often encounter challenges as they apply new devices and applications to their existing practices. However, the benefits of new capabilities and the resulting conveniences often outweigh the costs of adoption.

Another indication of the refinement of smart device apps, which occurs in response to the evolving use of these apps, is the feedback mechanism embedded in smart device infrastructures like the App Store or Google Play Store. When users provide feedback and reviews for applications, the developers of those apps have immediate access to customer comments so they can make updates to meet customer needs for capabilities and convenience.

Smartphones and tablets have access to an ever-growing selection of capabilities and applications that continue to replace many traditional objects in our daily lives. Examples of such traditional objects include clocks, remote controllers (e.g., for TV's, cameras), books, musical instruments, flashlights, fitness trackers, calendars, calculators, and GPS navigation systems to name a few. The list goes on and on, limited only by one's imagination. Our study participants valued this integration because it allowed them to travel lighter and still have everything they need at their fingertips. The biggest downside of relying on one device for all this functionality is that if the device were lost or damaged, there could be a serious impact and disruption in the owner's life, especially if the device contents were not backed up. One participant jested that losing his smartphone would bankrupt his lifestyle: "if I lose (my smartphone), I'll go live on the streets with my bike."

The convenience afforded by the integration of multiple capabilities in a smartphone or tablet device can lead to some compromise regarding individual capabilities. The quality of any individual function—for example, the camera, audio or video recorder, e-reader or email—may not be up to the standards of a stand-alone device or application on a PC. However, our study participants demonstrated that they were willing to compromise for the convenience of having these capabilities in one compact, easy-to-use device that is close at hand. Many participants used e-readers for reading books, but left them home and used their phone when traveling. One participant commented, "The Kindle is a much better reader … (but) I'm not going to carry yet another device." In another example, cameras on phones were used as scanners to capture images of documents, such as receipts, which business travelers submitted for expense reports. In each of these cases, smartphones provided a lower quality experience, but the convenience offset potential concern about quality.

An interesting side effect of the proliferation and use of mobile devices, smartphones in particular, is that they have become an appendage, always in hand or nearby. They don't seem to be carried in backpacks or bags any more, but reside in more accessible locations throughout the day and night. When not in hand or in a pocket, they wait on the table beside dinner plates during meals, stay close at hand (maybe even provide directions) in the car, and rest by the bed side, or even in the bed (Isaacs et al. 2012) at night. The close physical proximity of these devices is another indicator that they are interwoven into everyday practice. They are go-to devices for all sorts of activities throughout the day. However, this tight integration raises interesting questions about the potential over-reliance on and attachment to technology, the impacts on personal interactions, and implications for cultural change.

Personal Productivity

Personal productivity has been defined as "completing the actions that move you closer to accomplishing your goals in a manner that brings balance

Figure 5.3   Participant checking messages during a red light micro moment.

and ease into your life" (Riddle, 2016). Personal productivity was a recurring theme among study participants. Many participants struggled with an overwhelming amount of information arriving through multiple devices and channels (e.g., email, web links, text messages). As one participant noted, "I have 700 messages in my inbox. They're there because I have to do something with them." Smart devices were viewed as a way to increase personal productivity in the face of this information overload. Participants took advantage of the "always on" aspect of smartphones by completing tasks during micro-moments: small moments of free time during the course of the day (Watts-Englert et al. 2012). Because the phone was always close at hand, or in their hand, participants could easily swing it into view for calls, texts, or reminders. We observed participants checking email or responding to texts at red lights (see Figure 5.3), in parking lots, waiting rooms, or during meals. This allowed them to take care of things as they arose. One participant read articles on his phone while at breakfast, stating, "I have a few minutes while I'm eating breakfast and I want to use them productively" (see Figure 5.4).

By allowing participants to manage incoming information throughout the day, smartphones helped eliminate or reduce the need to catch up or review email at the end of the day. As one participant commented, "I think the beauty of these mobile devices is now it's even easier to keep up, and ... anything that needs my attention, it happens. It has made my life so much easier because I don't come home at night and have to read through all of the stuff. I easily save a couple of hours every day with the (smartphone)."

Figure 5.4   Participant reading on smartphone during micro moments.

The evolving network of always on, always connected devices has transformed the way we receive and process information. Information, once shared as static paper and electronic documents, is now received in more dynamic, nonlinear, often-fragmented content in formats such as electronic documents, web links, texts, and multimedia content. Devices provide on-the-spot information for individuals and groups. Everything is at your fingertips—food, rides, shopping, banking, notes, to-do lists, and entertainment. Cognition and problem solving have become distributed across people and their devices (Hollan et al. 2000, Zhang and Patel 1996, Woods 2003). For example, another way mobile devices increase personal productivity is by serving as an access point or personal portal, extending the reach of users to external information as well as to their own data on remote devices, such as the cloud. One participant scanned personal documents that he had previously carried in his wallet, such as his health insurance card. This practice came in handy during a doctor visit which he recalled, "I'm sitting in front of the receptionist. … And before she runs out of patience, I've usually found that group number, and I just show her the phone and say, 'Here, I'm insured.'" He relied on the ability to access whatever information he needed, whenever he needed it, with his smartphone.

Smartphones have changed the landscape of work, increasing personal productivity by allowing people to leverage micro-moments to manage information and accomplish tasks. Along with these advantages, the "always on" aspect of the phone has begun to include an expectation that people are "always available" to immediately respond to calls, emails, and texts. Perpetual connectivity poses an ongoing challenge for people to define and maintain a sense of balance. One participant expressed a need for more non-technology-mediated interaction when she said, "Everything is digital. It has its perks, but ... sometimes I don't want to be connected ... I just want to interact (with real people)," Several participants scheduled downtime from digital devices. For example, one participant mentioned, "Sundays are no-technology days for me."

Social Resources

As mobile devices have become entrenched in daily life, people have come to rely on them for communication, networking, and support for real-time social interactions occurring in their everyday lives. In our studies, participants referred to tablets as "talking pieces" that enrich conversations by providing Internet-based resources like facts, diagrams, YouTube videos, and slide presentations. One participant brought his tablet to share a brief presentation and demo with attendees who stopped at his booth during a trade show. He then used his phone to take photos of their business cards, jot notes and reminders in the note taking app, and send product brochures via email as a follow-up to their discussion. Not only did his smart devices enrich his conversations with attendees, but they also stored the information he needed to remember, and helped him immediately establish future connections with attendees through email.

Another participant, a professor, constantly used his phone and tablet to supplement his meetings with students by pointing them to information on the Internet or in specific applications. Yet another participant, a real estate agent, used her iPad to show her clients a preview of available properties while they were touring houses. She also used the camera on her phone to document needed repairs with contractors, and then used texting to discuss details, schedules, and costs. Because tablets can display information in engaging multilayered ways that allow users to interact dynamically with figures and illustrations, and provide hyperlinks allowing users to explore topics mentioned within the pages, people are increasingly weaving them into their everyday conversations.

Social media and cloud computing spaces also enhanced participants' ability to share information with colleagues, friends, and family. For example, social media enabled one participant, a pastor, to track his impact within his community of friends and followers by reading and responding to comments on his posts. During Sunday services, he used an iPad to refer to his notes and to project videos, which he created or found on the web, in conjunction with his sermon (see Figure 5.5). He also integrated text messages into the sermon, sending text messages to teen members of the congregation during the service

Figure 5.5 Pastor preparing for Sunday sermon using tablet and laptop to create sermon notes and video to accompany sermon.

to solicit their input and engage them in a conversation about the service. "We text a few questions and it will hit all the kid's phones during the service time ... keep their attention, because kids are always on their phones texting. If we keep up with the times, the church can remain relevant and current."

Other participants invested time and effort to ensure that their businesses were visible in social media channels like Facebook and Twitter, because they've learned that many customers prefer to follow and get automatic notifications rather than go to the business websites. Similarly, participants commented that cloud spaces made sharing very easy because the information was already "there," on the cloud, and they just had to send or share the link, rather than sharing the actual video or picture. This practice allowed them to save the time and bandwidth required to send large files, and share links to information during the course of a conversation, rather than wait until they had access to a computer. As such, it provided yet another anchor for the close adoption of these devices into everyday life.

Challenges for users sharing mobile devices.

In addition to being social resources, personal mobile devices were often shared with participants' family, friends, and sometimes colleagues. In the professional setting, sharing a device with others presented several challenges. We observed primary school teachers who shared their personal smartphones with students, so they could use educational applications they had downloaded onto their phones. We also saw teachers who shared a

Figure 5.6 Teachers discussing education apps for primary school students on their tablets.

community iPad (one purchased by the school for use in the classroom) with students or other teachers (see Figure 5.6). In both cases, teachers commented that it was difficult to manage the accounts for their devices since the applications had to be downloaded through someone's personal account. Obtaining reimbursement from the school for personal account purchases made on a shared device was difficult. Moreover, on the community device, where only one account could be created, the teachers had to coordinate the acquisition of apps, and be careful not to delete apps that other teachers had downloaded.

While we observed an increase in the use of personal mobile devices in the workplace, most participants commented that they still were not able to use tablets to do their "heavy" work. Participants said their tablets did not yet "plug and play" with everything they needed to use. Moreover, they said that with tablets, printing and typing with integrated keyboards was still difficult. They commented that while many of the work-related applications they use on computers are available for tablets, the tablet versions of the apps require completely different interaction styles. Menus have been rearranged, and participants said they had to relearn how to use the application on the tablet. In addition, tablets do not readily support the easy flow of information across multiple applications at one time. Consequently, the biggest barriers for replacing computers with tablets are the limited capability of some key applications and the difficulty of navigating back and forth between multiple applications.

Personalization

In the smart device landscape, people are the primary agents in assembling their digital lifestyle from both a device and a functionality perspective. The device is the tool that creates the foundation for select applications, chosen because they are relevant to that person's lifestyle. Interestingly, while the application is designed for a specific purpose, its actual use and applied usefulness are always determined by the person using the application. Whereas LinkedIn is a business- and employment-oriented social networking service, one participant treated it as his rolodex, enabling him to keep in touch with people he did not see often. In another case, Google+, an interest-based social network, served as a repository of restaurants that a social group wanted to try.

As smart devices store more and more of our information, people are increasingly depending upon—even building trust with—their device's ability to "know" what they need to know and do. One participant enabled this type of information access by custom designing his own home page that was full of links to medical information, bank accounts, and password hints. He could then access this information whenever and wherever he needed it. In another scenario, the TripCase application oversaw travel details which one participant said, "reduces a certain amount of the anxiety around, 'Did I remember to book that rental car? And when does the flight leave anyway?'"

Smart devices can track physical and digital activity to inform people about their practices around diet, exercise, personal productivity, and other activities. Tracked digital experiences are informing proactive customer support to help users avoid service overage fees and maintain their devices in working order as well as shopping recommendations tailored to users' preferences. This human-device collaboration is also changing how people manage their health and wellness. It enables proactive monitoring of actions that include contextual support and recommendations for behavior change (e.g., periodic alerts to stand up and take a break from stationary work, status updates on calorie or exercise goals, recognition when goals have been met). While this capability provides a way for people to gain insight into their own actions, it can infringe on personal privacy. For example, a user may agree to share his/her fitness data with a community of fitness application users, but may receive unanticipated feedback from members of the community. In other cases, users may inadvertently enable permissions to share their data or not read and/or fully understand how their data will be shared.

Overwhelmingly, we found that the augmented cognition and action tracking benefits provided by devices outweigh the concern for privacy risks. Some participants said they were careful not to post any confidential information in an environment where something "could go viral at any moment." However, others were more likely to take full advantage of the convenience brought about by sharing personal information, rather than choosing not to use these applications. When asked about privacy, one participant said: "It's a consideration ... But it's never stopped me from doing anything." This quote reflects what we heard from many other participants. They did not have experience with privacy breaches, and at the time, the scope and potential impacts of cyber security breaches were not as well understood or visible as they are today. Many people who enjoy recording their information and experiences in the digital landscape engage in sharing by broadcasting and posting on social media sites that chronicle their activities, which essentially creates a personal history over time.

The capacity for personalization—of phones, of apps—has facilitated the evolution of mutual relevance between users and their smart devices. Since these devices have become so interwoven into peoples' everyday lives, it is easy for them to share intimate details about their habits and practices with their smart devices; such devices now include smart watches and other wearable technologies, in addition to smartphones and tablets. As the devices track these details, they can provide services and information that are extremely relevant to their users. We see this mutual relevance as a strong factor initiating a trajectory of change that has already transformed our culture and from which it is difficult to retreat. For example, one participant, a salesperson, acknowledged that since her company owned her business car and credit card, her company could track all of the locations that she visited, as well as the timing for these trips, and all of the purchases that were charged to the card. Participants mentioned that while they may be uncomfortable sharing such intimate details, they feel they cannot live their current lives without this kind of sharing. "What really can you do? Do you go off the grid and only get cash? I wouldn't be able to have my job if I didn't have E-ZPass (an automatic electronic toll collection system for some US toll roads), or use the company gas card. Like I don't even know how I would do it."

DISCUSSION

One only has to remember the world before the introduction of smart devices to get a sense for the powerful impact these technologies have had on peoples' lived experiences. In less than a decade, these devices have disrupted cultural practice as they have rapidly begun to replace a wide array of everyday tools and technology: phone books, clocks, maps, watches, rolodexes, shopping lists, and even money, to name a few. This change is truly accelerated, as Toffler (1970) predicted, and as McCabe mentions in the introduction to this book. In a matter of a few years, these devices have replaced long-lived technology for people who use these devices regularly, some of which have existed for over 60 years. The first phone book was printed in 1878 (Keillor 2012), and Rolodexes were first sold in the 1950s (Diaz 2010).

Factors Facilitating Smart Device Adoption

In this chapter, we have described the agency of people in adopting smart devices and technology. Smart devices have become deeply interwoven into the everyday lives of the people who use them regularly, leading to a mutual identity of sorts—a new type of assemblage, in which the person and the device have become intertwined in a coevolving relationship. The evolution and refinement of these devices are driven by their usage and the choices their users make. The cultural practices they support are, in turn, impacted by the evolving design and development of the devices. Consistent with assemblage theory, the factors that have facilitated the adoption of these devices include interactions between the devices, their users, and their practices, as well as discourse and ideas shared with other people and groups (see Figure 5.7).

Convenience can only be defined in the context of a particular cultural practice or expectation. The notion of convenience refers to the way in which the device supports the particular needs of its user, in the context of the tasks and goals he or she is attempting to accomplish. Therefore, these characteristics are not external forces that impose cultural change. Instead, they contribute to change through a mutual resonance and coevolution between the

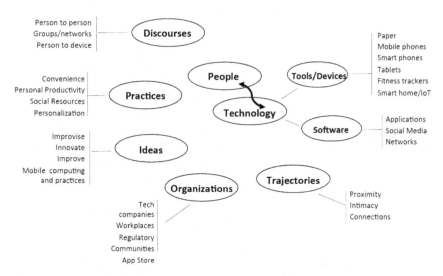

Figure 5.7 Assemblage of Factors that have Facilitated the Adoption of Smart Devices.

devices and the practices they support. Agency and innovation are therefore distributed between the devices and their users.

Trajectories of Cultural Change

This process of interwoven coevolution contributes to several trajectories of cultural change. The trajectory of proximity emerges from and is facilitated by the characteristics of convenience and personal productivity. Since these devices afford convenient access to many useful functions, people have begun to keep them within close physical proximity, thus opening the opportunity for further innovation, refinement, and adoption. This trajectory of proximity began when people started carrying their smartphones on their body, instead of in bags or briefcases, and has continued to evolve into smaller devices like smart watches that are worn on the body at all times. Already, we are seeing this trajectory continue through the development of smart clothes like bras and shoes that monitor and adapt themselves to biometric patterns detected through heart rate, breathing rate, and muscle activity (Edwards 2016).

The trajectory of intimacy is the second trajectory we have identified. It arises from the characteristic of mutual resonance and leads to an increasingly stronger bond between devices and their users. This trajectory began with isolated software applications that tracked behaviors like food consumption or exercise activities. These early applications required users to input information about their behaviors manually, and offered inherent leeway for users to filter and intentionally choose the information they provided. As the trajectory has progressed, early tracking technologies have evolved into systems that monitor a wider set of behaviors for a longer period of time. These new systems do not depend on manual input, and therefore make it more difficult for users to filter out patterns that they might want to keep private. At the same time, the ability to monitor this larger set of behaviors makes it possible for the tracking systems to identify and inform users of patterns they may not realize. For example, cell phone service companies monitor data usage and proactively send warning messages when users get close to their data limits. Looking into the future, we see predictions of even closer relationships between smart devices and their users, in which personal digital agents embedded in the devices will monitor a person's habits and practices and offer personalized recommendations (Levy 2015).

A third trajectory of change, emerging from the characteristic of social resource, is one of the interpersonal connections. Smart technology and the Internet have provided opportunities to establish detailed connections with people across the globe. Starting with text-based chat communities in the early days of the Internet, this trajectory currently manifests as a huge array of social networking apps, from Facebook, to musical.ly, to online multi-player games; all are supported by rich, visual, dynamic media that have the potential to facilitate connection over the Internet. As this trajectory continues into the future, we see predictions of holograms and other technologies that support three-dimensional, real-time interaction between people who are not colocated (Prigg 2014), as well as augmented reality applications that provide an overlay of social information to supplement conversations and other social interactions (Strickland n.d.).

CONCLUSION

These trajectories of change are underway and have already contributed to changes in cultural practices and expectations. Looking into the future, we are left with three concerns: (1) implications of the always-on, connected nature of the technology, (2) implications for non-digital interpersonal relationships, and (3) implications for privacy.

The close physical proximity that people establish with their smart devices can lead to a lifestyle in which they are constantly stimulated by technology. Before smart technology, people used their micro-moments as down time, which gave them periodic breaks from their work or activities throughout the day. Now that smart devices are always close at hand, we see people cramming work or other types of stimulation into every micro-moment they have. Patkar (2015) states that people pick up their smartphone an average of 211 times per day, and that the constant use of smartphones can cause problems for the human body, ranging from disrupted sleep to neck problems and increased anxiety. There is a growing body of research focusing on smartphone addiction and the impacts on our lives (Matthews et al. 2009, Roberts et al. 2014, Al-Barashdi et al. 2015, Goswami and Singh 2016).

The trajectory of change in interpersonal connection has also led to significant cultural change. Keller (2013) states that many people who use social networking tools tend to prefer online interactions over face-to-face encounters, which can lead to the tendency to spend more time with their smartphone than interacting with people in their vicinity.

When we examine the trajectory of intimacy, combining the impacts of constant connection and the possibility of being tracked via smart devices, a third concern arises: privacy. As people choose the benefits that can be gleaned from tracking applications, they do not always consider the potential implications of this tracking on their personal privacy. Once the intimate details of their habits and practices are documented digitally, this information can be used in a variety of ways, some of which may be detrimental to the person who was tracked.

Despite these concerns, we find hope in the notion of agency within assemblage theory. Our observations and studies in the domain of business anthropology lead us to believe that people can, and do, actively participate in the process of cultural change. As society evolves along the trajectories that emerged from our study findings, people will continue to make choices and innovate as they assemble resources to choreograph their lives. As technology continues to evolve rapidly, our key prediction is that people will adopt, use, and refine these technologies in unexpected ways, to support their requirements, behaviors, needs, and lifestyles.

NOTE

1. All authors formerly worked for Xerox and participated in conducting the studies on which this chapter is based.

REFERENCES

Al-Barashdi, Hafidha Suleiman, Abdelmajid Bouazza, and Naeema H. Jabur. 2015. "Smartphone addiction among university undergraduates: A literature review." *Journal of Scientific Research & Reports* 4, no. 3: 210–225.

Blomberg, Jeanette. and Mark Burrell. 2012. "An ethnographic approach to design." In *Human-Computer Interaction Handbook: Fundamentals, Evolving Technologies, and Emerging Applications*, edited by Julie A. Jacko, 1025–1052, Boca Raton, FL: CRC Press.

Domingo, Muriel. 2016. "Micro-moments: Are you designing for them?" Accessed March 13, 2016. https://www.interaction-design.org/literature/article/micro-moments-are-you-designing-for-them.

Edwards, Luke. 2016. "Best smart clothes: Wearables to improve your life." Accessed December 19, 2016. http://www.pocket-lint.com/news/131980-best-smart-clothes-wearables-to-improve-your-life.

Goswami, Vandana and Divya Rani Singh. 2016. "Impact of mobile phone addiction on adolescent's life: A literature review." *International Journal of Home Science*, 2: 69–74.

Grossman, Anna Jane. 2010. "The Life and Death of the Rolodex." Accessed December 19, 2016. http://gizmodo.com/5497511/the-life-and-death-of-the-rolodex.

Hollan, James, Edwin Hutchins, and David Kirsh. 2000. "Distributed cognition: toward a new foundation for human-computer interaction research." *Association for Computing Machingery (ACM) Transactions on Computer-Human Interaction (TOCHI)* 7, no. 2: 174–196.

Isaacs, Ellen, Margaret Szymanski, Yutaka Yamauchi, James Glasnapp, and Kyohei Iwamoto. 2012. "Integrating local and remote worlds through channel blending." In *Proceedings of the Association for Computing Machinery (ACM) Conference on Computer Supported Cooperative Work*, February 11–15, 2012, Seattle, Washington, pp. 617–626.

Johansen, Jens Petter, Petter Grytten Almklov, and Abdul Basit Mohammad. 2016. "What can possibly go wrong? Anticipatory work in space operations." *Cognition, Technology & Work* 18, no. 2: 333–350.

Jordan, Brigitte, and Peter Putz. 2004. "Assessment as practice: Notes on measures, tests, and targets." *Human Organization* 63, no. 3: 346–358.

Keillor, Candace. 2012. "The First Phone Book. Stories from American History." Accessed December 19, 2016. https://studiesinamericanhistory.wordpress. com/2012/12/08/the-first-phone-book/.

Keller, Maura. 2013. "Social Media and Interpersonal Communication." Accessed December 19, 2016. http://www.socialworktoday.com/archive/051313p10.shtml.

Kelly, Heather. 2012. "5 ways the iPhone changed our lives." Accessed March 13, 2013 http://www.cnn.com/2012/06/28/tech/mobile/iphone-5-years-anniversary/.

Levy, Heather Pemberton. 2015. "Gartner Predicts Our Digital Future - Smarter with Gartner." Accessed December 19, 2016. http://www.gartner.com/ smarterwithgartner/gartner-predicts-our-digital-future/.

Mathew, Jerin. 2015. "Apple App Store growing by over 1,000 apps per day." Accessed March 13, 2017. http://www.ibtimes.co.uk/apple-app-store-growing-by-over-1000-apps-per-day-1504801.

Matthews, Tara, Jeffrey Pierce and John Tang. 2009. "No smartphone is an island: The impact of places, situations and other devices on smartphone use." IBM Research Report #RJ10452. Accessed December 19, 2016. http://domino.research. ibm.com/library/cyberdig.nsf/papers/F5FD878B5B062ACA85257635004EC3F5/ $File/rj10452.pdf

O'Neill, Jacki, and David Martin. 2013. "Relationship-based Business Process Crowdsourcing?." In *14th IFIP International Conference on Human-Computer Interaction – INTERACT 2013*, Cape Town, South Africa, pp. 429–446.

Orr, Julian Edgerton. 1996. "Talking about machines: An ethnography of a modern job." Ithaca, NY: Cornell University Press.

Patkar, Mihir. 2015. "What Your Smartphone Is Doing To Your Body & Mind." Accessed December 19, 2015. http://www.makeuseof.com/tag/smartphone-body-mind/.

Prigg, Mark. 2014. "Home Researchers reveal the tech of 2025." Accessed December 19, 2016. http://www.dailymail.co.uk/sciencetech/article-2787330/Home-holo-decks-personalised-diets-clothes-3D-print-morning-Researchers-reveal-tech-2025. html.

Rangaswamy, Nimmi, and Payal Arora. 2016. "The mobile internet in the wild and every day: Digital leisure in the slums of urban India." *International Journal of Cultural Studies* 19, no. 6: 611–626.

Riddle, Joshua. 2016. "What is personal productivity?". Accessed November 19, 2016. http://workawesome.com/productivity/personal-productivity/.

Roberts, James, Luc Yaya, and Chris Manolis. 2014. "The invisible addiction: Cell-phone activities and addiction among male and female college students." *Journal of Behavioral Addictions* 3, no. 4: 254–265.

Sellen, Abigail J., and Richard H. R. Harper. 2003. *The myth of the paperless office*. Cambridge, MA, MIT Press.

Stappers, Pieter Jan, and Elizabeth B. N. Sanders. "Generative tools for context mapping: tuning the tools." In *Design and Emotion*, edited by Deana McDonagh, Paul Hekkert, Jeroen van Erp and Diane Gyi, pp. 77–81. Boca Raton, FL: CRC Press. 2003.

Statistica, 2016. "Global smartphone sales to end users from 1st quarter 2009 to 1st quarter 2017, by operating system (in million units)". Statistica.com. Accessed November 17, 2016 https://www.statista.com/statistics/266219/global-smartphone-sales-since-1st-quarter-2009-by-operating-system/.

Strickland, Jonathan. 2016. "Looking Ahead to Future Communication - What is the future of communication?" Accessed December 19, 2016. http://electronics.howstuffworks.com/everyday-tech/future-of-communication1.html.

Suchman, Lucy A. 1987. *Plans and Situated Actions: The Problem of Human-Machine Communication*. New York, NY: Cambridge University Press.

Suchman, Lucy A. 2007. *Human-machine reconfigurations: Plans and situated actions*. New York, NY: Cambridge University Press.

Szymanski, Margaret H., and Jack Whalen. 2011. *Making work visible: Ethnographically grounded case studies of work practice*. New York, NY: Cambridge University Press.

Toffler, Alvin. 1970. *Future Shock*. New York: Random House.

Urban, Glen L. and Eric von Hippel. 1988. "Lead user analyses for the development of new industrial products." *INFORMS Institute for Operations Research and Management Sciences* 34, no. 5: 569–582.

Wall, Patricia, Jonas Karlsson, Johannes Koomen, Tong Sun, Eric Bier, and Margaret Szymanski. 2010. "Capturing and sharing stories in virtual and interactive web environments: a cross-organizational case study." In *Proceedings of the 11th Biennial Participatory Design Conference*, November 29–December 3, 2010, Sydney, Australia, pp. 292–293. New York: Association of Computing Machinery.

Watts-Englert, Jennifer, Margaret H. Szymanski, Patricia Wall and Mary Ann Sprague. 2016. "Collaboration for impact: Involving stakeholders in ethnographic research." In *Collaborative Ethnography in Business Environments*, edited by Maryann McCabe, 60–79. New York, NY: Routledge.

Watts-Englert, Jennifer, Margaret Szymanski, Patricia Wall, Mary Ann Sprague and Brinda Dalal. 2012. "Back to the future of work: Informing corporate renewal." In *Proceedings of the Ethnographic Praxis in Industry Conference*, October 14–17, 2012, Savannah, Georgia, pp. 150–162. Hoboken, NJ: Blackwell Publishing Ltd.

Watts-Perotti, Jennifer, Mary Ann Sprague, Patricia Wall, and Catherine McCorkindale. 2009. "Pushing new frontiers: Examining the future of paper and electronic documents." In *Proceedings of the Ethnographic Praxis in Industry Conference*, August 30–September 2, 2009, Chicago IL, pp. 197–208. Hoboken, NJ: Blackwell Publishing Ltd.

Watts Perotti, Jennifer, Patricia Wall, and Gabriele McLaughlin. 2010. "The future of knowledge work: predictions for 2020." *On the Horizon Journal* 18, no. 3: 213–221.

Watts-Perotti, Jennifer., Mary Ann Sprague, Patricia Swenton-Wall, Catherine McCorkindale, Lisa Purvis and Gabriele McLaughlin. 2011. "Exploring Documents and the Future of Work." In *Making Work Visible: Ethnographically grounded case studies of work practice*, Edited by Margaret. H. Szymanski and Jack Whalen, New York, NY: Cambridge University Press.

Whalen, Jack, Marilyn Whalen, and Kathryn Henderson. 2002. "Improvisational choreography in teleservice work." *The British Journal of Sociology* 53, no. 2: 239–258.

Whalen, Jack and Marilyn Whalen. 2011. "Integrated Customer Service: Reinventing a Workscape." In *Making Work Visible: Ethnographically grounded case studies of work practice*, edited by Margaret. H. Szymanski and Jack Whalen. New York, NY: Cambridge University Press.

Woods, David D. 2003. "Discovering how distributed cognitive systems work." In *Handbook of Cognitive Task Design*, edited by Erik Hollnagel, pp. 37–53. Mahwah, New Jersey: Lawrence Erlbaum Associates.

Zhang, Jiajie, and Vimla L. Patel. 2006. "Distributed cognition, representation, and affordance." *Pragmatics & Cognition* 14, no. 2: 333–341.

Chapter 6

Technology Metaphors and Impediments to Technology Use at the Base of the Pyramid in India

Bhattacharyya and Russell W. Belk

Society is an assemblage or a "whole" that comprises "self-subsistent" heterogeneous parts (DeLanda, 2006 p. 5, 9). It is ever-morphing, given the inevitability of cultural change. Of the various facilitators powering a cultural change, technology is foremost today (Beard, 1927; Giddens, 1994; Heidegger, 1977; Marcuse, 1982; Marx, 1867; McLuhan, 1964; Mumford, 1970; Nye, 1996; Postman, 2011; Romanyshyn, 1989; Standage, 1998). In fact, technology is held as one of the greatest destabilizers (or "deterritorializers") of a societal assemblage for it offers people the power to unravel the internal homogeneity that an assemblage tends to have (DeLanda, 2006, p. 13). Thus, technology is positioned as a key enabler, helping people to enact their own cultural change both at the micro and macro levels (Asbell, 1963; Canham, 1950; Kurzweil, 2005; Lotan et al. 2011).

In today's world of technological "solutionism" (Morozov, 2013, p. 5), consumers are viewed as empowered beings, wielding technology to pick and choose the kind of cultural changes that they want to enact (Epp, Schau, and Price, 2014; Kozinets, 2008). When people do not pursue a cultural affordance, or a possibility of action, this phenomenon is seen as a voluntary choice made by empowered people (Askegaard, Arnould, and Kjelgaard, 2005; Kozinets, 2002; Oswald, 1999; Penaloza, 1994; Varman and Belk, 2009). In these studies, a deliberate lack of embrace of technological change has been seen as purposeful resistance. Yet the following excerpts from our field study highlight a different phenomenon among the poor in India:

Interviewer: You mentioned that your husband knows how to operate a computer. Can you operate a computer?
Taposhi: No. How can I know to do that?
Interviewer: Have you seen his computer?

Taposhi: Yes, he sometimes brings it home.
Interviewer: What does your husband do on it?
Taposhi: Don't know [Shrugs].
Interviewer: Has he shown you things in the computer?
Taposhi: No [Gets irritated]. Do people like us have the time to see stuff in things like those, tell me? I return home from work and then I have to run to collect water from the timekol [a timed water outlet], then I have to cook, then take care of our child. If people like us sit around with things like those, how will things [life] work, tell me?

From the field notes:

> Today, while waiting on the landing for the elevator, I saw Shyamoli (the maid from the apartment next door) head towards the stairs to go downstairs. I called out to her, indicating that the elevator was just about to arrive. She looked confused and shook her head. "That's not for us. The watchman will tell the management if I take the elevator and then I shall get into trouble," she said.

While various product features such as Relative Advantage of the product, its Triability, Compatibility, Complexity, and Observability (Rogers 2003) as well as the 4 A's of Affordability, Accessibility, Availability, and Awareness (Prahalad 2012) impact product TABLEpower disparity can have in decelerating or stopping the adoption of technological change by the poor. Yet with the exception of Berry (1980), this phenomenon has been largely overlooked in the literature on technological change. This oversight is notable since it ignores the variation in agency of various entities in the assemblage involved in technology adoption and use (Bode and Kristensen, 2016; Foucault, 1980; Marx, 1867). In this chapter, we provide the poor's perspectives on the barriers to the technological and cultural change vis-à-vis perceived domination in specific technology consumption assemblages.

The poor participating in this study were those living at the base of the economic pyramid (the BOP). The BOP is a metaphor for the majority of the world who survive on the lowest levels of income. Standards by which "poverty" are gauged are subjective (Karnani, 2007); arriving at a realistic "poverty line" has always been a contentious issue in India (Sangal, 2015). Drawing on the Indian government's 2014 definition of those who live below the poverty line in cities (Singh 2014), we focused on study participants whose meager income makes it impossible for them to spend more than 47 INR (0.72 USD) per day on their basic food requirements.

Our study involves an analysis of technology metaphors in relation to the poor in India. We begin by introducing our theoretical approach. We identify the various entities of the micro-assemblage in our study, detail the construct of forbiddance density, and discuss the use of metaphors as an analytic tool. We follow this introduction with a description of our study's method. Next, we present the study's findings. We argue that perceived domination critically impacts the technology perceptions of the poor in highly nuanced ways. We conclude with a detailed discussion of the implications of our findings and their relation to assemblage theory.

THEORETICAL APPROACH

The Poor's Consumption Assemblage

Humans are always part of an assemblage. The rhizome, on which assemblage theory is based, has "no beginning and end," with its fabric being "the conjunction, 'and . . . and . . . and'" (Deleuze and Guattari, 1987, p. 25). However, for the sake of simplicity, in the current study, we limit the micro-assemblage under consideration primarily to BOP consumers, the technology that they use or aspire to use (e.g., electricity, television, computers, fan, phone, cooking gas, kerosene, medicines), and what we have labeled the "dominating others." This group includes those who curtail BOP consumers' access to and use of technology either directly (e.g., landlords, technology providers, employers) or indirectly (e.g., education system designers, legislators, imposers of social rules such as dominant males in the household). In this micro-assemblage, we also include our ethnographic observations and the poor's perceptions of behavior that help them survive under continued domination. While the potential capacities of each entity in an assemblage border on the infinite (De Landa, 2006, p. 10), we describe how the poor's varied perceptions of technology dampen the human instinct to resent and resist oppression (Leach, 1977), thus curtailing the innumerable potential capacities of the BOP consumers.

Forbiddance Density

To explain the poor's perspectives on the barriers to technology and cultural change vis-à-vis power disparities in consumption assemblages, we invoke the construct of forbiddance density (Bhattacharyya, 2016, p. 50), which we define as:

> The study participants' perceived intensity of barriers from the human mediators associated with consumption as well as the types of forbiddance (whether easily negotiable, negotiable at a high cost, or completely non-negotiable) that these mediators exert.

While humans might mediate any consumption episode (Latour, 2005), in the current context, human mediators are those who have the power to bar, to varying degrees, the consumption of those who are poor. We use etic (i.e., researcher-based) metaphors to describe the poor's perspectives since metaphors are known to shape our perceptions and understandings of consumption objects (Gentner and Stevens, 1983; Lakoff and Johnson, 1990). They also inform and guide consumption, "the very arena in which culture is fought over and licked into shape" (Douglas and Isherwood, 1979, p. 57).

Metaphors as an Analytic Tool

Analyzing metaphors can be invaluable in understanding a phenomenon. Each metaphor can convey "a nexus of assumptions, concerns, values, and meanings" (Thompson, Pollio, and Locander, 1994, p. 435), and thus "holistically" describe something (Cotte, Ratneshwar, and Mick, 2004, p. 334). Importantly, metaphors arising from a phenomenon can reveal systematic differences in the phenomenon (Thompson, Pollio, and Locander, 1994). Metaphors can also explain how partnership cultures work (Briody and Trotter, 2008). Thus, metaphors help build theory (Lakoff and Johnson, 1980) and have been used to understand consumers' experiences (Belk, 1988; Belk, Ger, and Askegaard, 2003; Belk, Sherry, and Wallendorf, 1988, 1989; Fournier, 1998; Thompson, Pollio, and Locander, 1994). Metaphors and technology are inextricably linked (Levy, 2001; Wilken, 2013). Technology metaphors might reveal how and why consumers engage with a particular technology the way that they do (Kozinets, 2008; Mick and Fournier, 1998).

DATA AND METHODS

Sample

Our goal was to conduct an analysis of barriers to technology consumption among people living at the BOP (Prahalad, 2012). The participants were from the slums in and around Kolkata and New Delhi in India. The first author's house-help, a highly sociable person on good terms with many of the surrounding slum dwellers, found the first couple of study participants in Kolkata. Subsequent participants in this category in Kolkata as well as all the participants in Delhi were theoretically sampled. In this method for theory development, "the analyst jointly collects, codes and analyses his data and decides what data to collect next and where to find them, in order to develop his theory as it emerges" (Glaser and Strauss, 1967, p. 45). We found the

Table 6.1 List of Study Participants

Pseudonym	Sex	Age	Religion-Caste	Occupation	City of Residence
Aftaab	M	37	Muslim	Bus driver	Kolkata
Geeta	F	26	Hindu-Vaishya	Housemaid	Kolkata
Hiren	M	29	Hindu-Vaishya	Construction worker	Kolkata
Kaushik	M	30	Hindu-Kshatriya	Whitewashes houses	Kolkata
Leela	F	25	Muslim	Stay at home wife	Kolkata
Maro	M	52	Christian	Potted plant seller	Kolkata
Neel	M	30	Hindu-Schedule caste	Rickshaw puller	Kolkata
Pallav	M	41	Muslim	Daily wage laborer	Kolkata
Promila	F	27	Hindu-Kshatriya	Housemaid	Kolkata
Protima	F	30	Hindu-Brahmin	Housemaid	Kolkata
Raju	M	60	Hindu-Kshatriya	Rickshaw puller	Kolkata
Sangeeta	F	35	Hindu-Schedule Caste	Housemaid	Kolkata
Seema	F	28	Hindu-Brahmin	Sells flowers for puja	Kolkata
Shibu	M	32	Hindu-Brahmin	Sells subscription of cable TV	Kolkata
Suchitra	F	32	Hindu-Schedule Caste	Stay-at-home wife of an apartment caretaker	Kolkata
Taposhi	F	20	Hindu-Vaishya	Housemaid	Kolkata
Anurul	M	26	Muslim	Chauffer to a college professor	New Delhi
Jeet	M	34	Hindu-Kshatriya	Office boy	New Delhi
Nafisa	F	26	Muslim	Helps in a tailor's shop	New Delhi
Picku	M	32	Hindu-Vaishya	Auto-rickshaw driver	New Delhi
Praval	M	44	Hindu-Schedule Caste	Security guard of a small building	New Delhi
Rita	F	65	Hindu-Kshatriya	Minds a *paan-bidi* [beetle nut and hand-rolled leaf-based cigarettes] shop	New Delhi
Ronu	F	36	Hindu-Brahmin	Housemaid	New Delhi
Savitri	F	38	Hindu-Schedule Caste	Housemaid	New Delhi
Sushma	F	26	Hindu-Brahmin	Cook	New Delhi
Yaseer	M	45	Muslim	Auto-rickshaw driver	New Delhi
Yasmin	F	23	Muslim	Stay-at-home wife	New Delhi

remaining participants by using a nominated expert sample from the initial study participants. As Table 6.1 shows, of the 27 participants, 13 were male and 14 were female. The average age of the participants was 34.6 years. Approximately 70% of the participants were Hindus, 4% were Christians, and 26% were Muslims. In terms of caste, approximately 21% of the Hindus were Vaishyas, and 26% of the Hindus belonged to each of the other castes.

Data Collection

We collected the data through in-depth interviews, observations, and field notes. We asked participants grand tour questions about specific objects and services that we perceived as technology since we recognized their unfamiliarity with the concept. We observed that the technologies used by the interviewees varied and included electricity, cell phones (owned by all study participants), ceiling fans, hand fans, TV, bicycles, stoves, and kerosene/gas cylinders, among others. Our interviews usually began with the question, "Tell me about . . . [a particular piece of technology that we noticed in the participant's house]." Subsequent questions were asked based on how the particular interview unfolded and thus varied across the participants. All of the interviews were audio recorded and transcribed in Bengali, the language of the interviewees.

Data Analysis

Even though the first author's native language is Bengali, translating Bengali into English without losing the essential nuances is a difficult task. Ensuring that the meaning is retained through back translation did not help entirely, for the highly contextual nature of Bengali meant that someone else would do the English translation in a different manner when translating it back into the language. For example, *Oi* in Bengali can indicate different things, depending on the accompanying words, the tone with which it is said, the physical gestures that accompany it, the length to which the sound is dragged, the length of the pause between it and the next word uttered, and the translator's perception of many of these factors. The first author analyzed the data based on what was said in the original language, and coded for contextually based concepts and apt Bengali metaphors. These metaphors were translated into their respective closest English counterparts. These translations were then handed over to another person who was adept at both Bengali and English. The second person then checked for the validity of the translations. Given this approach to analyze data in Bengali, we exclusively hand-coded the data.

The metaphors that are proposed as emerging from the BOP consumers' experiences of technology arise from our holistic grasp of the "nexus of assumptions, concerns, values and meanings that systematically (emerge) throughout the interview dialogue" (Thompson, Pollio, and Locander, 1994, p. 435). This approach follows past research that has used etic metaphors (e.g., see Cotte, Ratneshwar, and Mick, 2004; Fournier, 1998; Thompson, Pollio, and Locander, 1994) to understand consumption experiences. The trustworthiness of etic metaphors is established through a "fusion of horizons" (Thompson, Pollio, and Locander, 1994, p. 434) between researcher and study participants. This fusion is particularly feasible when the researcher and the study participants are from the same culture (Thompson, Pollio, and Locander, 1994), as in the case of the first author.

FINDINGS

In this section, we present findings related to the focal research question for this study, namely: "How do those at the BOP experience technology?" We offer representative excerpts of the lived experience of our research participants, and we propose etic technology metaphors that emanate from our reading of these interview excerpts.

The technology metaphors that arose from among the BOP consumers were formed by combining the different effects of technology agency (as perceived by the study participants) and the varying degrees of "forbiddance density." "Forbiddance" refers to the actions and/or decisions of those in positions of power in the particular assemblage that prevent BOP consumers (either deliberately, or as a by-product of their own decisions and actions) from engaging in daily consumption practices freely within the limits of their income. Forbiddance can also be exerted by life situations arising as a by-product of the decisions and actions of those in positions of power in a particular consumption assemblage. Forbiddance density ranges from none (where study participant agency is at a maximum) to complete (human intermediaries completely dominate).

A Toy

The toy metaphor reveals how engagement with technology is playful, with the user (mostly males in this case) perceiving a gendered dominance in the interaction. Consider Anurul's engagement with his phone. According to his employer, he regularly changes his ringtone. On asking him how he does that, in contrast to his self-conscious single-line responses about other things related to technology, he enthusiastically elaborates:

> Here is my phone, sister . . . I go to the settings, sister, then I go to the ring tone, Ok? Then from the ring tone, I change the ring, I change the song. (He changes the ring during this demonstration. The song that plays is an incomprehensible, Asian version of "I am a gummy bear" and he starts laughing.) It's all stored in the memory chip. See here? . . . I get it all from Boo-loo Tuth (Bluetooth) . . . I got to know about it (Bluetooth) while tinkering around with my phone, his phone (indicates his cousin). I tried to find out how it sends the song, how it takes the song, how to save a song. I take songs from my cousin's phone . . . I also take songs from my friends' phones. I like it (he smiles). New, new day; different, different songs, my phone sings to me.

Anurul's joyous laughter at the incomprehensible mewing version of the gummy bear song emitting from his phone after he tinkers around with it (and the very fact that he even *has* this children's song in his phone) demonstrates that for him, his phone is a toy. His description of Bluetooth reveals his view of the phone as a free territory to explore, like a new game with unknown rules. Anurul's playful consumption of the phone, a piece of technology that he earlier claimed to have purchased "only for emergencies" (i.e., technology as a tool), highlights that his phone (or phones in general), is also a toy. He enjoys that his phone "sings to him" and that the Bluetooth in it allows him to connect with the pleasure-giving facets of his cousin and friends' phones. He takes pleasure in changing his ringtones frequently, making his phone "sing to him" differently each day (i.e., "new-new day").

Some technology is used to provide succor to those at the BOP. However, using technology as a toy is highly gendered. Without exception, the perceived playful aspect of technology was only present in male participants' responses. Women have to shoulder the main household responsibilities including bringing home money, bringing up children, seeing that food is available, and clothes and vessels are washed and dried despite the extremely limited essential resources like water. As a result, women have virtually no time for play. A few female study participants can access television or radio—either their own, their extended family's, or the neighbors'. Yet, such "play," if it can be called that, is passive, a stark contrast to the active play in which males at the BOP engage.

A Walled Garden

The poor's experience of certain technology is reminiscent of the children's experience of the walled garden in Oscar Wilde's story of "The Selfish Giant" (Wilde 1888). The giant had a beautiful garden that children could covet from beyond the garden walls but could not play in, for the giant had barred everyone's entry. Like the wall-scaling children in this story, our study participants are able to experience the pleasure that the technology provides, but illicitly, and are driven away when the resource owner is around. Consider Suchitra, a stay-at-home wife of the caretaker of a three-story apartment block in the heart of India's second most densely populated city, Kolkata. She, her husband, and their toddler are allowed to live rent-free in a small room on the ground floor of the apartment. The rest of the floor serves as a garage for residents' cars, restricting her family's access to the area outside their door. The owners of the apartments pay their own electricity bills as well as those for the garage. The residents and landlords affect Suchitra's use of electricity, as she explains:

The other day, K's father (one of the apartment owners) scolded my husband: "Why is the common area's bill so high? I am not going to pay this!" But wherever we live, whether there is an electric meter or not, we are careful about our electricity usage. My husband, he feels very bad. He loses face when he is told things like this. . . . There are many evenings when I am lying down alone in bed, I keep the lights off. I do the same if I go to the washroom, or take a bath. . . . Even if I wash my vessels (dishes), I do so in the dark. . . . It is not that I don't get any light at all, 'cause the street lights are over there, just across the road . . . 'cause I try to save as much as I can . . . I try to keep fans and lights off as much as I possibly can. A little TV, maybe . . . I know that the TV will hike up the electricity bill. That's why I keep the lights and other stuff off. Suppose something important has happened, then to see that. I also like to watch the news. That's when I watch TV.

Suchitra's repeated references to how she saves electricity reflects her consciousness about using a technology that someone else is paying for, a technology to which she and her husband do not feel entitled. It is a resource belonging to others (i.e., those in positions of power). The guilt that Suchitra feels in switching on her TV to use someone else's resource is evident in the myriad ways that she tries to save electricity from being used, thereby managing her guilt. Thus, electricity usage to watch television is a forbidden fruit that is only accessed by stealth and borne with guilt.

An Exclusive Club

Sometimes, those at the BOP simply cannot experience an essential component of technology without the patronage of those having greater power in a specific assemblage, and at a very high financial cost. Take the example of the shift from using a wood fire to kerosene to cook. Sangeeta reports her experience in trying to access kerosene:

That's a kerosene stove . . . the kerosene has to be bought in black (market) . . . we don't have ration card here. . . . That's why, we have to buy at INR 40–45 per litre . . . (To get a ration card) is very tough . . . one has to go talk to the Panchayat (local—self-government organization) one day, go to the BDO (Block Development Office) one day. One has to do this, one has to do that, run here, run there, feed this guy money, feed that guy money. One has to run around a lot. My ration card is in my village. . . . We get some kerosene from there, when we go to our village after one-two months, maybe. But in the village, we get one—one and one-half liters per month, unlike here in the city, where that amount is given every week. So here in the city, you all get more than double of what we get in the village. But what use is that to me? I don't have a ration card. So here, those among you people who have a card, I tell them from before maybe, to get their kerosene in their card and give it to me at the price that I would get (it) on the black market. You all get it at INR 15 per litre.

For poverty-stricken migrants to the city, access to kerosene is largely unavailable since they do not have the required credentials (i.e., a ration card) to gain access to it. However, they can get access through the patronage of those in the city who possess a ration card. The patronage occurs by paying these people—in this instance, those in a position of greater power—a fee that is three times what those with ration cards pay. The alternative, procuring a ration card, can only occur through navigating a bureaucratic maze and "greasing a lot of palms." In this sense, it is not a garden that they can access through the simple means of scaling the wall when the owner is not looking, but an exclusive club. Furthermore, the path to the necessary technology is through patronage. The fee paid is not a one-time fee, but rather every time access is needed—a never-ending impediment to maintaining this access.

A Nonarable field

Some technology might be legally owned by the study participants, yet the domination by some of those in the assemblage connected to the particular technology, makes reaping its benefits difficult; those in positions of power may put obstacles in the way. Consequently, benefiting from this technology is like trying to get a yield from a nonarable field that one owns or uses. Feelings of righteous indignation and frustration erupt when denied access to something one owns. The following is an illustration of this metaphor. Pallav speaks about using the cooking gas cylinder (supplied by an agency of the Indian government) to which he has a subscription:

> They make it very difficult, these people. You get the message on the phone that "the gas has been delivered," but you don't get the gas for 15 days after that. And then when you complain in the gas office, they say "Yes, yes, you'll get the delivery in the next two days." They do this so that people (i.e., customers) get bitterly irritated, so that people get angry. They don't have any work, these people (i.e., office staff). They just sit the whole day in the cool shade of their office. For us, who are daily wage labourers, one day's visit to the gas office means we don't earn anything that day. Yet we have to go to that office, day after day, smiling with our teeth out, talking gently, gently, trying to reason with them. Otherwise, if they wish, they can make things difficult and then there will be no cooking gas in the house for months.

In this situation, ownership of or subscription to a product does not automatically provide access to the product. While ownership might provide the consumer with some agency, in the sense that his ownership gives him the right to go and ask for the product, his ability to gain actual access is curtailed by those in power—those human actors who generate a thick Kafkaesque forbiddance density. Without emotional the labor (Hochschild 1983) of suppressing his "bitterly irritated" state, coupled with "smiling with teeth out," Pallav will not have access to the needed gas even though he technically owns it.

A Spare Tire

Certain technologies are not perceived as necessary since the old ways of doing things help the study participants cope with not being able to afford things. For instance, while those with greater economic resources go to doctors and use pharmaceutical drugs (e.g., technological innovations) for illness, many of the poor use traditional tantric methods. There are various factors at play in relegating medical technologies to the role of a spare tire, to be used only when other means fail; not least is the fact that their poverty makes the doctors' fees unaffordable. "These doctors, they are like leeches, the way the suck money out of you," is a common refrain. Illness is often perceived as the result of a "touch" (usually through the wind) of the "evil eye" of people who died in unnatural ways (e.g., by suicide, by being murdered). Many of the poor believe that recovery from illness is not contingent on a visit to the doctor and "swallowing down some pills." Instead, dissipating "the evil air that is touching the person" through the recitation of a mantra (i.e., words/verses perceived to have magical power), in combination with blowing on the ill person's head, leads to recovery. The poor's choice of modern technology in terms of medicines, surgery, and so forth, is normally a last resort due to both the money involved and cultural beliefs about the causes of illness.

An Albatross

Consider the following interview excerpt:

Interviewer: Do you have a computer?
Hiren: No, where is the money (for it)?
Interviewer: If someone gifted it to you, would you like it?
Hiren: No. We live in a rented house. Computer-Shumputer are not for us. . . . Any moment, the landlord will ask us to leave. Then where will we go, lugging things like computers around? It's also a tiny place. Should we live in the house? Or should the computer? And moreover, our house is made of mud, and my wife and I go out to work whole day. Are things like computer things that should be left lying around in the house when we are out for so long? Who knows when what thought will come to whose mind and what they will do (in our absence)?

An albatross refers to those pieces of technology that study participants at the BOP consider burdensome. Some BOP study participants exert agency in *not* acquiring these same pieces of technology, as evidenced in the hypothetical refusal of the gift of a laptop. They perceive that such technology in the assemblage of their everyday lives would slow them down. Other areas of their lives are more crucial to their survival given the immense precariousness that they face. Like nomads, valuable possessions can be a burden when day-to-day survival is the paramount concern.

A Mystery

In certain instances, the forbiddance density reduces interest in the poor's curiosity and knowledge about a technology. Taposhi's interview excerpt at the beginning of this chapter illustrates technology as a mystery. She asks, "Do people like us have the time to see stuff in things like those?" She spends her day working in other people's homes. On her return, she collects water from a timed water outlet, and then cooks and takes care of her child. "Life" will not "work" if she "sits around" with things like computers. For Taposhi, a cultural change harbinger like a computer is an impenetrable and frivolous mystery. The effort of everyday living takes precedence over learning anything new. The continued disinterest in technology is likely a strategy to conserve their energy so that our study participants can get through another day.

Taposhi's repeated references to "people like us," and "things like those," highlight her perception that her world (the world in which "people like her" live) is different from the one that others, including researchers, inhabit. Ours is a world where technology like computers belong. She perceives a distanced demarcation, underscored by her choice of using the adjective "those" things instead of "these" things. This difference is more salient in the actual language of her speech, Bengali (i.e., *oi shob jinish* vs. *ei shob jinish*) than in English. Energy and time depletion in the sheer grind of everyday life is especially harsh at the BOP. The poor often cannot be proactive about exerting agency to bring a "life-changing" technology into their everyday assemblage. Thus, they lose the potential of the technology to bring about an empowering cultural change in their lives.

Fort Knox

At times, the poor are not even aware of the existence of the technological resources available to enact a deterritorialization or disruption that would help them achieve a change in their social or economic status. The metaphor "Fort Knox" refers to a view of technology that is not available to the BOP study participants at all. The forbiddance density usually hides this technology from the poor's awareness. When awareness exists, such technology is seen as being completely out of reach; it may even repel the participants if they try to get close. Consider the following interview excerpt from Kaushik, a daily wage laborer who paints houses:

> I used to work at a place on a computer. I was capable of taking out prints of maps and things. But, if I had to earn more, I had to know to do more with the computer. That, there was no way for me to do . . . everything is in English, you see. We are poor people. We have studied in government schools. And you know how government schools function. Half the time, the teachers don't even come. So the little English that I knew wasn't enough to help me do more with the computer. So I quit that job and started whitewashing houses. This pays me more.

Lack of education, coupled with insufficient English language skills, made it impossible for Kaushik to progress beyond a certain level. While he felt there were riches to be made if he had more knowledge about using a computer, he realized that he would never be able to achieve that goal. The sheer impossibility of penetrating the Kevlarian walls that lack of education and lack of time and poverty erect puts certain technology in an impenetrable Fort Knox-like position for study participants like Kaushik.

A Stonewall

In certain instances, the harbinger of a cultural change from one aspect (e.g., watching television for fun vs. interacting with neighbors for pleasure) is perceived by some at the BOP as a stonewall that blocks the possibility of change in terms of bettering their lot. The interplay of the maximum forbiddance density offered by those in positions of power and certain "blocking" properties of technology preclude reaching one's life goals in this metaphor. As the following excerpt shows, Sushma views a TV as a stonewall that prevents her daughter from "doing well in life":

> No, we have decided not to own a TV. I want my daughter to study well and to grow big in life (do well in life). If we keep a TV in the house, that's it. When she returns from school, all she will do is sit in front of the TV. How will studies happen? How will she reach very high (do extremely well in life)?

Shylock/Jezebel

These two metaphors represent essential pieces of technology that those at the BOP can only adopt by sacrificing other essential resources. Consider Maro's case below:

Maro: Ooh! How hot it is growing already, sister! The hot months are coming and my head is being caught by worries. Again we have to reduce our food!
Interviewer: Why would you need to do that?
Maro: The fan will be running more, *na*? So much light (electricity) bill, where am I going to give it from? If I want this (the working fan), I have to give up that (food). That's why when the hot months come, we have to reduce our food.
Interviewer: How do you do that?
Maro: Ei, any fish-meat, that stops. We live on lentil-rice for those months.

The fan and its use of electricity for Maro is a money-grabbing, uncompromising mistress. For while he desires to be soothed by technology's ministrations in the hot summer months, he can obtain this respite only if he succumbs to technology's demands by paying for it. To get any relief from the heat, he must reduce his budget for food to pay for the fan and the electricity to run it.

A similar theme of technology as an uncaring master is seen in Promila's perception of her cell phone. Instead of needing something from the technology itself, and for herself alone, she needs the technology to provide an emotional lift for herself and her family. She sees the technology as a Shylockian hungry, grasping, unyielding, but not unfair, calculator. She speaks of the rare times when she gets to speak with her children in a distant village:

> Frequently-frequently we have to insert money into it (the phone). If it is fed money, then the communication (with the children) happens. Otherwise not.

She includes the word, *toh* when she speaks about this frequent feeding necessity to indicate something that should be known to the listener; she perceives that resource guzzling by technology is a well-known fact. On the other hand, she does not complain about the phone working, even though it falls apart when the rubber band holding it together breaks. Thus, she perceives the phone as an unemotional, but not unfair calculator, since it will work every time you feed it money and when you do not, it will not.

DISCUSSION

By refracting technology effects through the prism of forbiddance density, our study helps to bring in expanded and nuanced conceptualizations of technology as a harbinger of cultural change. These nuances have been masked by the conflations in the extant functional or symbolically oriented approaches that are implicit in the "product attribute" lens of product perception, adoption, or consumption (e.g., Kozinets, 2008; Mick and Fournier, 1998; Rogers,

2003). The nuanced reading of metaphors offered in our study pushes the conceptualizations of technology beyond ideologies, paradoxes, or utility (Kozinets, 2008; Mick and Fournier, 1998) to the role of perceived domination in influencing the BOP's perceptions of different culture-changing products. The variation in technology access stems from different densities of forbiddance. Place of residence, religion, and caste had no discernable effect on the technology consumption experience of the study participants and thus these demographic characteristics did not affect the naming of metaphors.

The variation revealed by our metaphors contradicts the binary conceptualization of "barriers" in extant technology adoption theorizations (i.e., either a barrier exists or it does not). It also shows the emotion-laden, quality-oriented, myriad perceptions of barriers to technology consumption experienced by those at the BOP. These qualitative, nuanced perceptions of barriers, in turn, affect feelings associated with certain products that have brought about cultural changes in the rest of the world (e.g., computers, TVs, electricity). For example, our study demonstrates that study participants do not have to master a particular technology for cultural change to occur (Kozinets, 2008; Mick and Fournier, 1998). Instead, our data reveals nuances in the consumer's power over the technology. Such nuances subsequently affect the BOP's use of the technology and their feelings of that experience—including guilt and emotional discomfort when using it, feelings understated in existing literature. Such attitudes can lead to the lack of use, or limited use, of an essential piece of technology, despite having access to it. Thus, in contrast to the implicit assumption of univocality in the meaning of "access" in access-based literature (Bardhi and Eckhardt 2012), our study highlights the fact that someone might have physical "ease of access," but not emotional access to a product, depending on one's role in an uneven exchange relationship. In such exchange relationships, one party (a landlord in the current context) has more power than the other party (a tenant in the current context), and thus can dictate the terms of the exchange.

REFLECTIONS: WHEN GLOBAL FORMS MEET ENTRENCHED POWER DISPARITIES IN AN ASSEMBLAGE

Technology is perceived as having a global quality, a quality that is "abstractable, mobile and dynamic, moving across and reconstituting 'society,' 'culture' and 'economy'" (Collier and Ong, 2008, p. 4). As a prime facilitator of cultural change, technology is often perceived to be the wind beneath the wings of agency, especially since its deterritorializing nature (De Landa, 2006, p. 13) is believed to have the power to force benevolence out of a structure that could have otherwise curtailed agency. However, while agency may be distributed among component parts of the assemblage (see McCabe's introduction to this book), there is inequality in this distribution.

This inequality holds in the assemblage—one that involves the people, objects, and attitudes that combine to result in particular actions (or in this case, that bar particular actions). The components in the assemblage in this context include tenants, landlords, watchmen, homes, electricity, money, electric connections, bureaucrats, and documents, among others. In such an assemblage, a major chunk of the population is socially and monetarily disadvantaged, and lives in "crystallized social relationships" or relationships that are "not simply occasional or capricious but have a pattern of some repetition and can to some degree be predicted" (Gordon, 1964 p. 31). Our chapter highlights the consequences of this unequal distribution upon the cultural trajectories among the poor, with the global form of technology being muted by entrenched power disparities. In contrast to the cultural pattern of blaming and blame avoidance among workers and management in a General Motors plant found by Briody, Trotter, and Meerwarth (2010), we find that among the poor in India there is often no named villain or external male-worthy agent or scapegoat. Rather, the poor often reveal their frustration in private, and simply accept that this is the way of the world about which they are powerless to do anything.

Beyond the constraints of money, education, and literacy, the poor that we studied face institutional constraints, corruption, gender bias, and perverse penalties imposed by bureaucracies and haughty landlords. These invisible injustices preclude access to technology even when it is affordable. For the rising tide of technology to lift all Indians, much must change. As with the e-choupal program aimed at providing poor farmers with computer access to gain information about crop prices so they will not be cheated, it is frequently the wealthy who benefit and the poor who are excluded and left behind (Varman, Skålén, and Belk, 2012). There is more to the trap of poverty than is clearly visible on the surface of structural arrangements. And the changes needed to ameliorate such injustices are often more social and cultural than technological.

CONCLUSIONS AND IMPLICATIONS

The different variations of technology use, as described in our metaphors, along with increasing degrees of forbiddance density, underscore the futility of envisioning the utility of a cultural change only through the technology's functionality or affordability among the BOP. Given that many consumers in this market experience disparities of class, finances, and power, the utility of a legally owned technology is grossly overshadowed by the ability of the

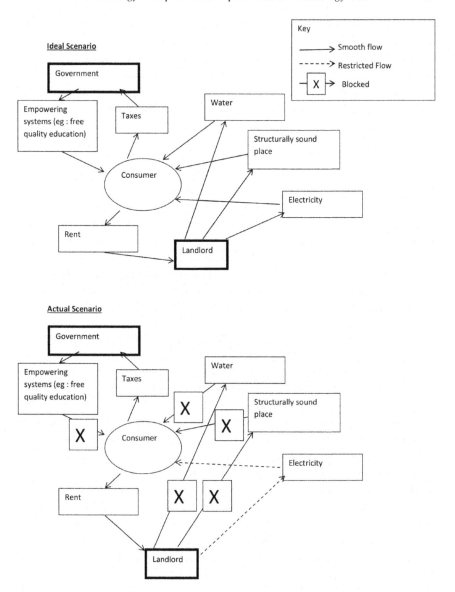

Figure 6.1   The Ideal Scenario of Consumption at the BOP, and the Actual Scenario.

BOP to use that technology. The offerings of affordable products to the poor are incomplete. Given an affordable product, Figure 6.1 portrays the difference between the ideal scenario of consumption at the BOP and the actual one. Systems are needed to ensure that affordability (both in terms of cost of the technology per se, and cost accrued in terms of loss of wages while chasing after the technology) is unchanged by the mediators in the technology consumption network.

The first crucial remedy to offset the power of the mediators is to bring into existence laws that protect those at the BOP from the precariousness that surrounds their lives, a precariousness often arising from power disparities. Those at the BOP are not protected either by a mandated minimum wage or by rental laws. With no employment contracts, the livelihoods of those at the BOP can disappear in an instant. Such situations put the BOP consumers at the mercy of those who have more power than they do.

The Indian government has tried to reverse social inequalities (e.g., forbidding caste bias) that have plagued India for centuries. Some success is apparent. For instance, the latest data from the Union Planning Commission of India show that the poverty level of indigenous Indians, whom the British considered to be historically disadvantaged and called the "depressed class" (now called Schedule Caste and Schedule Tribe), is no longer different from the poverty level of the rest of the country's population (Jha, 2014). Some studies have even observed that the caste and class relation in India is at times reversed (Varman, Skålén, and Belk, 2012), with the increasing spread of markets and market forces dismantling traditional status hierarchies (Vikas, Varman, and Belk, 2015; Jacquelot, 2011; Sheth, 1999). Yet, as evidenced by the continued prevalence of racism in first world countries (West, 1993; Blackmon, 2008; Alexander, 2010; Rankin, 2014; Coates, 2015; Cadogan 2016; Eversley, 2016), social injustice is difficult to overcome simply through legislation and greater economic resources.

Beyond laws, education is a possible route to empowerment for these BOP consumers. While India has made education free and compulsory, education that is offered "compulsorily and freely" in most states is not monitored. Unless the quality of education is consistently high, the next generation of BOP consumers cannot hope to compete with "the haves" in the job market. High-quality education at schools for the children of BOP consumers is extremely crucial for this competition, given that the kind of support that empowered consumers get at home after school (e.g., electricity, an environment conducive to completing their homework, opportunities to broaden cognitive skills) is not available to them. The fruition of the government's dreams of building an empowered India is difficult to foresee if the majority of the nation's population continues to be repressed, kept ignorant of its rights, and denied sufficient power to launch itself out of repression.

REFERENCES

Alexander, Michelle. (2010). *The new Jim Crow: Mass incarceration in the age of colorblindnes.,* New York, NY: New Press.

Asbell, Bernard. (1963). *The new improved American*. New York, NY: McGraw-Hill.

Askegaard, Søren, Arnould, Eric J., & Kjeldgaard, Dannie. (2005). Postassimilation-ist ethnic consumer research: Qualifications and extensions. *Journal of Consumer Research,* 32, 160–70, June.

Bardhi, F., & Eckhardt, G.M. (2012). Access-based consumption: The case of car sharing. *Journal of Consumer Research,* 39(4), 881–98.

Beard, Charles A. (1927). Time, technology, and the creative spirit in political sci-ence. *The American Political Science Review,* 21(1), 1–11.

Belk, R.W. (1988). Possessions and the extended self. *Journal of Consumer Research,* 15(2), 139–68.

Belk, Russell W., Wallendorf, Melanie, & Sherry Jr., John F. (1989). The sacred and profane in consumer behavior: Theodicy on the Odyssey. *Journal of Consumer Research,* 16, 1–38, February.

Belk, Russell W., Sherry, Jr., John F. & Wallendorf, Melanie. (1988). A naturalis-tic inquiry into buyer and seller behavior at a swap meet. *Journal of Consumer Research* 14, 449–470, March.

Belk, R. W., Ger. G., & Askegaard, S. (2003). The fire of desire: A multisited inquiry into consumer passion. *Journal of Consumer Research* 30(3), 326–51.

Berry, John. (1980). Acculturation as varieties of adaptation. In Padilla, Amado M. (Ed.). *Acculturation: Theory, models and some new findings.* Boulder, CO: West-view 9–26.

Bhattacharyya, A. (2016). Technology metaphors at the base of the pyramid. Unpub-lished Doctoral Dissertation, York University, Toronto, ON, Canada.

Blackmon, Douglas A. (2008). *Slavery by another name: The re-enslavement of Black Americans from the Civil War to World War II.* New York, NY: Random House.

Bode, Mattias & Dorthe Kristensen. (2016). The digital doppelgänger within a study on self-tracking and the quantified self-movement. In Canniford, Robin and Bajde, Domen (Eds.). *Assembling consumption: Researching actors, networks, and mar-kets.* London, UK: Routledge, 119–34.

Briody, Elizabeth K. & Trotter, II, Robert T. (Eds.). (2008). *Partnering for organiza-tional performance.* Lanham, MD: Rowman & Littlefield.

Briody, Elizabeth K., Trotter, II, Robert T. & Meerwarth, Tracy L. (2010). *Trans-forming culture: Creating and sustaining a better manufacturing organization,* New York, NY: Palgrave Macmillan.

Canham, Erwin D. (1950). *Awakening: The world at mid-century.* New York, NY: Longmans, Green.

Coates, Ta-Nehisi. (2015). *Between the world and me.* New York, NY: Spiegel & Grau.

Collier, Stephen J. & Ong, Aihwa. (2008). Global Assemblages, Anthropological Problems. In *Global assemblages: Technology, politics and ethics as anthropo-logical problem,* Aihwa Ong and Stephen J. Collier, Eds. Oxford, UK: Blackwell.

Cotte, J., Ratneshwar, S., & Mick, D. G. (2004). The times of their lives: Phenom-enological and metaphorical characteristics of consumer timestyles. *Journal of Consumer Research* 31(2), 333–45.

DeLanda, M. (2006). *A new philosophy of society: Assemblage theory and social complexity.* New York, NY: Continuum.

Deleuze, G. & Guattari, F. (1987). *A thousand plateaus: Capitalism and schizophrenia*. Translated by Massumi, Brian. Minneapolis, MN: University of Minnesota Press.

Douglas, Mary & Isherwood, Baron. (1979). *The world of goods*. New York, NY: Basic.

Epp, A.M., Schau, H.J. & Price, L.L. (2014). The role of brands and mediating technologies in assembling long-distance family practices. *Journal of Marketing,* 78(3), 81–101.

Eversley, Melanie. (2016). Justice Department: Baltimore police regularly violated constitutional rights. *USA Today*. http://www.usatoday.com/story/news/2016/08/09/justice-department-baltimore-police-regularly-violated-constitutional-rights/88489196/. Accessed 30th May 2017

Foucault, M. (1980). *Power/Knowledge: Selected interviews and other writings 1972–1977*. London, UK: Harvester Press.

Fournier, S. (1998). Consumers and their brands: Developing relationship theory in consumer research. *Journal of Consumer Research*, 24(4), 343–73.

Gentner, D & Stevens, A. (1983). *Mental models*. Hillside, NJ: Erlbaum.

Giddens, Anthony. (1994). Living in a Post-Traditional Society. In Beck, Ulrich, Giddens, Anthony, & Lash, Scott (Eds.). *Reflexive modernization: Politics, tradition and aesthetics in the modern social order*. Stanford, CA: Stanford University Press, 58–59.

Glaser, B. and Strauss, A. (1967). *The discovery of grounded theory: Strategies for qualitative research*. New York, NY: Aldine.

Gordon, M.M. (1964). *Assimilation in American life: The role of race, religion and national origins*. New York, NY: Oxford University Press,

Heidegger, M. (1977). *The question concerning technology and other essays*. Translated by Lovitt, William. New York, NY: Garland Publishing.

Hochschild, Arlie. (1983). *The managed heart*. Berkeley, CA: University of California Press.

Jacquelot, Patrick de. (2011). Capitalism over caste: The success of India's 'untouchable' CEOs. *Time*, http://content.time.com/time/world/article/0,8599,2103056,00.html, Accessed 30th May 2017

Jha, Somesh. (2014). Fewer poor among SC, ST, OBC. *Business Standard*. http://www.business-standard.com/article/economy-policy/fewer-poor-among-sc-st-obc-114031301232_1.html, Accessed 30th May 2017

Karnani, Aneel. (2007). The mirage of marketing to the bottom of the pyramid: How the private sector and help alleviate poverty. *California Management Review,* 49(4), 90–111.

Kozinets, R.V. (2002). Can consumers escape the market? Emancipatory illuminations from burning man. *Journal of Consumer Research,* 29(1), 20–38.

———. (2008). Technology/Ideology: How ideological fields influence consumers' technology narratives. *Journal of Consumer Research*, 34(6), 865–81.

Kurzweil, Ray. (2005). *The singularity is near*. New York, NY: Viking Press.

Lakoff, George & Johnson, Mark. (1980). *Metaphors we live by*. Chicago, IL: University of Chicago Press.

Latour, B. (2005). *Reassembling the social: An introduction to actor-network-theory*, Kindle Edition. Oxford, UK: Oxford University Press.

Leach, E.R. (1977). *Custom, law and terrorist violence*. Edinburgh, UK: Edinburgh University Press.

Levy, P. (2001). *Cyberculture*. Minneapolis, MN: University of Minnesota Press.

Lotan, G., Graeff, E., Ananny, M., Gaffney, D., & Pearce, I. (2011). The Arab spring| the revolutions were tweeted: Information flows during the 2011 Tunisian and Egyptian revolutions. *International Journal of Communication*, 5(31),1375–405.

Marcuse, Herbert. (1982). Some social implications of modern technology. In Arato, Andrew & Gebhardt, Eike (Eds.). *The essential Frankfurt school reader*. New York, NY: Continuum, 138–162.

Marx, Karl. (1867) [1990]. *Capital: A critique of political economy*. Volume I, (Das Capital Series). Translated by Fowkes, Ben. London, UK: Penguin Classics,

McLuhan, Marshall. (1964). *Understanding media: The extensions of man*. New York, NY: McGraw-Hill.

Mick, D.G., & Fournier, S. (1998). Paradoxes of technology: Consumer cognizance, emotions, and coping strategies. *Journal of Consumer Research*, 25(2), 123–43.

Morozov, E. (2013). *To save everything, click here: The folly of technological solutionism*. New York, NY: Public Affairs Books.

Mumford, Lewis. (1970). *The pentagon of power*. New York, NY: Harcourt Brace Jovanovich.

Nye, David E. (1996). *American technological sublime*. Cambridge, MA: MIT Press.

Oswald, Laura R. (1999). Culture swapping: Consumption and the ethnogenesis of middle-class Haitian immigrants. *Journal of Consumer Research*, 25, 303–18, March.

Peñaloza, Lisa. (1994). *Atravesando fronteras*/Border crossings: A critical ethnographic exploration of the consumer acculturation of Mexican immigrants. *Journal of Consumer Research*, 21, 32–54, June.

Postman, N. (2011). *Technopoly: The surrender of culture to technology*. New York, NY: Vintage.

Prahalad, C.K. (2012). Bottom of the pyramid as a source of breakthrough innovations. *Journal of Product Innovation Management*, 29(1), 6–12.

Rankine, Claudia. (2014). *Citizen: An American lyric*. Minneapolis, MN: Graywolf Press.

Rogers, E.M. (2003). *Diffusion of innovations*. 5th ed. New York, NY: Free Press.

Romanyshyn, R. D. 1989. *Technology as Symptom and Dream*. London: Routeledge,

Sangal, P.P. (2015). Defining a poverty line for India. *Financial Express*. http://www.financialexpress.com/article/fe-columnist/defining-a-poverty-line-for-india/74725/. Accessed on 30th May 2017

Sheth, D.L. (1999). Secularisation of caste and making of new middle class. *Economic and Political Weekly*, 34(34/35), 2502–2510.

Singh, Mahendra Kumar (2014). New Poverty Line: Rs 32 in villages, Rs 47 in cities., *Times of India*, http://timesofindia.indiatimes.com/india/New-poverty-line-Rs-32-in-villages-Rs-47-in-cities/articleshow/37920441.cms Accessed on 30th May 2017

Standage, T. (1998). *The Victorian Internet: The remarkable story of the telegraph and the nineteenth century's online pioneers.* London, UK: Weidenfeld & Nicolson.

Thompson, C.J., Pollio, H.R., & Locander, W.B. (1994). The spoken and the unspoken: A hermeneutic approach to understanding the cultural viewpoints that underlie consumers' expressed meanings. *Journal of Consumer Research,* 21(3), 432–52.

Varman, R. & Belk, R.W. (2009). Nationalism and ideology in an anticonsumption movement. *Journal of Consumer Research,* 36(4), 686–700.

Varman, Rohit, Skålén, Peter, and Belk, Russell. (2012). Conflicts at the bottom of the pyramid: Profitability, poverty alleviation, and neoliberal governmentality. *Journal of Public Policy and Marketing,* 31(1), 19–35.

Vikas, Ram Manohar, Varman, Rohit & Belk, Russell W. (2015). Status, caste and market in a changing Indian village. *Journal of Consumer Research,* 42(3), 472–98.

West, Cornel. (1993). *Race matters.* Boston, MA: Beacon Press.

Wilde, Oscar (1888), The Selfish Giant, in *The Happy Prince and other Tales*, Project Gutenberg, available online at https://archive.org/details/thehappyprincean00902gut

Wilken, R. (2013). An exploratory comparative analysis of the use of metaphors in writing on the internet and mobile phones. *Social Semiotics,* 23(5), 632–47.

Chapter 7

The Enigma of Innovation

Changing Practices of Non placed into an alcoholic Beverage Consumption in China

Dominique Desjeux and Ma Jingjing

When innovative products and services enter a consumer market, they are placed into an existing social system, and that social system may be undergoing cultural change. A social system is comprised of concrete action and actors who have converging and diverging interests, are involved in relations of power and of cooperation, and are seeking to survive, gain new territories or limit the hold of other actors in their everyday life. Recent theories of cultural change draw on the concept of assemblages as a tool to enhance understanding. This concept originates with the work of Deleuze and Guattari (1980), and was further developed by Latour (2005) and Akrich, Callon *et* Latour (2006). They use the term *acteur-réseau* (actor-network) to describe a network of animate and inanimate entities. They make reference to nonhuman entities as *actants*. In the version of assemblage theory, that we share for the most part, *agency* (conscious action) is ascribed to human (individual and group) entities, and *meaning* is ascribed to nonhuman entities and objects.

Understanding cultural change, and innovations in particular, often requires consideration of the whole assemblage, as a network of people, groups, practices, circumstances and objects. We can then understand better how the whole assemblage has a mutually-influencing effect and also changes together. Lack of stability or variation in an existing assemblage may be a sign of change that is underway. Innovation is related to cultural change, but distinct from it; as noted in the introduction to this book, innovation is planned and purposeful, unlike cultural change.

Understanding the social mechanisms that underlie the diffusion of innovations makes it possible to understand why a new technology, a new product or a new service is accepted or refused by the actors associated with it. For a doctor, a biologist, a chemist or an engineer, a new technology is neutral and rational. It should therefore be diffused without difficulty. However, there is no diffusion of ideas or material objects without resistance. Typically, "resistance to innovation" is explained by the "irrationality of actors." However, it is in this supposed irrationality that the enigma of innovation lies. The work of the anthropologist is to elucidate this enigma by illustrating the social mechanisms that seem irrational from the point of view of disciplines such as the natural sciences and economics.

Elucidating this rational-irrational tension means resolving the enigma of innovation. The objective of this chapter is to show how an anthropological approach makes it possible to deepen knowledge of the social mechanisms that underlie social customs and innovations. The example is based on the consumption of drinks in China. We examine the cultural changes occurring in Chinese beverage practices and how the introduction of an innovative soft drink beverage could fit within the changing set of practices.

THEORETICAL APPROACH

Anthropological Analysis Related to the Diffusion of Innovations

Innovation is a disruptive element in a more or less balanced social system just as much as it is a new idea, good or bad. The contribution of anthropology is precisely to show the relative organization of material, social and symbolic constraints in the system of action which we have to analyze as "total social facts," to use the expression of the French anthropologist Marcel Mauss (1925) in his famous article later published as a short book, *The Gift*. Here, we use the word "new technology" intentionally, to show that the problem is the same whether it is applied to a new agricultural technology, a new digital technology or a new drink, as we will see in the case of China below. In all of these cases, an innovation will affect the social organization which is in place, whether in a company or associated with the final user. It will benefit certain actors and disadvantage others. It will be liked by some and will shock others, particularly in terms of morality and social norms. It will resolve some problems and create others. An innovation is therefore never socially neutral.

This assertion neither means that nothing should be changed, nor that the engineers who propose a particular change are wrong. Instead, it means that we should not be surprised when some actors are opposed to the change and others approve of it. This interplay between those who win and those who lose can be analyzed by anthropology to minimize the losses and optimize the gains, and hence improve the chances of better negotiation and acceptance of a change, depending on the interests of various parties. Today we know that this objective is largely utopian, but we love this reformist utopia. A technical innovation that seemed to be beneficial for farming practices actually caused a loss of income for certain sections of the population (primarily women) and so understandably met with resistance (see *La question agraire à Madagascar* [The Agrarian Question in Madagascar], Desjeux 1979).

The important point to retain here is that a new technology, an innovation, is never socially neutral, and that there are actors who can gain and actors who can lose from it. Innovation is not only not limited to an individual and it not only develops within an interplay of collective actors; but it is also embedded in a political context which often depends on geopolitics and on globalization, and which surpasses the mere analysis of interactions among actors at the local level. The social conditions of the diffusion vary depending on the scales of observation of reality (see *Les stratégies paysannes en Afrique Noire* [Farmers' Strategies in Sub-Saharan Africa], Desjeux 1987).

Innovation and the Scales of Observation

Explanations of social and individual phenomena vary depending on the scales of observation, discussed in *Les sciences sociales* (Desjeux 2004). Scales of observation, like scales on maps or plans, refer to the focus applied to social phenomena to study them. The micro-individual scale makes it possible to observe individuals by placing an emphasis on their motivations, their cognitive processes and the meaning that they give to their actions. Causality comes mainly from meaning.

There are two interactionist scales: the microsocial scale (which most often applies to the interplay of actors organized around the utilization of consumer goods in the home and family space) and the mesosocial scale (which has to do with the interplay of actors mobilizing larger collective bodies, such as large organizations, companies or the market). These interactionist scales include the practices, the usages, the social interactions, the power relations and the networks that organize the interplay among the actors. Causality varies depending on the situation.

The macrosocial scale makes it possible to observe the correlations between effects of belonging (such as social class, gender, generation, or ethnic, political or religious culture) and social practices linked with consumption or the environment. Such correlations are an indicator that can be used to initiate consideration about what the true mechanism of causality is. The macrosocial scale is also the scale of observation of geopolitics, and of the major values that structure cultural areas throughout the world across history—as the German sociologist Max Weber showed in *The Protestant Ethic and the Spirit of Capitalism* (1904–5).

Observations conducted by Desjeux between 1969 and 2016 centered largely on diffusion processes related to the mesosocial scale (e.g., companies, NGOs, ministries), and the microsocial scale (e.g., families). An innovation typically goes through three major stages: (1) the invention of an idea, (2) its diffusion or its failure to diffuse through a system of action and (3) contact with an end user, whether it is a company or a household. Desjeux worked upstream, during the invention stage when he was in China.

All along the diffusion itinerary (here called the "drink itinerary"), the abstract idea to be transformed into an object or service circulates in a nonlinear manner and undergoes a process of continual change from an innovation-invention to an innovation-reaction, from one group of actors to another. It is transformed each time it passes from a system of invention, which may be in a company within the R&D department, to a system of production associated with a factory, to a system of marketing transformation, and subsequently to a system of "hard" distribution or digital distribution ("click and mortar"), then to a system of use and consumption with the final user before potentially entering once again into a new system of transformation by recycling. It can disappear at any moment—which is what happens most often. Very little invention/innovation finally emerges.

In this social process of innovation, consumption involves trying out an invention as an innovation. At this stage, the innovation may be the result of a new idea transformed into new technologies, or the result of an old technology in a new milieu. At this stage innovation may be either "high-tech" or "low-tech." Paradoxically, the fact that it is new in a new place is important, not the novelty of its technical content. It is equally complicated to gain acceptance for new mass consumer products, introduce existing agricultural techniques into a region in which they are unknown and promote new, environmentally friendly practices. The latter are particularly difficult to promote because they make daily life more complex, not simpler, as when new consumer technologies (e.g., refrigerators, washing machines, quilts, ready-made meals) were introduced.

In this chapter, we focus on understanding and explaining the drink itinerary, defined as the innovation, production, consumption and disposal of nonalcoholic drinks in China. In particular, we consider people's drinking practices, and examine how a company may respond (or fail to respond) to the changing beliefs and expectations surrounding traditional and commercial beverages.

METHODOLOGY

The Innovation Trigger

It is not always possible to follow the entire path of the production of an idea, then of its transformation into an action or a concrete object. It is a fraction of this process that we wish to present in this chapter. The point of departure was a question asked by the R&D department of an international food group operating in China. The data are derived from our anthropological research project designed to understand the practices, norms and mental representations related to the consumption of drinks in China. The project was based on a collaboration between Desjeux, CIRAD (the French association for agronomic research and international development cooperation), Danone Waters China and Danone Nutricia Research.

However, instead of centering on the brand and its territory, and looking at the end consumer to see what might correspond to this territory, the company agreed to look first at the end user. We explored end user practices throughout the day, over the course of weeks, and during holidays, as well as while those users were at home, at work, or in transit. We considered different stages in the consumer life cycle and generation effects, thereby illustrating consumption diversity pertaining to drinks. This microsocial approach centered on the consumer, not only from a personal point of view based on his/her experiences, but also with respect to consumption in different rooms in the home, the way in which the consumer produces or purchases and consumes drinks, social interactions and power relations between members of the family, and the conception of the body and health in China. We mobilized our team of French and Chinese anthropologists created with Zheng Li Hua and Yang Xiao Min in Guangzhou (Canton) in 1997.

Methods and Sampling

We carried out a qualitative investigation involving 76 people (39 male and 37 female, from 7 to 58 years of age) in four cities situated in the north and the south, on the coast and in the center of China: Beijing, Shanghai, Guangzhou and Chengdu. These investigations took place between November 2014 and June 2015, and involved semi-directive interviews lasting between one and three hours, some of which were carried out where the drinks were consumed (i.e., the kitchen or living room). This investigation sought to discover all of the possible practices related to drinks, the material, social and cultural dimensions of their use, the acquisition and consumption of these drinks, and the effect of life cycles on the diversity of use of these drinks.

Practices and Methodological Principles

Our study is based on five practices and methodological principles. The first is *induction*, a method enabling a cultural exploration without testing specific hypotheses. Our study focuses primarily on the microsocial and mesosocial scales.

The second principle is that of *ambivalence*. All social phenomena have a positive and a negative side.

The third principle has to do with the *qualitative generalization of results* in a different way from quantitative or experimental approaches. In qualitative investigations, we generalize the functional mechanisms of society, such as power relations being organized around areas of uncertainty. In most societies, uncertainty is present; in the Congo, it surrounds "sorcery" (Desjeux 1987). The most important and least expected generalization is that related to the diversity of practices, and not their frequency. Very often, within a given domain, this diversity can be reduced to four or five major usages. In particular, this diversity of use is generalizable when working on the consumption practices of the global urban middle class. What may vary, however, is the importance of particular practices in a certain culture. Statistical frequency has no meaning here since in a qualitative study we work with samples of about 20 to 70 individuals.

The fourth principle is based on an *emic perspective*: understanding the social logic of actors from their point of view without judgment or accusations. The method consists of reconstituting and understanding the constraints that organize the calculations of the actors.

The fifth principle is *symmetry*, which assumes that it is equally relevant to work on an innovation that has succeeded or one that has failed.

FINDINGS

Taking the Customer, His Usages and His Culture as a Point of Departure

To understand the social conditions of the diffusion of a new drink in China, it is important to recognize that there is no drinkable tap water in large Chinese cities. One of the daily practices is boiling water. In 1997, Desjeux lived for three and a half months at the Guangdong University of Foreign Studies, in Guangzhou. Every morning, with his two thermos flasks, he went to fetch boiled water so that he could make his tea during the day. Today mineral water tanks (large tanks which dispense drinking water) are probably in the process of replacing thermos flasks because they make daily life easier. In many families, boiling water remains a major daily practice.

In China, water occupies an important place in the daily lives of families, since it is situated at the crossroads of five major practices in the management of drinks. The first has to do with the physical management of the body, which is associated with hydration and thirst. Consumption of nonalcoholic commercial beverages (e.g., soft drinks, bottled water) varies greatly depending on the season, peaking in the summer. The second is organoleptic management, which requires a choice between a bland drink and a drink with a taste. The third practice involves materials management and logistics of the production, sales and subsequent use of drinks, depending on their practical use and the concrete system of material items that promote their use. The fourth has to do with the social management of drinks—in other words, the social context of consumption (e.g., with companions, special social occasions). The fifth practice has to do with symbolic management in terms of "cold" and "hot" associated with the balance of the circulation of energy, *Qi*, 气and health. Commercial beverages are part of a more general system of management of traditional and modern drinks—intended to preserve health or promote the return to good health, offering a variety of tastes and restoring energy.

The Transition from Domestic Production to Commercial Consumption

Traditional Beliefs and Practices

Access to drinking water is problematic in the city. Chinese families have to produce their own drinking water at home using tap water or buy bottles or tanks of water. Traditionally, people drink boiled water from morning until evening, lukewarm or at ambient temperature, on its own or with infusions, or for tea. Additives to the water may give it a certain taste or promote health. These practices occur particularly in southern China.

Cold water and iced drinks are not recommended. They are linked with a ban that is particularly internalized by women from puberty onward and associated with the beginning of their periods. Ice cubes do not seem to be a key aspect of Chinese drinks culture. However, the refrigerator is a form of domestic technology that is used in the management of cold drinks. Today commercial drinks are in competition with, or exist side-by-side with, the traditional ways water is prepared and consumed at home. In fact, bottles and tanks of water ease the lives of Chinese families at home, on the move and at work.

Current Practices

Today there is easy access to mineral water and to purified bottled water, as well as most other commercial beverages. At home, the Internet seems to play an increasingly important role in ordering consumer goods, especially commercial drinks. Some Chinese can spend the whole week without leaving home, and order everything they need on the Ali Baba website, which has become the most important Internet shopping venue in the world. When on the move, consumers can easily find most drinks in supermarkets, boutiques, kiosks or machines in the metro stations.

The drink itinerary forms a system and conditions what people drink. It is related to a set of concrete objects. In the home, we note the tap, the filter, the electric kettle, the thermos flask, the jug, glasses, cups, the refrigerator, an Internet connection, water tanks or bottles and cans of various beverages that are commercially produced. While on the move, Chinese consumers typically take a plastic bottle, a thermos flask or other flask with them; knapsacks feature a special pocket where the bottle or thermos flask can be put. Consumers find different sorts of drink machines that sell cold drinks in summer and hot drinks in winter; they may include heating cupboards, cans and trash cans. At work, there are water fountains and electric kettles. All of these items are tied to the preparation, consumption and disposal of nonalcoholic drinks. They do not determine usages related to drinks, but without them the consumption of commercial drinks is more difficult.

Seasonal Beliefs about Beverages

Beverage consumption varies strongly depending on the season. In winter, Chinese consumers avoid consuming drinks that are physically and symbolically cold. Instead they look for hot drinks. During seasonal transitions, the body needs help in getting used to the changing conditions. For example, as the weather gets warmer in spring, cool drinks help to compensate; conversely, herbal teas and hot drinks are used to compensate for the cooler environment of autumn. In summer, it is important to keep the body hydrated and cool to cope with the summer heat.

The meaning and therefore the positioning of commercial beverages with respect to heat are not clearly fixed by the norms of Chinese consumers. Commercial beverages tend to be classified as cold and are therefore seen rather negatively by some Chinese—those who are sensitive to the symbolic system of the traditional management of cold and hot. Any bans or stipulations on commercial drinks within Chinese families remain vague and flexible, and are a regular source of conflict.

Taste Preferences

Choosing a drink for its taste often equates to a decision-making process between what seems natural, bland and healthy and something that may have a bitter taste, is artificial, and has unknown ingredients. The taste of water is often considered bland, or even bad, when it comes from the tap. However, when it is boiled, it is considered healthy. Blandness is associated with being healthy.

The tastes of the Chinese vary from drinks perceived as nauseating (e.g., "too sweet," containing milk), and those that are pleasing (e.g., "light, mild and refreshing," cool acidic taste [酸爽 *Suān shuǎng*]). These pleasing drinks are good to drink (好喝 *Hǎo hē*) and slip down (滑 *Huá*) the throat. The "light, mild" taste (清淡 *Qīng dàn*) is positive, distinguished from a "bland" taste (淡 *dàn*). Bland is considered a neutral word, although it can be used in a negative meaning when applied to drinks. The negative meaning of the word bland partly explains why drinks that taste good are sought after—in particular sweet commercial drinks—but are not considered healthy. The important thing is not to drink them too often since that often results in an accumulation of unhealthy ingredients in the body (e.g., sugar, coloring agents). Sugar may be perceived positively (e.g., having a good taste, creating a social link, restoring energy) but may also be viewed negatively if it is consumed in excessive quantities and leads to obesity or diabetes.

Sugar, which adds taste but can become unhealthy, has a particular relationship with blandness, which has no taste but which is healthy. Here we simplify a complicated but significant association in Chinese culture—that opposites are both in tension and in harmony, just like Yīn is associated with Yáng (阴阳), and female with male.

Other Effects on Consumption

Generational Differences

Studying the development of commercial beverages has parallels with how Chinese families function, including the divisions and tensions within them. We see the effects of agency on the "consumption" assemblage—that people of different ages favor different consumption practices with respect to drinks, and in some cases impose their practices on others. These divisions reflect a generational effect. Three major generations can be identified in Chinese society.

The first is the *generation of scarcity* born before 1980. Its norms of consumption are often much more austere than those of younger generations, and hence infrequently linked with pleasure. This generation is associated with the symbolic norms of hot and cold linked with traditional Chinese medicine. This generation generally takes care of the grandchildren and conveys its norms to them.

The second is the *generation of economic reform and the single child family*. This generation began about 1980 (*Bālíng Hòu* 八零后, born "after 1980"). As the sandwich generation, it is caught between the traditional norms of its parents, and the demands of its children (i.e., for a drink with more taste).

The most recent generation is the *generation of abundance*. Born around 1995–2000, the parents of these children have greater purchasing power at a time when there is significant development in the commercial drinks market and its infrastructure. This generation is subject to strong pressure in school, at least for children of the upper middle class. School pressure works against the consumption of commercial drinks, which are viewed negatively by teachers and some parents.

Life Cycle Differences

The diversity and divisions related to the use of nonalcoholic drinks also vary depending on life cycle effects; we identified four major stages in China. The first stage in the life cycle includes *young non-adults* (未成年人 *Wèi chéng nián rén* "people who are not finished") from 7 to 18 years. This group can be subdivided further. Elementary school students between the ages of 7 and 12 are only supposed to drink water. Middle school students between the ages of 13 and 15 begin sneaking soft drinks despite prohibitions from their parents, grandparents and teachers. High school students between 16 and 18 years are under significant pressure because they are preparing for the national competitive examination, the *Gāo kǎo* (高考), which enables them to go to university afterward. They increasingly feel the need for such high-sugar drinks to boost their performance during examinations.

During this stage of the life cycle from age 7 to 18, commercial beverages are generally forbidden. They represent moments of relaxation that compete with school time. However, they are allowed (or even required) after sports, as a social activity to make friends, or while preparing for examinations. During this same stage, girls learn about the ban for them on cold drinks. The "young non-adults" are considered children (*hái zi* 孩子). This term formally signifies that children owe obedience to adults including grandparents, parents and teachers.

The second stage of the life cycle is that of *young adults* (青年人 *Qīng nián rén* "green, immature person"). This stage begins at the end of high school, around the age of 18 and lasts until the birth of the first child, between the ages of 25 and 35 years. This life cycle stage is much more flexible in terms of social norms and bans, except for young women who wish to have a baby. And, when young women are pregnant, commercial drinks may be entirely forbidden. It is likely that this life cycle effect overlaps with the generational effect. The most recent generation, born after 1995/2000 and already accustomed to commercial beverages during childhood, is more open to these drinks—say, when they go to university.

The third stage is that of *older adults* (中老年人 *Zhōng lǎonián rén*), those who are older than 35/40 years; most were born before 1980. They are beginning to pay attention to their health and set a good example for their children by limiting their consumption of commercial beverages. Some older adults consider these drinks off limits.

The fourth stage of the life cycle includes *retired people* (老年人 *Lǎonián rén*). They are very concerned about their health problems, and for some of them, care related to traditional Chinese medicine. They prefer hot drinks such as soups rather than commercial drinks that are "cold" symbolically, and hence seen as a poor choice, particularly for women.

These different life cycle stages correspond to three major phases in understanding the relationship with health and nutrition. During childhood, it is important to pay attention to "nutrition" (营养 *Yíngyǎng*), in the sense of encouraging growth and giving children a good start. Young adults need to "maintain their health" (保健 *bǎojiàn*), in the sense of keeping active. For adults and the retired, it is necessary to "feed life" (养生 *yǎngshēng*), in the sense of slowing down the loss of energy. These three mental representations of health, which develop as a function of stage in the life cycle, correspond to changes in human energy over time. First energy grows, then it is maintained and finally it is reduced.

Gender Effects

Consumption of commercial nonalcoholic drinks is also affected by gender. The pressure seems to be stronger for young women than for young men than on young men to refrain from cold drinks, particularly when young women are pregnant.

It also seems that commercial drink consumption is sensitive to the effects of social class and income. However, our data at the microsocial scale does not permit us to examine this likely pattern in any detail; a quantitative survey with a larger sample size would be necessary.

Tensions Arising at Home

Through our study of commercial beverage consumption, we have been able to document tensions in China. Sometimes the tensions are high, involving some combination of paternal and maternal grandparents, the two parents, and the only child. These tensions involve supporters of traditional Confucian authority, often designated using the term "filial piety" (孝 *xiào*). Those adhering to the principles of Confucianism are generally against sweet commercial drinks containing sugar, and are generally in favor of a traditional, strict educational system based on memory rather than creativity. They differ from those who have a more flexible view of parental authority and an educational system that fosters creativity. These tensions also vary depending on the priorities that families have related to success at school, good health and the proper socialization of their only child.

However, a new social norm, which is implicit and diffuse, is emerging in China. It authorizes the expression of emotions and pleasure. This norm appears to be similar to one experienced in the West between the 19th and

20th centuries, as shown by the sociologist Eva Illouz (2012) in her book *Why Love Hurts: A Sociological Explanation*. A roundtable discussion carried out in 2014 with Ma Jingjing and Wang Lei (Desjeux et al. 2014) certainly showed the erotic dimensions of pleasure, which were nonexistent in the first roundtable discussion that we carried out in 1997 (Zheng and Desjeux 2002). This new norm goes against the norm of unquestioning obedience. As a result, there are many more negotiations between parents and children than 20 years ago, and hence a potential opening for the commercial beverage market. However, comparatively speaking, parental authority seems to be much stricter in China than in France, Brazil or the United States (Desjeux et al. 2016). Similarly, in a recent 2017 study, Desjeux found the same debate in São Paulo, Brazil on family's authority and flexibility.

The Role of Social Norms

Integration of commercial beverages into family life is likely to occur when parents allow it. Some young people adhere to the ban on commercial drinks imposed by their teachers and parents. However, this norm becomes less and less applicable the older the young people get, particularly as they approach the end of secondary school. Other young people may ignore their parents' rules about consuming commercial beverages. Peer groups may tolerate, encourage or even promote such beverage consumption after sports or before an exam, when it increases students' energy or allows them to make friends.

Beverage consumption becomes a game between parents or grandparents and the children. One of the ways in which parents exercise control is by limiting their children's pocket money. However, this method of control can only be an occasional practice. Maneuvering by the parents and grandparents is limited because the child is an only child; no one wants to have a poor relationship with his/her only child. Children control a strategic area of uncertainty with respect to their parents; they can give or withhold love, as observed in France (Desjeux 1991). Their agency is therefore an important factor in the changes that are underway in beverage consumption.

The analysis of power relations between adults and the child shows that there is sales potential due to the social transgression linked with the consumption of commercial drinks, if this consumption is not too strongly opposed to the goals of success at school and good health. There is also sales potential associated with the progressively-seeking independence of young people.

If the norm surrounding commercial beverage consumption is relaxed, the drinks market for children can be developed. The market is subject to a field of forces, including changing norms, practices and behaviors. Our interpretation differs from those that are purely individual-oriented, centered on desire and motivations, such as the approaches of marketing and psychology. We are not suggesting that these approaches are incorrect, only that they are different from an anthropological approach. Marketing and psychological approaches may be quite relevant when one is facing a store shelf or computer screen (i.e., at a particular moment in the acquisition of goods and products). Anthropology adds context to our understanding of beverage consumption. It provides the framework or cultural overlay for beliefs and expectations, including their changing patterns and hence the collective constraints guiding individual choices on which marketing focuses.

Variation in Beverage Consumption

Beverage consumption practices vary. They depend on the time of day (i.e., between the morning and the evening), "sedentary" times or times of transportation, and ordinary periods versus exceptional occasions. Since water from the tap is not potable, the Chinese boil all tap water before consuming it. Boiling water is often done in the morning. Water is a way of purifying the body and "feeding life" at the moment of getting up. There are two kinds of breakfasts: the traditional kind based on soup or soy milk, and the modern kind based on coffee, fruit juices and milk. Breakfast involves making a decision between traditional and modern dishes or drinks. Traditional breakfasts require a certain amount of time for preparation; they are perceived as being healthy. Modern breakfasts require no preparation and are not always perceived as being healthy.

Breakfast may be eaten at home, on the way to work or school, in school or the office, and at the *Dān wèi* (单位, work department) for those who work in the public sector. Water must be boiled for breakfast when one eats at home. For those who stay at home, that boiled water can be used all day, including for making tea. Commercial soda-style drinks are generally forbidden during breakfast.

While on the move, some of the Chinese drink traditional and/or modern beverages. They may put them in their thermos flasks or buy them at shops or from machines in the metro stations. Commercial drinks are considered acceptable.

At school, young people have easy access to drinking water. Commercial drinks are strictly forbidden at primary school. In middle school or high school, it is possible for students to buy commercial drinks in the small shops located next to schools, and then drink them—usually in secret. At work, the beverage consumption norm is flexible. The workplace is often equipped with a kettle and/or a water fountain for use with a thermos flask.

At lunchtime, commercial beverages are generally forbidden for everyone—particularly sweet drinks such as soda. As a rule, it is not common to drink anything at meals except soups, hot water or tea. The evening is a more flexible time for consuming drinks other than traditional drinks, especially when returning from work and after dinner.

The drinks permitted at home are those that are perceived to be healthy, nutritious, and purifying for the body (e.g., boiled water, cereal soups, home-made soy juice). Chinese families try to address the uncertainties linked with the quality of the drinking water on their own; they are concerned with every-thing that could threaten the health of their child or other family members. Sweet commercial drinks are generally not allowed. On the other hand, they are permitted in the workplace, when one is in transit, and in the evening.

However, when we observed the size and number of the supermarket shelves devoted to commercial beverages, we noticed a gap between stated norms and actual practice. Interestingly, in the few home refrigerators that we saw, we did not see many commercial drinks perhaps because sweet commer-cial drinks are a source of concern for some Chinese families. Today, each member of the family maneuvers around the rules, trying not to exceed the social limits so as to avoid sparking too many conflicts.

Beverage consumption and its meaning also vary depending on the occa-sion. Water is generally stipulated on ordinary family occasions throughout the day, unlike commercial beverages, which are forbidden or only tolerated.

However, water—whether hot or lukewarm—is not allowed during social gatherings away from the home. Instead, commercial drinks or alcohol, become the beverages of choice. These beverages become part of the face-saving strategies (*Miàn zi* 面子) of the Chinese. The notion of blandness comes from analogical reasoning, which is strongly present in traditional Chinese culture. It associates a bland taste with a bland social relationship, bringing the risk of loss of face for the host. The risk of having a bland social relationship makes it obligatory to consume commercial drinks with a strong taste, symbolizing a strong social relationship. Commercial drinks are considered acceptable before an exam or after playing sports. As a gen-eral rule, everything that promotes success on exams is allowed in China. On the other hand, in the event of illness, traditional herbal teas are gener-ally stipulated.

In qualitative research, the analytic criterion is not frequency or quantity, since these elements cannot be demonstrated statistically. Instead, qualitative researchers emphasize the existence and diversity of practices that are situa-tion-dependent. The context, the actions people take and the objects associ-ated with them, represent variables that can explain practices and meaning. We do not consider the product's image and its symbolic dimensions as explanatory variables that trigger a decision. Instead, we use them to explain the meaning that consumers employ to justify their purchase decisions. In a counterintuitive manner, the meaning ascribed to a practice at the microsocial scale of observation is not independent of it. Meaning is constrained by social norms, whether that involves accepting them or breaking the rules. Meaning reinforces the effect of the situation, which leads to action.

The Symbolism of "Hot" (热 *rè*) and "Cold" (冷 *lěng*)

For some of the Chinese, the symbolism of health and what is healthy revolves around two key notions: that of "cold" (冷 *lěng*) and that of "hot" (热 *rè*). All of this is known to specialists (Yang 2006). What is less well known, and more difficult to estimate, is the proportion of the Chinese who live in accordance with the principles of traditional medicine. Previous research on body care practices and use of cosmetics in China (Lei 2015) shows that some Chinese adhere to traditional principles, while others are opposed to them; still others adhere to both traditional and western medicine principles and practices. Agency features here again in the existence of alternative cultural models. Human actors can decide which principles and practices they will adopt.

In traditional medicine, the basic principle is that the body is in good health when energy (*Qi* 气) circulates correctly inside it. It circulates well when hot and cold are balanced in the body. The categories of hot and cold are symbolic and do not correspond to some actual temperature. These categories are not entirely constant across China. The categorization of a particular foodstuff as symbolically hot or cold may vary depending on family or region.

Women are thought to have colder bodies due to their monthly loss of blood; they are also supposed to have less energy. Therefore, they have a heat deficit and need to consume more foods and drinks categorized symbolically as hot to restore the body's balance. They must avoid "cold" products, and hence to some extent, commercial drinks; while such drinks may be neutral, they may be categorized as cold products. However, for some Chinese, commercial drinks are not part of categorization system of hot and cold. Commercial drinks are seen in an ambiguous way in that they have both positive and negative associations.

The symbolic category of cold is of particular importance to body and health care, especially for women. Women believe they run a higher risk of illness or infertility than men if they drink cold beverages. Cold drinks may simultaneously threaten the proper functioning of organs such as the heart, liver or lungs. Symbolically, these organs contribute toward the proper circulation of energy (*Qi*), the ability to have children, and the aesthetics that their body and face represent. This belief explains why boiled lukewarm water is a way of dealing with the problem of cold drinks and righting the balance of *Qi* for women. Boiled water has a strong positive symbolic charge, while commercial drinks can have a negative symbolic charge.

Yet, commercial beverages, one way or another, are becoming integrated into the care of the body and the regulation of hot and cold. The meaning ascribed to commercial drinks is neither stable nor automatic, but rather follows the dynamics of the development and divisions of Chinese society.

Some of the Chinese attach great importance to the symbolism of hot and cold, while others do not and categorize it as a "superstition," and still others are somewhere between the two positions. Thus, even though Chinese women are not equally sensitive to cold products, the symbolism behind them, which is often associated with commercial drinks, remains problematic today.

If we look at the relationship between the life cycle and beverage consumption, we can see that the commercial beverage market is structured with little left to chance. Some adolescents partake during exam periods and while playing sports. The market is much more open to young adults who do not have any family pressures (even if they already experience work pressures) since they are generally in good health, are financially independent, and like the taste of commercial drinks. With middle-aged adults, market share is lower compared to young adults. For older people, the market seems to be relatively limited, and China's population is aging. However, it is entirely possible that in the years to come, some of the beverage consumption practices associated with young non-adults and young adults may extend to the older generations.

DISCUSSION

The Social Framework for Innovation Success

Our anthropological study shows that drink choice is subject to significant social constraints in terms of what is stipulated, allowed or forbidden. This choice varies as a function of tensions crossing the generations, between those who adhere to the traditional Chinese system of beverages and those who prefer to make compromises by drinking modern commercial beverages. Here again we see the importance of agency, with the consumers themselves deciding which cultural model they will adopt.

These tensions require a negotiation between the cultural goals of good health and of pleasure linked with taste: boiled water is healthy but bland while a commercial drink has taste but may be bad for one's health. A compromise, for the Chinese, typically involves choosing the commercial drink that is perceived to be the least detrimental to one's health, but while having a pleasant taste. This compromise takes into account price, particularly when the consumers are young and have little money, and brand, an indicator of quality and taste. Choosing a particular brand is often a way for consumers to identify the quality for which they are looking. However, the satisfaction drawn from the product is more important than the love of the brand.

Our anthropological investigation makes it possible to identify those social groups able to purchase commercial drinks. The primary group, consisting of young people between 18 and 35 years of age, is positioned to allow themselves this treat. Another group includes those adults who are on the move in the metro, on trains, in cars or on foot, regardless of age. A third group includes those who are outside their home at work, at a restaurant, or have just finished playing a sport.

Diffusing Anthropological Findings within the Firm

It is within the triangle of social norms, practices and the effect of the life cycle that Chinese consumers make decisions between hot and cold, natural and artificial, light and sickly sweet, pure and impure, healthy and unhealthy, and bland and strong tasting. This emic classification is significantly different from the one proposed by marketing, whether in terms of motivation or revenue. The diffusion of anthropological data from anthropological consultants to the R&D department to the marketing department may face a variety of issues (e.g., data reliability, representativeness). Yet, the anthropological methodology prides itself on its validity. The difference in disciplinary approaches lies at the heart of the enigma of innovation.

This situation forced us to reflect on how to proceed so that the company would use our results. We were not content with simply presenting our results. We organized an activity (the nature of which is confidential) to stimulate reflection on the part of all the anthropologists and the in-house teams of the company.

Saying that there is a difference between the information produced by anthropologists, by R&D, or by marketing does not mean that one of the three actors is better than the others. It simply means that information is not socially neutral because it is produced within specific cognitive frameworks. Our anthropological framework emphasizes practices—what consumers do given certain constraints. It also emphasizes the social forces leading consumers to act and places less stress on consumer needs and wants.

However, marketing focuses first on consumer needs. References are frequently made to the famous hierarchy of needs created by Maslow (1934), which poses many problems today due to the evolution of what is considered a primary need. In the 1940s, the period in which Maslow was writing, food was thought to be a primary need. Since the year 2000, electrical energy and mobility may also be considered primary needs.

Thus, for inventions/innovations (produced by anthropological investigation) to be "diffused," they need to be transformed, "reinterpreted" or "translated" (Callon 1986) using the mental frameworks of marketing specialists who review and react to anthropological findings and recommendations. Working meetings involving diverse disciplinary backgrounds and professions allow the information to be translated from one professional universe into another.

We participated in such a working meeting. After it was over, the company proposed a series of key findings of the study. At this point, the anthropological data was transformed and reduced to a slide with six columns. Crucially, this simplification enabled the data to be reinterpreted by company employees. As a result, an invention was produced—an idea had the potential to be transformed into an innovation and ultimately end up with consumers.

However, data reduction by itself is not sufficient, because the cognitive models or frameworks of marketing experts do not correspond to those held by anthropologists. Briefly, the framework for marketing is organized around three questions: What are the needs? What do I like? What are the motivations? These three questions can also be phrased: Why do I like something? What meaning do I give to it? What are the psychological barriers that prevent me from getting it? Desire is central for marketing professionals. For anthropologists oriented to explaining cultural practices, it is the set of constraints and the interplay of actors that are central.

This disciplinary difference was so great that the Chinese firm's general management had difficulties understanding the "insights" from the anthropological study. We found some basic similarities between the two approaches. We settled on the following: Consumption practices corresponded generally to individual needs, motivations corresponded to trigger events, and the combination of occasions for use, Chinese symbolism related to management of the body and health, and the constraints corresponded to the social norms which promoted or forbade consumption.

SUMMARY AND CONCLUSIONS

Figures 7.1 and 7.2 display the overall findings. They represent the cultural change in progress in the area of drinks via two assemblages, one representing the old *status quo*, and the other representing the current situation. The effect of agency is apparent in a number of areas. First, people choose whether or not to adhere to the old traditional systems of beliefs about symbolic hot and cold. Second, taste plays a role in their choice of drink. Third, children have greater bargaining power with their parents than previous generations of children had with their parents. Consequently, only children are more likely to be successful negotiators in being allowed to consume commercial drinks. They may also transgress any bans in secret. Such agency-related changes interact

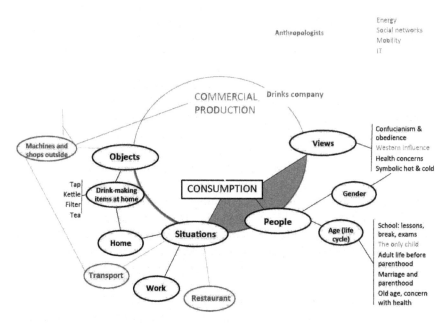

Figure 7.1   Traditional Pattern of Non-alcoholic Beverage Consumption.

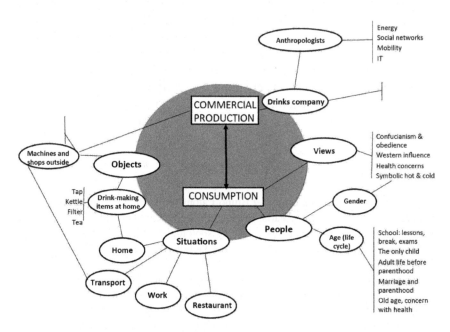

Figure 7.2   Trajectory of Change in Non-alcoholic Beverage Consumption.

with changes in other areas involving larger groups (e.g., school authorities), social circumstances (e.g., a rise in the use of restaurants, increased travel time to work) and inanimate actants (e.g., drink machines). It is the assemblage as a whole that changes over time.

A great deal of time and energy was required for our anthropological ideas to diffuse within the company. The diffusion process was not purely mental, but involved a great deal of energy, mobility, computers, budgets, mobilization of internal networks in the company, and work carried out in French, Chinese and English. The findings produced within the company corresponded partly, but only partly, to the sociocultural framework proposed in the anthropological conclusion. This outcome was expected, given the normal path followed in the diffusion of innovations. Our anthropological investigation was reinterpreted with respect to the objectives and the constraints of actors within the company. This reinterpretation made it possible for them to create an invention that could be diffused within the company. Otherwise, we would not have known whether our results were useful to either the firm or the end user.

Innovation will always be an uncertain phenomenon; in this sense there will never be an answer to the enigma of its success or failure. However, based on the example of nonalcoholic drinks presented here, it is possible to lift part of the veil masking this enigma. Some, but not all, of this unknown derives from the ability of actors to agree to a reinterpretation, transformation and translation of their ideas all along the collective process of innovation. This process begins with an invention and, with luck, ends with an innovation for the end user. It is a process on the microsocial and mesosocial scale that incorporates actors and objects, meaning and interest, relations of power and cooperation, and both material and imagined attributes. The resolution of the enigma of innovation is to be found by taking into consideration this uncertain combination.

REFERENCES

Akrich Madeleine, Michel Callon *et* Bruno Latour (éd.), 2006, *Sociologie de la traduction: textes fondateurs,* Paris: Presses de l'Ecole des Mines.

Callon, Michel. 1986. "Éléments pour une sociologie de la traduction. La domestication des coquilles Saint-Jacques dans la Baie de Saint-Brieuc", in: *L'Année sociologique,* no. 36.

Carré, Jean-Michael. 2013. *Chine le nouvel empire. De l'humiliation à la domination (1911–2013).* DVD documentary. Arté éditions.

Desjeux, Dominique. 1979. *La question agraire à Madagascar.* Paris: L'Harmattan.

———. 1987. *Les stratégies paysannes en Afrique Noire.* Paris: L'Harmattan.

———. 1991. *Comment les enfants manipulent les parents.* http://bit. ly/1991-desjeux-enfant-manipulation-parents

———. 2004. *Les Sciences Sociales.* Paris: PUF.

———, Wang Lei and Ma Jingjing. 2014. Confidental report for Danone. 85 pages.

———, Yang Xiaomin and Hu Shen. 2016. "Classe moyenne et consommation ou les mutations silencieuses de la société chinoise, depuis 1997", in: Bouvier Lafitte, Béatrice and Pauzet, Anne (dir.). 2016. *Art et intercultures ou les mutations silencieuses de la Chine contemporaine.* Paris: L'Harmattan.

Deleuze, Gilles and Gatari, Félix. 1980. *Mille Plateaux.* Paris: Les Editions de Minuit.

Illouz, Eva. 2012. *Why Love Hurts: A Sociological Explanation.* Cambridge: Polity Press.

Latour, Bruno. 2005. *Reassembling the social. An introduction to Actor-Network Theory.* Oxford: OUP.

Lei, Wang. 2015. *Pratiques des soins du corps en Chine. Le cas des cosmétiques.* Paris: L'Harmattan.

Maslow, Abraham. 1943. "A Theory of Human Motivation." *Psychological Review,* Vol. 50 #4, pp. 370–396.

Mauss, Marcel. 1925. "Essai sur le don. Forme et raison de l'échange dans les sociétés archaïques", in: *L'Année sociologique.*

Weber, Max. 1904–5. "Die protestantische Ethik und der Geist des Kapitalismus." *Archiv für Sozialwissenschaft und Sozialpolitik.*

Yang, Xiaomin. 2006. *La fonction sociale des restaurants en Chine.* Paris: L'Harmattan.

Zheng, Lihua and Desjeux, Dominique. 2002. *Entreprises et vie quotidienne en Chine.* Paris : L'Harmattan.

Chapter 8

Relationship Building

Nigerian Entrepreneurs, Business Networks, and Chinese Counterparts

U. Ejiro O. Onomake

In the spring of 2012, the International Fire and Security Exhibition and Conference-West Africa (IFSEC) held its second annual conference at the upscale Eko Hotel in Lagos. The hotel was full of Nigerian and international patrons. Eko is one of the most expensive and well-known hotels in Lagos. Although some say it is living on its past laurels and newer competition (e.g., Radisson, Sheraton) will outpace it, the Eko still hosts events like the security conference. The security industry in Nigeria is growing as Nigerians spend more money on safety ranging from personal safety at home and on the road to security for businesses and institutions. Itoro (a pseudonym), the managing director of an international private security firm headquartered in Nigeria, was one of the conference attendees. Itoro is one of an increasing number of Nigerian entrepreneurs who have made business connections with China. His business expansion and links to China were initiated and maintained through the help of brokerage and networking.

This chapter discusses the historical and contemporary role of social networks and brokerage in Nigerian business. Brokerage and social networks play a crucial role in Nigerian-Chinese business relationships. There is an emerging cultural shift from individual brokers to a growing number of organizations that serve as brokers. This chapter focuses on the resulting mixed model approach to brokerage consisting of individual and organizational brokers that help foster Nigerian-Chinese relationships. When these relationships are examined using ethnography, the agency of Africans is visible. The human-centered analysis I present allows exploration of Africans' agency, in this case the role of Nigerian brokers and entrepreneurs in these relationships. Through the analytical framework of assemblages, we can understand the cultural shift in brokerage that is influencing Nigerian-Chinese relationships.

The first part of the chapter describes the application of assemblage theory to my data set, along with my methodological approach. These sections are followed by an examination of the theoretical concepts of brokerage and networking and their importance to Nigerian entrepreneurs, particularly those attempting to conduct business with Chinese counterparts. I describe brokerage and its role in Nigeria in a brief historical analysis. Next, I present a contemporary discussion of Nigerian-Chinese networking associations with insights into the role of brokers using an example of a former ambassador to China who plays a prominent role in a networking association. Finally, I discuss the challenges of initiating business with China and the role of networking in the life of Nigerian entrepreneurs based on the example of Itoro.

ASSEMBLAGE THEORY

Assemblage theory focuses on the bonds between multiple actors and groups that represent diverse and sometimes seemingly divergent interests. Deleuze and Guattari first proposed this theory in 1980 (Deleuze and Guattari 1980). DeLanda (2016, 2) has continued to analyze and interpret their philosophical thought: "two aspects of the concept are emphasised: that the parts that are fitted together are not uniform either in nature or in origin, and that the assemblage actively links these parts together by establishing relations between them.

Assemblage theory allows for analysis of relationships between people who on the surface have nothing in common. Since its original proposition, assemblage theory has been applied to various situations including global networks, cities, and policy studies (Collier and Ong 2005; Clark et al. 2015; Kamalipour and Peimani 2015). One question that continues to arise in these analyses is the issue of consistency and coherence. "How do things take on consistency? How do they cohere?" (Deleuze 2007, 179). Coherence and consistency are important for keeping the assemblage together, but how long assemblages remain coherent depends on the purpose of the formation. Members of an assemblage choose to maintain the bonds of the relationship as long as it benefits them. This chapter examines the cultural changes related to brokerage in Nigeria. The change in brokerage from precolonial to contemporary Nigeria highlights the evolving nature of assemblages.

METHODOLOGY

Fieldwork for this research took place from February 2011 to April 2012 in Nigeria, which is located in West Africa. I conducted my research primarily in the southwestern Nigerian States of Lagos and neighboring Ogun. Lagos State is the birthplace of several Nigerian presidents and artists while Ogun State boasts more universities than any other state. Both states are home for a growing number of Chinese firms operating in Nigeria. Most of my time in Lagos State was spent in Lagos city and Lekki. As the commercial capital of Nigeria and the most populous city in Nigeria, Lagos city was the perfect place to conduct research. As of 2014, Lagos city was estimated to be the home of 21 million people (Kaplan 2014). My major research questions included:

- What is the relationship between Chinese and Nigerian elites?
- Why do Nigerian entrepreneurs choose to conduct business with Chinese counterparts?
- How do these entrepreneurs initiate contact with Chinese counterparts?

Research participants included a range of aspirational and elite Nigerian and Chinese actors involved in shaping the growing relationship between Nigeria and China. I met entrepreneurs through individual or organizational

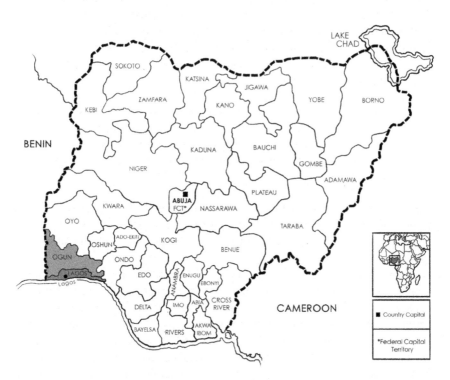

Figure 8.1 Map of Contemporary Nigeria Highlighting the States of Lagos and Ogun Where the Research was Conducted.

brokers. While attending a conference on foreign direct investment, I met a variety of Nigerian businesspeople, one of whom introduced me to a Nigerian entrepreneur who conducted business with Chinese counterparts. Through that entrepreneur, I was introduced to another entrepreneur; from there it snowballed and I was subsequently introduced to other entrepreneurs via individual or organizational brokers. As a doctoral researcher with an MBA and experience working in business, entrepreneurs felt comfortable discussing business concepts with me.

I interviewed nine entrepreneurs and focused on five of them for this chapter. Data was gathered through interviews and participant observation. Business participants generally had constricted schedules with little leeway so there was considerable focus on engaging in their activities as far as permitted and conducting "ethnography by appointment," basically doing research when my research participants could allocate time in their schedules (Kemmitt 2008). Therefore, research into Nigerian entrepreneurs took place throughout a wide variety of places including offices, restaurants, in cars, at an industry event, and on social media as they used various platforms to promote their businesses. Sometimes our meetings were scheduled a few weeks in advance, and other times I would receive a call the day before an entrepreneur was available.

When conducting ethnography, general practice is to anonymize the names of research participants and other identifying features such as the names of organizations to which they are related. Woods (2012) argues that there are three challenges to anonymizing elites:

> elite subjects are by definition drawn from a relatively small group of individuals; elite subjects are often interviewed because of the position that they hold, and the reporting and analysis of their comments cannot be easily divorced from their office or organization; and some (though not all) elite subjects are public figures. (2012, 4)

I anonymized all the entrepreneurs' names, but I did not anonymize the names of organizations or public figures related to these organizations. Despite my efforts, some of the research participants and organizations are easy to determine due to their prominence in Nigerian society.

I employed two particular analytic techniques to understand the ethnographic data: content analysis and discourse analysis. These techniques helped in the identification of cultural themes and patterns (Bernard 2011; Fetterman 2010). Since this study was exploratory (rather than confirmatory), I anticipated that the key analytic themes and patterns would emerge from the data. My coding of the interviews and conversations, and my experiences during data collection generally, resulted in a set of categories that enabled me to make sense of and explain the relationship between brokerage and social networks.

Additionally, I used an array of documentary materials, which included historical works and past studies of brokerage in West Africa. I also examined the government's public discourse regarding Nigerian-Chinese relationships. To understand this discourse and document the overarching context and environment in which Nigerians operated, I analyzed bilateral trade agreements and related public relations campaigns.

BROKERAGE IN CONTEXT: PAST & PRESENT

Precolonial Times

I define *brokerage* as the use of an intermediary (a broker) to assist in gaining access to a tangible or intangible object or process. The obtained object or process is wide ranging and can be anything from knowledge, to a relationship, to an introduction to someone. Brokerage can be traced back to precolonial times (pre-1800s) when it was utilized in various parts of Africa including Nigeria. Brokers had various duties including putting "technical knowledge and linguistic skills at the service of inexpert prospective traders and supporting traders who needed help finding customers in new places" (Jones 1970, 189). Brokers were primarily used for trade and government business. In an economic history of 19th century Africa, Zeleza (1993) described the reliance upon intermediaries by international merchants. In North and West Africa, traders that did not have links to local networks or diasporic communities used local brokers. Diasporic communities consisted of groups of expatriates who came from the same country and lived together in neighborhoods in another country. The benefits of these communities include access to social and financial capital. As Zeleza (1993) writes:

> Using these intermediaries had several advantages, especially in the light of the restriction on the foreigners' freedom to move and trade locally. Moreover, the local traders and brokers were more likely to be better informed about local consumption trends and tastes. (1993, 271)

Additionally, brokers helped with logistics such as accommodations and storage facilities. They also found local sellers from whom traders could purchase goods (Zeleza 1993, 281).

Colonial Times

Initially during the colonial period, Nigeria was divided into three areas: Northern protectorate, Lagos colony, and Southern protectorate. In the early 1900s, Lagos colony was incorporated into the Southern protectorate.

Colonial times (1800–1960) brought a different form of brokerage. Elite Nigerians in both Northern and Southern protectorates with higher levels of education and connections acted as intermediaries between Nigerian citizens and British officials. Colonial forces in the Southern protectorate worked with local intermediaries, but faced challenges in leveraging the help of these intermediaries in collecting taxes. Intermediaries worked primarily as interpreters, translators, and clerks. A smaller number served as traditional rulers.

Brokers of this era were "perceived within a dichotomy of collaboration and resistance" (Pratten 2006, 221). Working with colonial forces branded brokers as collaborators because they worked with the very forces that subjugated their fellow citizens. Conversely, brokers were viewed as subversive agents who worked within the colonial system to weaken it and find ways to help themselves and others. For example, in the latter half the 1860s, African intermediaries well versed in Western life came to the forefront. These intermediaries were a small group of formerly enslaved Africans and their family members who returned to Freetown and Libreville, and worked in positions associated with middle/upper class status. "Essentially, their role was that of cultural intermediaries, men who straddled the frontier between Europe

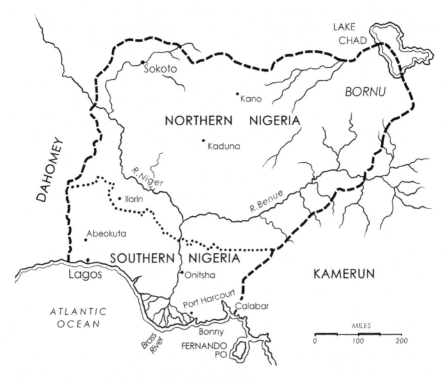

Figure 8.2 Map of Nigeria During Colonial Times.

and Africa, interpreting, in the broadest sense of the word, one to the other" (Hopkins 1973, 153). Although, both Europeans and Africans viewed these brokers negatively, Hopkins asserted that they served a necessary role by mediating the flow of cultures between Westerners and Africans.

Precolonial times in the land we know as contemporary Nigeria was ruled according to ethnic groups and corresponding kingdoms. Under British rule, a particular British administrator was assigned to govern a set of ethnic groups. Despite colonialism, many traditional kingdoms remained virtually intact. Those with "chiefs who presented themselves as being open to the new were regarded as important partners on the supposedly long way to self-government and independence" (Eckert 2006, 259). Chiefs were utilized to help with administrative duties such as tax collection and other local government affairs. Chiefs brokered peace and engaged in daily governance on behalf of colonial officials. Today traditional rulers still play an important role in some communities due to their influence in people's lives and access to community resources such as land. Additionally, rulers served as patrons that helped their people solve a variety of disputes including land and familial and inheritance issues. Rulers also helped their subjects find employment and gather money during financially difficult periods. Figure 8.1 highlights the shifts along with

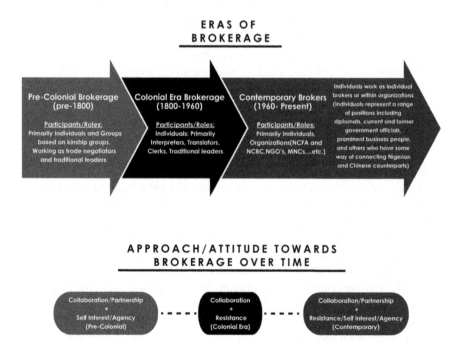

Figure 8.3   Changing Eras of Brokerage and their Related Approaches.

the participants involved in brokerage during three eras: precolonial era, colonial era, and contemporary era.

Historically, brokers mediated primarily between the village and the national capital. In the contemporary context, their role is not immediately obvious (Lindquist 2015, 9). The boundaries between areas for mediation have blurred. Brokers now serve as mediators for communities and conventional parties such as local and national governments, as well as new players such as local and international firms, development agencies, local charities, and other civil society groups (e.g., labor unions, community groups, nongovernmental organizations).

Contemporary Brokerage

Contemporary brokerage, particularly in the context of international development, is "any social process that brings localized low-level actors or groups into relationship with global structures (the town, the state or the market being the most obvious of these) [that] requires the service of go-betweens or mediators who occupy a clearly strategic function" (de Sardan 2005, 173). Situations that require brokers do not solely center on connecting "low-level actors" with "global structures." Therefore, my definition of brokerage relies upon de Sardan's definition of the facilitation of relationships between two parties but with the caveat that the people being discussed have greater power and access to resources than "low-level actors." Brokerage organizations have board members who come from elite business and political circles. Additionally, James (2011) argues that although in the past brokers were maligned for acting with greed and interfacing between "powerless people and the externally imposed power of the modern state," brokers are more complex than this commonplace caricature portrays (2011, 335).

Geographically speaking, contemporary Nigeria is now divided into 36 states and accommodates the complexity of the over 200 ethnic groups that make up the country. The contemporary development landscape in Nigeria includes private business, professional and business associations, government ministries, media consultants, and traditional large and small donors (Dada and Oyediran 2016; Dibie and Okonkwo 2000). Lindquist discusses the reemergence of the broker as a person of interest in anthropological studies in relation to a number of areas including the international development aid industry, transnational activism, tourism, finance and transnational migration (Lindquist 2015). I argue that the emergence of brokers also highlights both the new role of individual brokers and the emergence of brokerage organizations that draw on the connections of their prominent individual members to provide help to other members.

In the South African example of brokerage, James finds that "elements of state, market, and patrimonial/patriarchal-style political authority intersect" (James 2011, 318). This intersection highlights how brokers must have connections to multiple areas and in turn, those utilizing brokerage services must have access to intermediaries in various arenas. The role of brokers in the contemporary landscape of international development and foreign investment is inevitably an entrepreneurial one. As Boissevain explains, brokers should be seen as acting not only in the interest of others but also fundamentally for their own benefit (Boissevain 1974 cited in Bierschenk et al. 2002). Boissevain goes further in describing brokers as entrepreneurs whose power comes not from ownership of capital (e.g., property, land, money), but from the mobilization of people who own resources (Boissevain 1974, cited in Bierschenk et al. 2002). This entrepreneurial dimension is the key to brokerage and highlights the capacity of successful brokers to seize opportunities by staying attuned to others' needs and demands. Alongside this social capital and the less tangible resources of opportunism and power, the brokers discussed here also have significant levels of financial capital which they leverage in their international role and parlay into greater income.

Boissevain's definition simultaneously reflects similarities and changes in contemporary brokerage from colonial days. Contemporary brokers tend to come from elite positions just as colonial brokers worked as clerks, interpreters, and in other administrative jobs. Contemporary brokers have the capital (e.g., education, financial, social) essential for working as a broker. Most importantly, the dichotomy of collaboration and resistance has been transformed into an opaque continuum with collaboration and partnership merging together and resistance flowing into self-interest. Against this analysis of historical and contemporary brokerage, I now move on to discuss brokerage in relation to Nigerian-Chinese networks.

BROKERAGE AND NIGERIAN-CHINESE NETWORKS

The Ambassador and His Network

A new assemblage of brokerage organizations is emerging in the Nigerian-Chinese relationship. Actors include Chinese and Nigerians who are current and former diplomats, and business people. There are a growing number of organizations that aim to broker Chinese-Nigerian business relationships; these organizations are instrumental in helping entrepreneurs travel to China. Nonetheless, few Nigerian entrepreneurs belong to a business association that can broker on their behalf (NBS and SMEDAN 2010). Thus, these networks are extremely exclusive. Two of the most well-known organizations are the

Nigerian-China Friendship Association (NCFA) and Nigeria-China Business Council (NCBC). The founder and president of the NCFA was Victor Chibundu, a former Nigerian ambassador to China. Ambassador Chibundu's relationship and long-standing history with China highlight the role of his organization in helping to build Nigerian-Chinese relationships.

When I visited the late Chibundu's home office, the ambassador was busy reviewing a large stack of papers on his desk. Other stacks of papers and books surrounded the desk. Along the walls were pictures and art from China and Nigeria along with certificates and letters from government officials. Throughout our discussion, Chibundu pointed to items along the wall and described the history behind them, or indicated from whom he had received them. Each item held a story; for instance, a traditional Chinese drawing that he had received as a gift from a group of Chinese officials. Chibundu valued these gifts not because of their monetary value but because of the relationships behind them. Chibundu placed a high premium on relationships. During his ambassadorship and over subsequent years, Chibundu championed the relationship between Nigeria and China, which he viewed as a good fit for political and business relationships. As high context societies, reliance on relationships and social networks are common in Nigeria and China.

> In an HC (high context) culture, people tend to rely on their history, their status, their relationships, and a plethora of other information, including religion, to assign meaning to an event. LC (low context) cultures typically value individualism over collectivism and group harmony. (Nishimura et al. 2009, 785)

Long before his post to China in the early 1980s, Chibundu began his career as a civil servant. After college, Chibundu entered the Civil Service and after a sabbatical to study in the UK, he returned to Nigeria to resume work. When the Foreign Service was created in the 1950s near the end of British rule, Chibundu was chosen as one of its first members. He worked his way through the ranks and was posted in various regions including Angola, Sudan, and Iran. Chibundu ended his diplomatic career as the director of Nigeria's diplomatic affairs for Eastern and South Africa. After retiring from the Foreign Service 1996, Chibundu worked as a consultant. Chibundu is most known for his time as Nigeria's ambassador to China from 1981 to1984. Ten years later, in 1994, Chibundu founded the Nigerian-China Friendship Association (NCFA).

NCFA's mission is "to promote friendship, political, socio-economic, cultural, educational, trade, industrial, technological, scientific and sporting collaboration between the government, corporate bodies and citizens of both Nigeria and China on the basis of equality and mutual benefits" (Omegoh 2016). NCFA is a member of a larger, international body of friendship organizations that focus on cultivating relationships involving China and other countries. Chibundu was frequently interviewed and quoted in the media discussing Nigerian-Chinese issues and the NCFA. In his public statements and speeches, both in Chinese and Nigerian media, Chibundu often referred to the historical ties shared by China and Nigeria. On the 40th Anniversary of Establishment of Diplomatic Relations between the two countries, Chibundu made a speech to a crowd of government officials and business people from Nigeria and China. The speech highlighted Nigeria's support of China's campaign to join the United Nations in the early 1970s. "This achievement was by no means a simple task. Indeed, the labors of our past heroes were not in vain" (Chibundu 2011).

During preparations for the Beijing Olympics, NCFA sent out a press release urging the media, the International Olympic Committee, and others to support China's efforts "to have a peaceful Olympic Games as no country should be upset that the Chinese will host the Games" (Xinhua 2008). Chibundu's advocacy for Nigerian-Chinese relationships extended to the business realm; a number of NCFA members are business people. One of the main services NCFA provides to its members is help with the Chinese visa application process.

Brokerage Organizations

Chibundu called the NCFA the only "authentic organization to secure information about China." Brokerage relies upon legitimacy and authenticity; Chibundu continuously parlayed his experience as a diplomat into a performance of authenticity. His diplomatic experiences were a critical asset in his role as a broker. Despite Chibundu's references to authenticity, NCFA is not the only well regarded organization that helps build connections between Nigerian and Chinese business counterparts. The Nigeria-China Business Council (NCBC) was developed in the early 2000s. Its mission is:

> To serve as a bridge connecting people with genuine interest in trade and investment. This is to be achieved through various events (trade and investment missions, expert conferences, match making events) and personal deal brokerage between investors, manufacturers and project developers. (NCBC 2011)

This business-focused mission is evident in many NCBC objectives such as this one that focuses on mutual economic growth for Nigeria and China: "To change our perception and place more emphasis on manufacturing, production and the processing of most raw materials into finished products exportable to China and other West African Countries" (NCBC 2011). NCBC emphasizes Nigeria's economic growth through building relationships among business people.

Because of NCBC's business mission, it tends to be portrayed in the media as having a strong focus on business, while NCFA is portrayed as being a mixture of diplomacy, social concern, and business. Nonetheless, the NCBC has a number of former ambassadors and politicians in its ranks. Furthermore, one of its members is the former president Obasanjo who serves as the organization's grand patron. In this position, Obasanjo has attended events on NCBC's behalf in China and Nigeria. The organization also has a few Chinese expatriates as members. Both NCFA and NCBC present themselves as authentic vessels for the Nigerian-Chinese relationships, yet they do not overtly compete. Moreover, they cooperate with each other by hosting joint events and sharing members who belong to both organizations.

On another occasion, Chibundu credited NCFA with encouraging Nigerians to visit China:

> We blazed the trail for Nigerians to go to China. Today, if you go to the embassy you would see several people wanting to go there for business. This is because Nigerians have found China as a fertile ground to do business, unlike their experiences in America and other parts of Europe, China because of its orientation and economic capabilities produces things that are akin to what Nigerians wants [*sic*]. (Okoh 2011)

Ambassador Chibundu's statements highlighted a promising view of Nigerian-Chinese relationships based on respect, success, and mutual understanding.

Chibundu's interviews and speeches portrayed him as a powerful public proponent of Nigerian-Chinese relationships. His reputation as a former diplomat alongside that of other patrons, including government ministers, bolstered Chibundu's assertion that NCFA was the "only authentic [Nigerian-Chinese] organization." A key component of brokerage is to make oneself indispensable by simultaneously showing a proximity to power and a disinterest in personal gain (Bierschenk et al. 2002, 17). Indispensability guarantees parties will come back to a broker when the need arises or send others to the broker. This need to focus on indispensability is entrepreneurial because the broker has found a way to be crucial to the formation of new relationships. Without the broker, these relationships would be challenging if not impossible to establish. Chibundu served as broker by providing a conduit for easy Chinese visa applications, sponsoring visits to China for Nigerians (e.g., journalists), and attending cultural and diplomatic events in China and Nigeria. Chibundu and NCFA were linked to both Chinese and Nigerian elite within the public and private sectors.

Drawing on Chibundu's history is a way to portray the organization as indispensable and unique. Not only does NCBC draw upon the prestige of prominent members, including ambassadors on its board, and the participation of a former president (President Obasanjo), but a Chinese board member, Jacob Woods, also works with both NCBC and NCFA. Chibundu's assertion that NCFA is authentic stems from the NCFA role as the first Nigerian organization to receive official approval from the Chinese alliance organizations. This "authenticity" is also deeply linked to having Chibundu as its founder, as a former diplomat with close to 40 years of relationships with Chinese counterparts.

The shift toward organizational brokerage is rooted in the Nigerian government's increasing relationships with China and its related public discourse that seeks to enlist the cooperation of Nigerians. The government's mobilization of diverse actors, each with individual brokerage power, into associations is a response to developing relationships. These actors have different motivations and backgrounds, but they all have agency that they use to further the Nigerian-Chinese relationship. For instance, Chibundu was a former diplomat whose focus was on alliances between nation states (Nigeria and China) and individuals. Conversely, Woods is a businessman with expertise in running successful companies in various sectors.

Networking: Visas & Connections

The authenticity of NCFA and NCBC are parlayed into helping the members of their associations create relationships with Chinese counterparts. The application process for both organizations is not overly complicated. Current members introduce prospective members to the organization. To apply, a prospective member is usually either currently engaged or seeking to be engaged in a relationship with Chinese counterparts. Prospective members range from business people to current or former government officials.

Organizational membership fees are not exorbitant. However, the cost to join these associations could deter some potential members. For example, in 2012, the annual application and membership fees for joining NCFA was ₦82,300 [$416 USD]. NCBC's membership fees were in three categories: Women: ₦25,000 [$126 USD]; Men: ₦50,000 [$250 USD]; and Corporate Organizations: ₦200,000 [$1,010 USD]. These organizations host forums where Nigerian and Chinese business representatives meet; government officials from both countries also attend these events. Additionally, these organizations lobby the Nigerian government to create policies that allow for Chinese business investment. The prominent members (including former Nigerian ambassadors to China and international business people) have links to both the Nigerian and Chinese governments, which bolster the credibility of any member applying for a visa.

One of the most popular forms of brokerage that networking associations like the NCFA and NCBC provide their members is help with obtaining

Chinese visas. Members apply for visas under the auspices of the respective organization. Obtaining a visa to travel to China was a relatively easy process for African entrepreneurs until 2005 (Lyons et al. 2013, 94). Over time, applying for a visa became more difficult due to stricter regulations from the Chinese government. These regulations sought to crack down on the increasing number of African traders who visited China and delayed returning home, either in an attempt to reside in China or to conduct further business before returning home. The entrepreneurs I interviewed described a complex visa process that has both elements of ease and difficulty. In Nigeria, applying for a Chinese visa is not as simple as going in person to the consulate or embassy, purchasing an airplane ticket, and flying off to China. The Chinese visa application process sometimes requires that applicants purchase or place a hold on an airplane ticket before applying for a visa, along with a certain level of available bank funds.

In 2012, the Chinese government created an exit-entry law that sought to "combat illegal entry, residence, or work in China—the so-called 'three illegals' (san fei)" (Haugen, 2015). Foreign nationals who overstay past their visa expiration date are subject to penalties and detention. "The fines will not exceed 100,000 RMB ($16,290 USD), as opposed to 50,000 RMB ($8,145.00 USD) in the previous law" (Lefkowitz, 2013, 13). While African visitors are welcomed to China, their return home is equally welcomed in China. In recent years, there have been clashes between the police and Africans in southern China. One highly contested incident was the death of a Nigerian national in police custody; a protest by Africans in the city of Guangzhou followed. The Chinese government's push for visitors to return home is demonstrated through the exit-entry fines and the high amount of money first-time business visa applicants from Nigerian applicants must supply. These applicants must show a minimum of ₦4 million ($20,000 USD) in their bank accounts (Consulate General of the People's Republic of China-Lagos 2013).

Visa applicants rarely apply directly for visas. In fact, the majority of the entrepreneurs I interviewed, and other Nigerians I met, had applied for a Chinese visa with the help of an intermediary. The minority that tried to apply directly encountered difficulties. The Nigerian persons with whom I spoke described Chinese consulate representatives as "not friendly and not so nice when it comes to (their) visas; they won't talk to you." Therefore, business people turn to brokers.

When applying for a Chinese visa through an organizational broker, entrepreneurs pay a price close to those quoted on the Chinese government's official website. As of 2013, the website for China's Lagos consulate quoted prices for business visas in the range of ₦5,000–₦11,000 ($25–$55 USD) depending on the speed of service and number of entries allowed (Consulate General of the PRC-Lagos 2013). This price is significantly less than what one entrepreneur paid for his first trip to China in 2008. He applied for a visa through individual intermediaries to whom he paid ₦130,000 ($656 USD) for a single-entry, 30-day visa. The entrepreneurs as well as other Nigerians with whom I spoke usually mentioned "agent fees" in relation to visas procured via individual intermediaries. Agent fees are the payments that people along the chain between the applicant and the visa officials receive. No one is quite clear how many people are involved along the chain since it changes depending on the applicant's initial connection.

The rules for the visa application itself are universal. However, one applicant could have direct contact with a broker who works for the consulate or embassy, while another applicant could have a broker whose connection to the consulate is via other people. Nonetheless, it is thought that there are Nigerian and Chinese sub-intermediaries along the way, particularly when an applicant does not have direct contact within the embassy. For sub-intermediaries to profit from their work, the price listed on the website is vastly different than the actual price an applicant using an individual broker can pay. The visa application process for an organizational membership can be cheaper than using individual intermediaries, even including the cost of membership. Additionally, the stress of finding a credible and honest intermediary is eliminated.

As discussed earlier, organizational membership fees are not extremely expensive. On the one hand, business people who cannot afford these fees are denied the ease of access to visa applications which organizational membership confers. Conversely, business people who do not know about the NCFA or NCBC can potentially spend more money and time searching for and locating unofficial brokers. Unofficial agents have a range of prices that are dependent upon how close of a connection the agent has with someone working at the Chinese consulate. If there are multiple intermediaries in between the broker and the consultant, there are more people to compensate which results in higher fees to the individual entrepreneur.

Applying for a Chinese visa through an organization is simple. The applicant completes all the necessary paperwork and submits the paperwork to the organization. In turn, the organization submits the completed application to the Chinese consulate along with a letter of recommendation from the brokerage organization with, as Ambassador Chibundu termed it, a "clear vision" of the entrepreneur's plans for the trip to China. The organization's representative handles all the details and maintains contact with the Chinese consulate on behalf of the applicant.

Organizations like the NCFA and NCBC are conduits for Nigerian entrepreneurs to conduct business in China. As Ambassador Chibundu described to me, "What we do here is to open the door for what type of activity you want to do in China. We don't say (what you should do). It's up to the individual."

For businesspeople to receive a Chinese visa, they have to meet a certain financial threshold, such as proof of savings, and have a stated purpose for their visits. Neither NCFA nor NBCB helps members arrange individual trip details. Because of the NCFA's connection to Chibundu, members' visa applications were given priority. The ease of applying for visas by virtue of their NCFA and NCBC memberships is a strong selling point for business-people to join these business networks. The organizations also have strong relationships with both the Chinese and Nigerian governments. For instance, NCBC has hosted Chinese trade delegations, encouraged Chinese firms to open up manufacturing plants in Nigeria, and provided forums for Nigerian entrepreneurs to meet with potential Chinese partners. NCBC's connections and visa application help was a key factor for Itoro, the owner and head of an international Lagos-headquartered security firm, to join the NCBC.

Leveraging Brokers and Networks

As a child, Itoro dreamed of joining the military but his mother did not approve so he decided to attend university. When he graduated in the 1990s, Itoro's degree in agriculture did not garner many job opportunities. At the time, Nigeria was under military rule and the only employment Itoro could find was in the security industry. One of his first security jobs was as a secu-rity guard for a church. Throughout the years, Itoro moved from providing personal security to managing an entire security firm.

After his experiences working for others, Itoro decided to open his own firm in 2009. Currently, he is both the owner and managing director of Pres-tige Security. Itoro operates the firm alongside his wife, a writer, who serves as the firm's executive director of communications. Prestige also conducts business in other countries throughout Africa, Europe, and the Middle East. When I conducted my research, Prestige had a variety of contracts to provide security for companies, hotels, schools, and individuals. A crucial component of the firm's security services are electronic security systems. These systems, used to secure houses and buildings, are purchased from China. Working with a Chinese partner is essential for Itoro's business.

The firm offers personal security for clients ranging from individuals to families, to groups on diplomatic missions. Prestige's roster includes real estate moguls, managing directors and chairmen. Itoro describes some cli-ents as "people you read about every week; we're not talking of small fish." As such, clients are promised top services including swift pickups from airports consisting of a swift immigration process and retrieval of luggage within 15 minutes. The average person can wait at the airport upward of one and one-half hours. Prestige's services extend to offshore oil and gas firms where the firm provides security to clients round trip, from land to sea.

Itoro's philosophy is that the "comfort of the principal (the client) must not be compromised."

The firm's high level of service has led to a positive reputation in the security industry and created opportunities for Itoro to speak at various conferences such as a maritime security and piracy conference in Nigeria. Additionally, his firm helped build a facility for the Nigerian Navy to monitor pirates off the coast of Nigeria. Although many of his clients are a part of the upper echelons of Nigerian society, Itoro believes that security is an important issue for everyone in Nigeria. Prestige provides free "security clinics" to teach the public about staying secure and ways to analyze risk in a variety of situations. As Itoro states, "Security is not only for the good; it's for the bad (too). Good people also get involved in bad (situations)."

Itoro initially explored options from the United States and South Africa in his quest to purchase alarm systems to suit his company needs. However, the low prices from China swayed him to purchase from Chinese manufacturers. Itoro reviewed hundreds of products on Alibaba.com, an online marketplace for business-to-business commerce that is headquartered in China. Alibaba.com has offices in various countries including Japan, India, the United Kingdom, and the United States. A large number of the website's transactions have one party in China as either the buyer or seller. Itoro finally chose an alarm system from a firm based in Shenzen. The firm sent him test samples. Despite Itoro's appreciation of the quality, other Nigerian businesspeople advised him to go to China to meet with the manufacturers and confirm product quality before making a large investment. Most Nigerian entrepreneurs who conduct business with China do not travel to China due to the lack of financial and social capital or time. Itoro utilized NCBC to help him travel to China to meet his prospective business partner.

During his trip to China, Itoro visited the factory in Shenzen and found that "they (the firm) had good personal relations and were very friendly." He spent over $15,000, which included the costs for an expert technician to come from Shenzen to teach Prestige employees how to operate the alarm systems from the firm's headquarters in Lagos. Itoro recalled that "they (the firm representatives) didn't have good English but they had a manual in Chinese" which the firm had translated into English.

The technician's visit went well despite the technician's initial fears over safety given Nigeria's reputation for being unsafe. During the visit, the technician trained a number of Itoro's employees on how to use the system and provide services for Prestige's customers. This training was the key, because these employees operated the control room that monitored the security systems for the firm's clients. Itoro and his employees also took the technician out on the town to experience Lagosian life. Despite the language challenges, the Prestige team and the Chinese technician were able to get to know each other and build trust. The combination of good professional interactions coupled with socializing boosted Itoro's confidence in his Chinese business counterparts. He argued that quality products can be bought from Chinese manufacturers as long as one is willing to pay for them. Itoro credited both his visit to China and the technician's visit to Nigeria with cementing the relationship between Prestige and its Chinese supplier.

DISCUSSION

Continuity and Change in Brokerage

Brokerage is a crucial component of Nigerian-Chinese relationships, particularly in the business sphere. The necessity of brokerage to help form these relationships has not been previously discussed in an in-depth manner, particularly in regard to these relationships. Historically, brokerage has been a part of Nigerian society since before colonization. Precolonial forms of brokerage mostly focused on aiding trade between Africans and Europeans (Havik and Green 2012). During colonial times, individual local brokers mediated between local communities and colonial rulers (Boissevain 1974). Contemporary brokerage includes individuals and organizations. Brokers such as Ambassador Chibundu use their long-standing relationships with Chinese counterparts to promote Nigerian-Chinese relationships by aligning themselves with associations. Nigerian-Chinese relationships are fostered through the emerging importance of organizations that leverage their connections to the benefit of their clients and members. One of the more easily accessible services these associations provide is a smooth Chinese visa application process for Nigerian members.

Individual brokerage remains an option for Nigerian business people seeking Chinese visas. In these cases, visa seekers are more likely to utilize the services of a number of individual brokers depending on the initial broker's connection to the Chinese embassy. The chain of brokers also represents another form of assemblage, but one that has a different mission than brokerage organizations. A cultural shift toward brokerage organizations, and away from individual brokers, is only possible if individual brokers leverage their power and link it with organizations. Additionally, entrepreneurs must consider the services of these organizations valuable enough to enlist them. As entrepreneurs make connections with Chinese firms, they will need to determine if these Nigerian brokerage associations are still useful.

These same associations must also determine if their exclusive nature is sustainable. Myhre (2016) draws upon Strathern's caution to not get bogged down in tracing the seemingly never-ending connections within an assemblage, but to instead explore the "occasions, events, persons, or things, where connections are severed and networks cut in order to actualize specific and definite forms" (2016, 2). The exclusivity of brokerage organizations helps to exclude and deny connections to those unable to meet their requirements to join. Additionally, examining brokerage in the context of Nigerian-Chinese relationships helps in understanding the relationship between domestic and international interests. This cross-national context is in line with Lindquist's argument that contemporary analysis of brokerage "moves beyond a static conceptualization of the relationship between the "local," "national," or "global" (Lindquist 2015, 1). I take this argument further and assert that understanding contemporary brokerage through the lens of assemblage theory allows us to understand the role and motivations of brokers within assemblages. These roles and motivations are often complex and have various local, national, and global links.

Assemblage Theory in Practice

Assemblage theory is useful in helping to deconstruct the various members that contribute to brokerage in the context of contemporary Nigeria, specifically Nigerian-Chinese entrepreneurial relationships. These members, who include government officials and business people with various and sometimes-contradictory interests, come together to facilitate brokerage. Marcus and Saka (2006) assert that "assemblage functions best as an evocation of emergence and heterogeneity amid the data of inquiry, in relation to other concepts and constructs without rigidifying into the thingness of final or stable states that besets the working terms of classic social theory" (2006, 106). Members of the brokerage assemblage are not in a fixed or "stable" state. They are free to alter the assemblage as needed. The cultural shift toward organizational brokerage is made clearer through the framework of assemblage, as is the agency of assemblage members. Most members, whether they are entrepreneurs who seek the help of brokers, or brokers themselves, exercise a level of agency. This agency allows members to decide if they want to become a part of the assemblage. Unlike past forms of brokerage, individual brokers who join a brokerage organization utilize their connections and social capital to help bolster the reputation of the organization and thus their individual reputation. Additionally, members of a brokerage organization socialize with each other; their connections can be analyzed using assemblage theory.

However, assemblage theory's weakness lies in the difficulty of deciphering the relationships among members of the individual brokerage chain. There are a myriad of individual brokers along brokerage chains that some business people use. These brokers are often intermediaries who are not directly linked to the initial client who sought brokerage. Therefore, while these actors are connected, they are unknown to each other and unable to interact directly with each other in the manner that members of brokerage organizations interact. This individual form of assemblage is more tenuous than the organizational brokerage assemblage. Moreover, the social component prevalent among members of a brokerage organization is missing from the chain form of brokerage, which can have a transactional feel.

CONCLUSIONS

The emergence of brokers, both individuals and organizations that draw upon the connections of their prominent individual members, is crucial to the development of Nigerian-Chinese relationships. Brokerage organizations have a level of exclusivity and are not financially accessible to the majority of Nigerian entrepreneurs. Those who are able to afford to join brokerage organizations depend upon the ability of these organizations to work on their behalf. Organizational and individual brokers leverage their authenticity and indispensability to appeal to clients and access the tangible or intangible objects and processes required by clients. Agency was a part of previous eras of brokerage; it is visibly embedded in the contemporary brokerage as well. Brokers join the assemblage and work to meet their own needs, those of their clients, and those related to the greater good. Agency can help to hold the assemblage together if member needs are met.

A crucial component of Nigerian-Chinese relationships is relationship building. These relationships encompass the various members of the assemblage and result in a range of permutations. For example, these relationships can exist between brokers and clients or between the parties that brokers help to connect. As the relationship between Nigeria and China grows, the emerging practices and beliefs will reflect an accommodation between both Nigerian and Chinese cultures. Assemblages will continue to evolve in brokerage and in other domains.

REFERENCES

Bernard, H.R. (2011). *Research methods in anthropology: Qualitative and quantitative approaches, 5th ed.* Lanham, MD: AltaMira Press.

Bierschenk, T., Chauveau, J-P. and de Sardan, J-P.O. (2002*). Local development brokers in Africa: The rise of a new social category.* Working Paper 13, Mainz, Germany: Johannes Gutenberg-University.

Boissevain, J. (1974). *Friends of friends. Networks, manipulators and coalitions.* Oxford, UK: Basil Blackwell.

Chibundu, V.N. (2011). Speech - 40th Anniversary of Diplomatic Relationship between Nigeria and China. Lagos, Nigeria.

Clarke, J., D. Bainton, N Lendvai, and P. Stubbs. (2015). *Making policy move: Towards a politics of translation and assemblage*. Bristol, UK: Policy Press.

Collier, S.J. and A. Ong. (2005). Global assemblages, anthropological problems. In S.J. Collier and A. Ong (eds.) *Global assemblages: Technology, politics, and ethics as anthropological problems*. Malden, MA: Wiley-Blackwell, 3–21.

Consulate General of the People's Republic of China in Lagos. (2013). *Notice for Applying Chinese for Visas*, Accessed January 20, 2014, http://lagos.china-consulate.org/eng/lszj/zgqz/t1090583.htm 18 November 2013

Dada, M.O. and O.S. Oyediran. (2016). The state of public private partnership in Nigeria. In A. Akintoye, M. Beck, and M. Kumarasawamy. (Eds.). *Public Private Partnerships: A Global Review*. Abingdon, UK: Routledge, 248–265.

de Sardan, J-P. O. (2005). *Anthropology and development: Understanding contemporary social change*. London, UK: Zed Books.

DeLanda, M. (2016). *Assemblage theory (Speculative realism)*. Edinburgh, UK: Edinburgh University Press.

Deleuze, G. (2007). *Two regimes of madness: Texts and interviews 1975–1995*.

Deleuze, G. and Guattari, F. (1980). *Mille plateaux* (Paris, France: Minuit); tr. as *A thousand plateaus*. (1987). B. Massumi, Minneapolis, MN: University of Minnesota Press.

Dibie, R. and Okonkwo, P. (2000). Aligning private business development and economic growth in Nigeria. *Journal of African Business*, 1(1), 83–111.

Eckert, A. (2006). Cultural commuters: African employees in late Colonial Tanzania. In B. N. Lawrance, E. L. Osborn and R.L. Roberts (Eds.). *Intermediaries, interpreters, and clerks: African employees in the making of Colonial Africa*. Madison, WI: The University of Wisconsin Press, 248–269.

Fetterman, D.M. (2010). *Ethnography step-by-step, 3rd ed*. Applied Social Research Methods Series, (Vol. 17). Los Angeles, CA: Sage.

Green, T. and Havik, P.J. (2012). Introduction: Brokerage and the Role of Western Africa in the Atlantic World in T. Green (ed.) *Brokers of Change: Atlantic Commerce and Cultures in Pre-Colonial Western Africa*. Oxford, UK: Oxford University Press, 1–26

Haugen, H.Ø. (2015). 4 March, 2015. Destination China: The country adjusts to its new migration reality. *The Online Journal of the Migration Policy Institute*. http://www.migrationpolicy.org/article/destination-china-country-adjusts-its-new-migration-reality

Hopkins, A.G. (1973). *An economic history of West Africa*. Abingdon, UK: Routledge.

James, D. (2011). The return of the broker: Consensus, hierarchy, and choice in South African land reform. *Journal of the Royal Anthropological Institute,* 17(2), 318–338.

Jones, W.O. (1970). Measuring the effectiveness of agricultural marketing in contributing to economic development: Some African examples. *Food Research Institute Studies*, 9(3), 175–196.

Kamalipour, H. and Peimani, N. (2015). Assemblage thinking and the city: Implications for urban studies. *Current Urban Studies*, 3, 402–408.

Kaplan, S. (2014). What Makes Lagos a Model City, *New York Times*, January 7, 2014. Accessed November 2, 2016. https://www.nytimes.com/2014/01/08/opinion/what-makes-lagos-a-model-city.html.

Kemmitt, A. (2008) *Ethnography by Appointment: Negotiating Access in a Social Entrepreneurial Media Organization*. Paper presented at the National Communication Association 94th Annual Conference. http://www.allacademic.com/meta/p260557_index.html

Lapoujade, D. (ed.), A. Hodges and M. Taormina (translators), New York: Semiotext(e).

Lefkowitz, M. (2013). Strike hard against immigration: China's new exit-entry law. *China Brief*, 13(23). https://jamestown.org/program/strike-hard-against-immigration-chinas-new-exit-entry-law.

Lindquist, J. (2015). Brokers and brokerage, anthropology of. *International Encyclopedia of Social and Behavioral Science*. 2nd edition, Amsterdam, The Netherlands: Elsevier.

Lyons, M., A. Brown, and Z. Li. (2013). The China–Africa value chain: Can Africa's small- scale entrepreneurs engage successfully in global trade? *African Studies Review*, 56(3), 77–100.

Marcus, G. and Saka, E. (2006). Assemblage. *Theory, Culture& Society*, 23 (2–3), 101–106.

Myhre, K. C. (2016). Introduction- Cutting and Connecting: 'Afrinesian' Perspectives on Networks, Rationality, and Exchange in K. C. Myhre (ed.) *Cutting and Connecting: 'Afrinesian' Perspectives on Networks, Rationality, and Exchange.* Oxford: Berghahn, 1–24.

NBS (National Bureau of Statistics) and SMEDAN (Small & Medium Enterprises Development Agency of Nigeria). (2010). *Survey report on micro, small and medium enterprises (MSMEs) in Nigeria.* Lagos, Nigeria.

NCBC. (2011). 17 March 2011. *Overview,* Accessed February 12, 2015, http://www.ncbcng.org/overview.html

Nishimura S., A. Nevgi, and S. Tella. (2009). *Communication style and cultural features in high/low context communication cultures: A case study of Finland, Japan and India.* http://www.helsinki.fi/~tella/nishimuranevgitella299.pdf

Okoh, C. (2011). 12 February 2011. Nigeria-China trade relations hit US $7.5 billion in *come to Nigeria.* Accessed http://www.cometonigeria.com/travel-news-and-events/nigeria-china-trade-relations-hit-u-s-7-5-billion/

Omegoh, C. (2016). 20 April 2016. Why we can't leave Nigeria, by Chinese nationals in *The Sun Newspaper* (Nigeria Accessed http://sunnewsonline.com/why-we-cant-leave-nigeria-by-chinese-nationals/

Pratten, D. (2006). The district clerk and the "man-leopard murders": Mediating law and authority in Colonial Nigeria. Lawrance, B.N., E. L. Osborn, and R.L. Roberts (Eds.). *Intermediaries, interpreters, and clerks: African employees in the making of Colonial Africa.* Madison, WI: The University of Wisconsin Press, 220–247.

SMEDAN. (2014). 4 March 2014. *President Jonathan Launches NIRP, NEDEP.* Accessed http://www.smedan.gov.ng/index.php/latest-news/119-president-jonathan-launches-nirp-nedep

Thornton, P.H, D. Riberio-Soriano, and D. Urbano. (2011). Socio-cultural factors and entrepreneurial activity: An overview. *International Small Business Journal,* 29(2), 105–118.

Woods, M. (2012). Anonymity and Elite Research in Anonymisation in Social Research WISERD Methods Briefing Series: 4–7.

Xinhua. [Staff Writer] (2008). 13 April 2008. Nigeria-China friendship association condemns disruptions over Olympic torch tour. *English People's Daily Online.* Accessed http://en.people.cn/90001/90776/90883/6391518.html

Zeleza, P.T. (1993). *A modern economic history of Africa: Nineteenth century.* Vol. 1. Dakar, Senegal: CODESRIA.

Part III

CONSUMER AND
ORGANIZATION INTERFACE

Chapter 9

Designing Disruption

The Neoliberal Nonprofit Industry Makes Room for Holistic Approaches

Kevin M. Newton

Some form of poverty has been a constant for many human groups throughout history. Views of poverty, however, have waxed and waned over time from the medieval idea that poverty gives Christians an avenue to express their "good works" (Weber 2003, 120) to the early 20th-century understanding that poverty needed "not pity, but justice; not a prayer, but a claim" (Munsterberg 1904, 339), and back to a belief that "the institution of poverty is under attack," highlighted in a satirical piece by Weeks (1917, 779). Back and forth, the debate has continued through most of modern history. Today in the United States, attempts to end or reduce poverty are great, but nevertheless the poverty rate in the US has remained stagnant for at least the past three decades (US Bureau of the Census). This stagnation, when viewed through the lens of both assemblage theory and Foucauldian theories of power, highlights cultural changes in the nonprofit industry that have contributed to this ongoing stagnation.

I offer an explanation of how nonprofit culture has changed over time as a function of the assemblages or "heterogeneous, contingent, unstable, partial and situated" (Collier and Ong 2005, 12) elements of the nonprofit industry. I provide a brief history of modern poverty and theories used to understand it, as well as recent policies and programs created to reduce or eliminate it. Using Foucault's (1978) idea that power is not held by one person or persons, but rather is something that creates knowledge through discourse and is then expressed through institutions, networks and expectations, I analyze how changes in the assemblage of the nonprofit industry had the power to create cultural shifts within the industry as a whole.

The case study I describe is a nonprofit tech company called "Lighthouse" (a pseudonym) that attempts to use smartphone technology and behavioral economics principles to enhance the efforts of other nonprofits interested in combating poverty. Lighthouse encourages its partnering nonprofits to embrace the most recent public policy shift away from individual responsibility to a more holistic approach. Throughout the chapter, I emphasize the ever-changing assemblage that makes up the poverty-oriented subsector of the nonprofit industry and its role in encouraging and facilitating cultural change.

RECENT HISTORY IN FIGHTING US POVERTY

US Nonprofits Prior to 1970

Although there are only two broad legal categories (i.e., charitable and noncharitable) within the current US nonprofit industry, there are in practice three major divisions—charitable, religious (e.g., Christian churches, Muslim mosques) and noncharitable (e.g., labor unions, sororities) entities. The charitable division houses two major distinctions—nonoperating (e.g., Bill and Melinda Gates Foundation) and operating (e.g., Feed America, Make a Wish Foundation). Nevertheless, the charitable nonprofit "industry" is still in its infancy.

Certainly, religious organizations in the US have been responding to poverty for centuries, but the idea of nonprofits as part of a "unified and coherent" industry only began in the 1970s (Hall 2010, 3). As Table 9.1 shows, in the 1940s, the composition of the 252,242 nonprofits was 5% charitable (12,500), 71% religious (179,742), and 24% noncharitable (60,000). Although a handful of charitable nonprofits existed before the 1970s, they were not seen as part of a cohesive sector. By 2006, however, the make-up of the then 1.6 million nonprofits had shifted to become 38% charitable (600,000), 25% religious (400,000) and 38% noncharitable (600,000) (Hall 2010).

The question becomes: why such a shift toward charitable nonprofits? The answer to this question lies in the assemblage of the nonprofit industry. The high-level assemblage that makes up the nonprofit industry includes (but is not limited to) the US government, the laws, the grant funders, the donors, the American public, the policies guiding the programs, those working at the organizations, the theories of poverty and those in need of poverty-relief services.

Table 9.1 Breakdown of Registered Nonprofit Categories over Time

Year	Charitable	Religious	Non-charitable	Total
1940s	12,500	179,742	60,000	252,242
2006	600,000	400,000	600,000	1,600,000

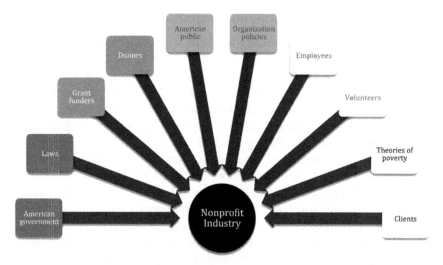

Figure 9.1   Nonprofits Industry Assemblage (ca. 1970).

Funding Charitable Nonprofits

Nonprofit categories began to shift after the 1960s because of the drastic changes in American life. Two key changes in the assemblage fostered great change and proliferation of nonoperational charitable nonprofit organizations, which in turn led to increased operational charitable nonprofits. First, the combination of "white flight" by the American public from the cities to the suburbs, and overall appeal of suburban life, decreased membership in communal organizations and activities such as choral societies, football clubs and bowling leagues, which have been linked to healthy civil societies (Putnam 2000). This decreased membership also reduced the standby volunteers who were, until then, available through community-based organizations (e.g., Masons, Rotary Club).

The other key shift came from US government and law. Government funds became increasingly available for nonprofits as part of the War on Poverty and the Great Society Programs during the Johnson administration (Kerlin and Pollock 2010). These aspects facilitated the growth of nonprofit foundations (Jones 2006) and led to a major cultural change for charitable giving. These changes boosted and solidified a dying vehicle (i.e., nonoperational, grant-giving foundations) through which charitable organizations could be funded. Up to this point, much of 20th-century charity was without a clear pattern (Jones 2006) and had relied on the kindness of individuals and the goodwill of millionaires (Hall 2010). The growth in the nonprofit industry was hastened by the incoming 1980 Reagan administration.

Neoliberalism Takes Its Toll on Nonprofits

Although the fight against poverty had been waged for more than a decade, the drastic shift in the political climate of the 1980s set off a series of changes that would rock the nonprofit industry. Specifically, Paul Volker as head of the Federal Reserve, along with President Ronald Reagan "plucked from the shadows of relative obscurity a particular doctrine ... [called] 'neoliberalism' and transformed it into the central guiding principle of economic thought and management" for the US (Harvey 2005, 2).

At its base, neoliberalism is a political-economic theory. In practice, however, it is a force for privatization, decreased government involvement and increased personal responsibility regardless of systemic hindrances. Ultimately, neoliberalism posits that the government's only role is to create and maintain institutions (e.g., military, police, courts) that support private property laws and the free market. The government should have minimal involvement with the free market because it would be impossible for the government to outperform market signals and because governments can be "bought" (Harvey 2005). One key element of neoliberalism important for nonprofits is its attempt to replace the term "common good" or "community" with "individual responsibility." Reagan's English counterpart and staunch promoter of neoliberalism, Margaret Thatcher, illustrates this viewpoint in a 1987 interview with *Women's Own* magazine. According to the Margaret Thatcher Foundation website, Margaret Thatcher famously said:

> There is no such thing as society. There is living tapestry of men and women and people and the beauty of that tapestry and the quality of our lives will depend upon how much each of us is prepared to *take responsibility for ourselves* and each of us prepared to turn round and *help by our own efforts* those who are unfortunate. (emphasis added)

There was no room in the neoliberal approach of the 1980s for the government as society to expand aid for those suffering from poverty. Indeed, the government "launched an offensive against social welfare and used a tax policy to widen the gap between the rich and the poor" in what had been called "the war on welfare" (Katz 1996, 283). The adoption of neoliberalism by the US government had a "trickle down" effect for businesses. It helped accelerate the already increasing number of nonprofits, calling for individuals to assist through their own efforts.

This belief in neoliberalism was reinforced and strengthened by the administration of George H. W. Bush. According to The American Presidency Project website, Bush claimed in his Inaugural Address that America had "more will than wallet, but will is what we need ... a thousand points of light." This stance severely injured the social contract between citizen and government. That contract once included, among other features, a promise of a government-provided "safety net." It also solidified the "volunteer" as the new political subject (Hyatt 2001, 205). Certainly, volunteerism has long since been a large part of the American way (for historical overview see Hall 2006). Nevertheless, volunteerism "has never met most of the needs of dependent Americans. Some public assistance has always been crucial" (Katz 1996, 289).

Training Programs Launched by Nonprofits

The foundation laid by neoliberal adoption, the "thousand points of light" promotion and the newly christened "volunteer as citizen" led seamlessly into the mid-1990s Clinton-led US government vowing to "end welfare as we know it." The big idea that eventually emerged was workfare, which is the belief that welfare recipients must work for what they are given, a belief that resonated with conservative and liberal voters alike (Bailey 1995). As a result, many nonprofits during the late 1990s and early 2000s based their programs on some sort of training that would increase personal responsibility; it was this increase that was supposed to lead to a better life (see Goode and Maskovsky 2001 for examples).

The assemblage of the nonprofit industry changed significantly. It now included four new components permeating through each existing element: the neoliberal ideals described above, the increased burden of individual responsibility, a shrinking safety net, and a sea of volunteers. This substantial shift in the still ephemeral assemblage began yet another cultural change—that of increased individual responsibility, circular reasoning and victim blaming. This circular reasoning turned on the idea that people are not thriving because they have failed as individuals; a nonprofit can help them increase personal responsibility and work ethic. If they subsequently fail after receiving help from a nonprofit, it is because they, once again, failed as individuals. Importantly, according to this reasoning, people did *not* fail because the nonprofit was unsuccessful or ineffective in achieving its goals (Goldstein 2001).

This ideology (1996–present) shifted the focus away from the government's responsibility, from the agencies' actual performance and from the structural violence created by years of institutional racism and neoliberal politics. Instead, it placed emphasis squarely onto the shoulders of the already suffering individual (i.e., victim blaming). I use the phrase "structural violence" as Galtung (1969, 171) explains it: "violence [that] is built into the structure and shows up as unequal power and consequently as unequal life chances." Without a focus on the systemic issues, a focus on personal responsibility is always a necessary, but not sufficient condition, in solving many client-related issues. Moreover, the networks of power created through a lifetime of capitalism [and decades of neoliberal reform] ensure that those

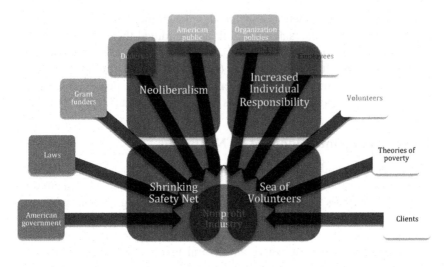

Figure 9.2   Nonprofit Industry Assemblage (ca. 1996).

suffering from poverty continue to blame themselves and that those who do not suffer continue to shame those who do (Gramsci 1971). These shifts together create what Foucault (1978) would refer to as a panoptic instantiation of power, which is power that is decentered and relies on the use of both self-surveillance and surveillance by citizens on other citizens. Indeed, it is the expectation that individuals will fit perfectly as a cog in the wheel of capitalism set forth by society that exerts this Foucauldian power over the lives of those subjected to structural violence. Such power almost guarantees no occurrence of a large-scale movement for sustainable change in "economic and racial inequality" (Lyon-Callo 2001, 304). Nevertheless, over the past five years, a noticeable shift in the assemblage of the nonprofit industry appears to be happening once again.

CURRENT APPROACH TO POVERTY ALLEVIATION

Return on Investment (ROI) Necessary on Nonprofit Training Programs

Beginning around the turn of the century, the cultural shifts created by the ever-changing nonprofit assemblage have pulled the focus of *why* poverty happens to the forefront. Bradshaw (2005) offers one of the most recent categorizations of the guiding theories by grouping them under five labels, indicating that poverty is caused by:

1. Individual deficiencies
2. Cultural belief systems that support subcultures of poverty
3. Economic, political, and social distortions or discrimination
4. Geographical disparities
5. Cumulative cyclical interdependencies (i.e., as barriers to economic participation increase, opportunity decreases exponentially).

Although there are other categorizations of poverty theory (see Egendorf 1999; Epstein 1997; Morrill and Wohlenburg 1971; Rogers 1991), there seem to be only slight variations on Bradshaw's five categories. No agreement on a single explanation for poverty exists. However, personnel at nonprofits or government agencies know and make policy decisions based on a particular theory (or theories) of poverty.

The decades of neoliberal ideals have changed the way in which charitable nonprofits are expected to function. They also have altered their approach for offering help insofar as funding is often directly connected to the volume of help and not its quality. Market principles have permeated the nonprofit industry such that grant funders and foundations must be able to measure ROI. This focus on ROI puts nonprofits in a situation that can be hard to navigate. Moreover, it creates interests that must be served before and above the clients that nonprofits purport to be helping (see Naples and Desai 2002; Wright 2013). This emphasis on ROI effectively places nonprofits under surveillance from funders and government agencies that constantly seek measurable results (Walden 2006; Wies 2013). In turn, nonprofits often rely on surveillance of their clients to measure compliance to their training programs and meet the growing demand of evidence-based outcomes.

Systemic Issues Evident in Behavioral Economics Approach

Another recent cultural shift, the adoption of behavioral economics within the nonprofit industry, opens the door for a more holistic approach. This shift may provide an opportunity to guide elements of the assemblage (i.e., organizational policies and employees required to express this power of surveillance) toward cultural change that may result in more effective approaches to poverty alleviation. However, nonprofit organizations must be given the proper tools and design.

Behavioral economics is the use of psychological findings around human limitations to explain economic decision-making (Mullainathan and Thaler 2001). Behavioral economics takes a holistic view of the individual and recognizes that the environment almost always has a profound effect on behavior. One of its key concepts is libertarian paternalism. This concept suggests that individuals can make design decisions that will affect the lives of others while still ensuring their autonomy (Thaler and Sunstein 2003), and that understanding the predictable irrationality of human behavior can be harnessed to promote a particular action.

One application of behavioral economics principles involves the use of "choice architects," people who design their own or someone else's environment to encourage a certain behavior (Thaler and Sunstein 2009). For example, behavioral economists have shown that the design of a cafeteria affects the purchasing behavior of those who frequent it; putting the fruits before the unhealthy snacks increases the consumption of fruit and decreases unhealthy snacks (Hankset al. 2012). Therefore, the lunchroom should be designed in a way that promotes health. Criticism based on anti-paternalistic motivations is addressed by arguing that there are three options for cafeteria food layout: designing for good (e.g., health), designing randomly, and ignoring the knowledge, or intentionally designing for bad (e.g., obesity) (Thaler and Sunstein 2003). Design affects those who interact with it. Importantly, the above example is relevant for health-related outcomes, but the concepts behind it could be used to design environments and interventions that decrease the friction between those experiencing poverty and anti-poverty behaviors (e.g., eating in, saving money).

When applied to poverty alleviation, the behavioral economics concepts merge individual responsibility with systemic causes. Specifically, understanding the behavioral barriers to receiving assistance and the systemic hindrances to self-sufficiency can help providers of products and services design interventions that will be well received by those they seek to serve and more effective in providing services (see examples in Thaler and Sunstein 2009). Adoption of behavioral economics interventions (e.g., defaults, pre-commitments) alters the assemblage of the nonprofit industry and creates a cultural shift toward increased recognition of the systemic issues mentioned earlier.

LIGHTHOUSE, NEEDLE AND THE COLLEGE PREP COMPANY

I now present a case study of the nonprofit Lighthouse. During my employment there in 2015, my colleagues and I attempted to increase the effectiveness of programs run by other nonprofit organizations operating in the same city as Lighthouse. The motivation behind this venture was simple— philanthropists have gifted millions of dollars to anti-poverty programs and yet poverty remains stagnant or increases. Findings in the field of behavioral economics provided a new hope for increased effectiveness. We used a behavioral economics approach to create a mobile application that focused on the client as a whole (e.g., family commitments, social obligations, barriers to transportation) and encouraged these nonprofits to embrace the recent

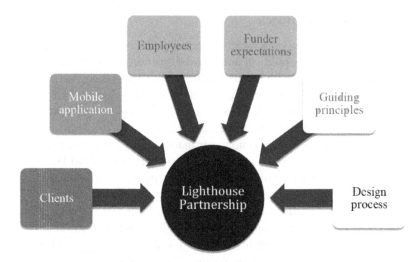

Figure 9.3 **Assemblage of the Lighthouse Partnership.**

culture shift toward increased recognition of systemic issues. Specifically, we partnered with another nonprofit, College Prep Company (CPC, a pseudonym) to create a microlevel assemblage that included the guiding principles of each nonprofit, funder expectations, employees, mobile application, design process and clients. CPC was interested in working with us because they saw the potential for more personalized attention for their clients and increased accountability across all aspects of their operation.

Background Information

Lighthouse was a startup nonprofit with five employees: an executive director, a tech lead, a developer, a content creator and me, a user researcher. A large, local philanthropist group interested in reducing poverty funded it. Lighthouse's mission was to reimagine social services in a way that shifted the focus back toward what worked best for the client while still remaining consistent with industry expert knowledge. Lighthouse developed a mobile application called Needle (a pseudonym), designed with three goals in mind:

- Offer help to those currently suffering from poverty, or likely to suffer from it in the future
- Evaluate the effectiveness of nonprofits that choose to partner with Lighthouse
- Increase the effectiveness of nonprofit agendas by promoting a holistic view of the client's current situation and utilizing behavioral economics principles

The Lighthouse Approach

At Lighthouse, we drew on a variety of poverty theories including individual deficiencies; economic, political and social distortions or discrimination; and cumulative cyclical interdependencies. We believed, as others do (see Goode and Maskovsky 2001), that there are systems in place that create barriers to upward mobility (e.g., unrealistic workloads, unreliable transportation, lack of Internet access). We also adopted the idea, put forth by others, that some nonprofits express their power, however inadvertently, in a way that creates barriers rather than access to help (see Fisher 1997; Naples and Desai 2002; Wright 2013). Certainly, nonprofits cannot be blamed outright; to survive, they typically must respond to increased pressure from funders for high-volume help and surveillance (see Adams 2004; Weis 2013). At Lighthouse, we believed that low-income individuals might experience lower levels of motivation and more frequent instances of forgetting than those with higher income. Our belief was based on recent evidence suggesting that those in poverty have fewer cognitive resources available to them due to the constant worry, stress and calculations in their lives, in addition to the typical stresses of modern life (Daminger et al. 2015).

We also believed that the cognitive and physical barriers were made worse by deficiencies in discipline, commitment and follow-through activity. Indeed, some of our beliefs seemed to echo and largely validate the "culture of poverty" (Lewis 1966), a culture that lacked the necessary structure and discipline to fit into mainstream society, and thus encouraged poverty. While we did not support Lewis' theory per se, we believed that there was a cognitive tax associated with being poor in the modern world, particularly for those experiencing longstanding poverty. While I was initially uncomfortable with this model, it appeared to be a necessary and logical premise for our argument and for the mobile application we were building. If a problem were caused entirely by systemic barriers and lack of available cognitive resources, there would be very little action individuals could take to make self-improvements. Therefore, it was our view that if individuals were given the proper tool, they could begin to make noticeable, if small, changes in their behavior.

We hypothesized that data collected on individual usage of Needle, along with other mobile-enabled activity (e.g., the user's location, the distance traveled over time) and Needle could qualitative investigation into its effectiveness, would lead to pertinent and potent recommendations for nonprofit partners. If other nonprofits adopted such recommendations, a cultural shift in ideology might result within institutional systems in the surrounding region. Although relying solely on the agency found within the other nonprofits, this approach positioned Lighthouse to affect change at the systemic level—within the nonprofit organization that chose to work with us. I use the word agency to mean "the socioculturally mediated capacity to act" (Ahearn 2001, 112).

Needle had a specific hierarchy through which a user could navigate to discover goals *he/she* wanted to complete. There were *categories* (e.g., health, education, family) that when chosen would lead to *goals* related to particular categories (e.g., lower my cholesterol, get into college, spend more time with my baby). When a user selected a *goal, behaviors* that supported that goal would be suggested (e.g., exercise, increase ACT score, talk to my baby). After deciding on a *behavior* of interest, the user had the opportunity to schedule reminders (i.e., smartphone notifications) for specific *actions* (e.g., walk for five minutes, schedule a study session with friends, tell my baby about my day). When the user took action, she would advance toward successful goal achievement, which would increase the quality and success for the overall category.

The plan was for Lighthouse to use Needle's architecture to deliver the agenda of the partnering nonprofits. The nonprofit became the category, the goals of the nonprofit became the goals, the way the nonprofit believed the goal could be achieved became the behaviors, and the steps needed to support the behaviors became the actions. Lighthouse worked to create a general library of goals, behaviors and actions for each category independent of the nonprofits with whom we hoped to partner.

I approached education-based nonprofits with a partnership proposal. A partnership resulted between Lighthouse and CPC, due to numerous commonalities including leadership personalities, funding requirements, lifecycle, agendas, client base, location, guiding principles and desired outcomes of both organizations. The partnership created a unique assemblage. Indeed, it emerged seamlessly, though it was the only substantial partnership that resulted during my tenure despite proposals to many nonprofits.

Needle offered hope of improved client outcomes based on its holistic approach. Although still in its beta form, Needle was beginning to provide an efficient means of self-reported and continuous tracking of client behavior. Such tracking was required by the changes in nonprofit approaches in the late 1990s. More importantly, Needle also could (1) provide a chance to make changes in a timely manner based on data collected from clients without negating the terms of current funding, and (2) offer on-time triggers to encourage greater compliance with the user-selected plan.

In addition, Lighthouse was positioned to offer other services because of its status as a nonprofit. For example, as an applied anthropologist, I was able to conduct a program evaluation related to the activities delivered through Needle. Consequently, our nonprofit partner could learn what worked and did not work for users, a task that was usually costly and time consuming; neither funds nor significant time were necessary. Lighthouse, in turn, improved Needle's functionality, including the timing of the triggers, and tapped into the influence held by CPC and the high school in which it worked to make small but substantial change. Ultimately, the goal of the partnership was to discover whether clients would utilize Needle even if their usage resulted in altering CPC's content or approach.

The Partnership

CPC worked with high school students in low-income areas to help improve their success in high school and increase their college acceptance and scholarship awards. Lighthouse used Needle to aid CPC in its specific program agenda, which was loaded into Needle and made available to its clients. The action/steps in the hierarchy were smartphone notifications that CPC clients would receive as reminders to complete a particular step necessary for moving toward their goals.

CPC had been highly influenced by the neoliberal ideals described above and focused solely on individual responsibility. Its leaders believed that with enough work and self-awareness, successful college admission, scholarships and a happy life would follow. CPC promised increased ACT scores and a higher number of scholarship awards through extensive self-discovery and practiced discipline. Its approach was similar to those of the late 1990s; if the client failed to achieve the desired outcome, it could be explained as a failure

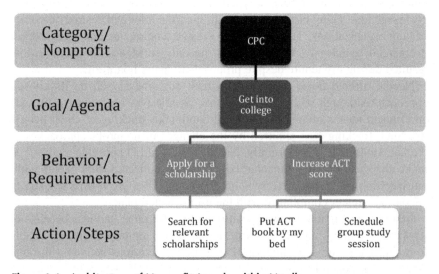

Figure 9.4   Architecture of Nonprofit Agenda within Needle.

to adopt or correctly enact the principles the program taught, and not a failure of the program itself. Lighthouse focused on one tangible step at a time that had the potential to lead to success.

TEST, PIVOT, TEST

Participants

Next, we conducted a pilot test of Needle to understand how it aligned with CPC's goals, and how it might fit into or change student lives. CPC recruited high school seniors and juniors to participate in the CPC program. I recruited students to participate in the Needle pilot from CPC's pool of 86 students (57% seniors). The pilot ended up with a total of 52 participants (62% seniors) due to limited interest, noncompliance and/or being dropped from the CPC program. All participants lived and attended school in a rural, low-income town.

Procedure

The procedure Lighthouse followed included: (1) asking participants to download Needle and go through the onboarding process, while I documented in notes instances of frustration and confusion, (2) electronically recording actions of users' responses to notifications within the application, (3) conducting two follow-up focus groups with student participants about their use of Needle, their feelings, any complications they experienced, and how Needle's content fit into their lives, and (4) meeting with the CPC staff to inform them of our findings.

Six high school seniors participated in the two focus groups. The purpose of these focus groups was to discover how the CPC content fit into the students' lives. The focus groups were held after school; I had to make special arrangements for several of the students to miss practice for the sport they played.

High Attrition but High Participation

The action notifications delivered to participants included four options: "Yes/I did it," "No," "Later" and the ability to swipe and dismiss the notification entirely. Over about five months, 52 students downloaded the app. Approximately five months later when the study ended, only nine students remained (17% retention). Those nine students recorded 466 actions. During the pilot, students began to drop out for unknown reasons and the

Table 9.2   Breakdown of Notification Categories in CPC Pilot

Month	# of Students	# of Notifications	CPC-Related	General Library
First 2 weeks	9	23	43%	57%
1st month	7	77	32%	68%
2nd month	5	34	38%	62%
3rd month	6	32	53%	47%
4th month	3	50	42%	58%
Last 2 weeks	2	15	13%	87%

number of students receiving notifications began to decline with attrition (see Table 9.2). A total of 231 notifications occurred (after a technical error was controlled), with 62% related to the general library of content not specific to CPC. As Table 9.2 shows, the ratio stayed relatively stable over time. The CPC content slowed down during the last two weeks.

The breakdown of how participants responded to these smartphone notifications is important. Of the 88 CPC-related notifications, the majority (54%) were marked "Yes/I Did It," a sizeable amount (39%) were dismissed, and almost none of them was marked either "Later" (6%) or "No" (1%). Of the 143 notifications from the general library of content, the pattern was quite similar. The majority (64%) marked "Yes/I Did It," fewer (30%) dismissed and almost none was marked either "Later" (3%) or "No" (3%) (Internal Report 2016). Had we looked only at the quantitative data, we may have concluded that not only was the CPC agenda mildly successful for the students who remained in the pilot, but also that Needle was a relatively successful delivery system. Fortunately, we planned for qualitative investigation.

No Room for Extra Homework

The students who eagerly joined the pilot program and agreed to participate quickly found that more urgent matters required their attention. The vast majority of CPC content was to be completed after school hours. Yet, when I asked participants about their lives outside of school, it was clear that this model would not fit easily into their busy schedules. Five out of the six students mentioned only sports, personal grooming, helping family members, homework and sleep. One student described, "After school, I take care of my three little sisters, take care of my grandmother, take care of my godson." Another explained, "I have practice 'til 5:30, shower. Then I do (specific teacher's) homework because she does not play (is very strict). Then I go to bed." Student responsibilities and activities appear to leave little time to complete additional assignments.

The students felt comfortable enough with Lighthouse to complain and criticize CPC, probably because Lighthouse was a third party organization.

Specifically, the students explained how they felt betrayed. They had agreed to participate in the CPC program because they believed they would increase their ACT scores and win scholarships. Instead, the program focused on self-improvement and self-awareness, program aspects that the students did not find valuable. Moreover, the students believed that the work related to CPC was going to be done during school hours, rather than scheduled as homework. The key takeaway from this initial investigation was that the CPC approach of assigning additional homework on topics seemingly unrelated to ACT scores or scholarships (i.e., personal development) was structured in a way that did not fit easily into the lives of the participants.

The second focus group confirmed the findings of the first focus group. When CPC advertised the pilot program, the students understood that CPC would help them increase their ACT score by two or three points and help them get into college. However, during the first month or two of the CPC program, assignments and classes involved exploring participants' interests, strengths and weaknesses. Needle effectively became, as one participant in the focus group claimed, "a pocket mom" (Internal Report 2015). Essentially, CPC wanted students to complete self-discovery homework with Needle sending a smartphone notification: "Don't forget to do your CPC homework." Moreover, the students found emphasis on self-discovery unnecessary. They already had their regular homework, household and childcare responsibilities, and the ACT/college prep. In addition, many students were members of sports teams.

Lighthouse scheduled a meeting with CPC approximately two and one-half months after the pilot began to discuss these findings in detail. I conveyed to the CPC staff, including the Operations Officer, what the students told me about feeling betrayed and overworked. CPC leaders responded by shifting their approach at the pilot school from personal growth homework exercises to a collaborative, peer-to-mentor, in-school focus on ACT scores and scholarships. The final follow-up email I received from CPC before my time at Lighthouse ended indicated that the new approach was well received by the few students who remained in the program. This was a major shift for a nonprofit focused so heavily on personal responsibility with the implicit beliefs that if you want something bad enough, no amount of work is too overwhelming. To recognize the situational barriers in completing the CPC curriculum is to accept that there is more to avoiding poverty than a strong will, and that is the beginning of a distinct cultural shift within, at least, this single nonprofit.

DISCUSSION

The rhetoric of individual responsibility in a vacuum is an inadequate approach to poverty alleviation. No level of responsibility can completely

overcome systemic and situational issues that many individuals find themselves subjected to in their everyday lives. A mentor once told me something
like, "When you go on to graduate school outside of your hometown you will
be much better off because you will escape the familial responsibilities that
hold you back and prevent you from reaching greater success." I was at first
shocked and somewhat angry, but this person was not wrong. The system in
which we live demands complete focus on singular goals for maximum success. The ability to give complete focus to any one thing is a privilege and
one not afforded by many people. The students I worked with through this
pilot could not even focus completely on their current schoolwork because
of familial obligations and sports commitments. It is not necessarily that the
students did not want to do the work required to be successful, but rather the
work necessary was a luxury they could not afford. Once the approach shifted
to in-class work, the students remaining were happy to do it. This finding
highlights how a holistic approach is necessary to have a substantial impact.
In this case, holism offers perspective on understanding the historical context
guiding efforts to alleviate poverty.

After examining the cultural shifts created by the ever-changing assemblage of the nonprofit industry, and the factors cited in the five dominant
theories guiding poverty-related policy, it is clear that poverty can change
as a whole when both systemic change is made and individuals are empowered. Change must happen within systems such as public transportation,
laws governing minimum wage, the valuation of housing, how education is
approached, and the list continues. Additionally, individuals who have been
victims of the current systemic inadequacies explained above must somehow
be given hope for a better tomorrow and a sense of empowerment that comes
with knowing that if you work hard, that work will actually be rewarded at an
appropriate level. Fortunately, for professionals working to combat poverty,
the cultural change happening due to changes within the assemblage seems to
offer an avenue through which a holistic approach could be taken.

My case study illustrates this new approach to charitable nonprofit activity. The approach aligns with the recent shift in the nonprofit industry toward
systemic issues and the adoption of behavioral economics, specifically
libertarian paternalism. As an applied anthropologist trained in feminist
anthropology with a focus on political economy, it was at first a mental feat
to reconcile any form of paternalism with the word "good." My training had
exposed the flaws of paternalism in favor of participatory action research
(Whyte 1991), activist anthropology (Hale 2006) and engaged anthropology (Low and Merry 2010), as well as promoting community-based
approaches in general. I was an applied anthropologist trained in giving
voice to the voiceless, empowering the disempowered and representing the
underrepresented.

Simultaneously, I had to reconcile my own cognitive dissonance in working on a project that attempted to control or guide the behavior of unsuspecting clients. My only source of comfort was that my employer, Lighthouse, had intentionally hired me as an applied anthropologist. So I set my sights on including those we claimed to help and wrapped my head around one simple truth: *Everything is designed to do something regardless of intention.* I hoped that the product we designed would help in ways that clients wanted to be helped. Moreover, I saw the potential to influence the nonprofit organization that adopted our technology to increase its efforts in understanding those it wanted to help. By providing a tool through which evaluation could be done easily and relatively cheaply, we were able to demonstrate how important it was to take a holistic view of the services offered. In this way, the paternalistic approach was not just applied to the vulnerable served by the nonprofit but also to the nonprofit itself.

Nonprofits are under constant surveillance by funding sources and as a result must keep a close watch on their clients. This mandate highlights the power expressed by nonprofit organizations over the clients they hope to serve. Still many nonprofit organizations have an issue with compliance and accountability; Lighthouse is not the first to wrestle with this issue. Lighthouse utilized its partnership with CPC to investigate Needle's design and efficiency, as well as client compliance, accountability and alignment of expert content with clients' lives. The goal of the pilot was to discover whether clients would utilize Needle even if their usage resulted in altering CPC's content or approach. Consequently, those designing Needle demonstrated agency and in a small way guided the power that lay in and was ultimately expressed by the institutions and networks with which they interacted.

In the pilot phase of an application, the key activity involves talking to users while they use the app. It is important to understand how the app is being used, what is not working in the way it was intended and how any issues with the app can be fixed. The quantitative data was less than flattering because it suggested a steady attrition rate. However, it is likely that this attrition was an artifact of the lack of engagement with the nonprofit partner's content and less an indication of problems with the Needle architecture or design. Ultimately, the quantitative data highlighted the requirement of talking to users to assess the reception of Needle.

Speaking with users illuminated the major issues. Completing exercises that did not have a direct relationship with getting scholarships or college acceptance letters seemed to be a waste of time in their view. Therefore, the students expressed their own agency and did not complete their CPC assignments, and many did not want to be reminded to complete them. Lighthouse interpreted participant reaction to mean that no matter how compelling or clever Needle became, an increasing rate of CPC completion was not likely.

For CPC, the implications were critical. Fortunately, CPC was open to this information about student reactions and through its own agency quickly shifted its focus almost exclusively to the ACT, college applications and securing scholarships. Because CPC was a nonprofit with an established relationship with an institution—the school—its power over students was significant and had the potential to improve their lives. It also had the power to force a program agenda that was inadequately aligned with student lives and resulted in little or no benefit for them. Nevertheless, it is the agency of those who participate in the assemblage (i.e., the employees of all three institutions) that is the driving force behind how the institutional power is expressed. By acting as a third party voice for the students, Lighthouse was able to use the temporary but powerful interconnectedness of CPC, the high school and itself to increase the benefits offered and shift CPC culture.

CONCLUSION

The power expressed through institutions (e.g., schools, organizations, funding groups) has the potential to change lives for the better. However, that power relies on the "heterogeneous, contingent, unstable, partial and situated" (Collier and Ong 2005, 12) elements, and the assemblages created from those elements (e.g., discourse created, guiding principles, funders' expectations), to embrace innovation and catalyze change. Moreover, those assemblages rely on guidance based on the agency of the individuals that make up yet a small part of the assemblage. Importantly, the assemblage of the Lighthouse Partnership illustrated in Figure 9.3 is expected to change continuously through the life of Needle. There will always be new and different partners with different guiding principles, funders and clients. This unstable aspect of the assemblage offers continuous opportunity for the employees of Lighthouse to use their agency to guide the power that these institutions hold and express.

The idea that assemblages form and reform is one that has implicitly influenced not just Lighthouse, but also the nonprofit industry as a whole. I agree with Foucault's claim that "power produces knowledge (and not simply by encouraging it because it serves power or by applying it because it is useful), that power and knowledge directly imply one another; that there is no power relation without the correlative constitution of a field of knowledge" (1978, 27). As such, power creates the field of knowledge that is most likely to ensure the power dynamic persists untouched. Neoliberalism in the nonprofit industry is a fitting example. The US government created a field of knowledge around neoliberal ideals and volunteerism, which created the idea that Americans are nothing if they are not volunteers. As the nonprofit industry grew, the power over those that the organizations were to help produced the discourse necessary for justifying mediocre results or even failure. Indeed, the power dynamic created the "knowledge" that a lack of personal responsibility and personal failure to adopt the principles provided by the organization prevented individuals from rising out of poverty. This worldview helps to ensure that when you ask someone experiencing poverty how to escape it, that person will respond as those in Lyon-Callo's (2001) work did—by citing increased personal effort as the key to escape—despite citing systemic issues for the reason poverty persists.

Nevertheless, there is cause for hope. Ultimately, the assemblage of a given industry, government or organization holding the power and creating the knowledge is fluid and unstable. My optimism aligns with Foucault when he said,

> My optimism would consist rather in saying that so many things can be changed, fragile as they are, bound up more with circumstances than necessities, more arbitrary than self-evident, more a matter of complex, but temporary, historical circumstances than with inevitable anthropological constants. (1988b, 156)

The instability of a given assemblage is the avenue through which innovation and change is possible. Foucault could easily be described as persistently pessimistic, with some calling his theories fatalistic. However, in his own words, he describes the opportunity for change, "as soon as there is a power relation, there is a possibility of resistance. We can never be ensnared by power: we can always modify its grip in determinate conditions and according to a precise strategy" (1988a, 123). The instability of an assemblage can be utilized to create resistance and change the knowledge being created. Therefore, it is the shifts in the assemblage that provide the "possibility of resistance" and the potential to create change. Importantly, it is not often, if ever, that paradigm-level changes happen, but rather, as Deleuze (1979, xi) explains, "small lines of mutation" feed one another and eventually shift the focus. This idea was, if implicitly, the hope behind the design work conducted by Lighthouse.

When innovation and change are embraced, a design process that includes the voice of users can be utilized to produce a new approach to seemingly old problems such as behaviorally-based mobile applications. This user-focused approach requires the knowledge and insight of those who will experience a product or service, combined with the knowledge and insight of those involved in designing and creating the product or service. The ever-changing assemblages created by this interplay between consumers and creators are but a small part of the larger cohesive assemblage of the industries in which they operate (in this case the nonprofit industry). However, it can be used to guide established dialogues and knowledge, produced by networks of power, in a way that offers hope for sustainable change within systems often in need of new life and innovation.

REFERENCES

Ahearn, Laura. M. 2001 "Language and agency." *Annual Review of Anthropology* 30: 109–37

Bush, George H. W. 1989. "Inaugural Address." The American Presidency Project website. Accessed February 18, 2017. http://www.presidency.ucsb.edu/ws/?pid=16610.

Bailey, Cynthia A. 1995. "Workfare and Involuntary Servitude—What You Wanted to Know but Were Afraid to Ask." *Boston College Third World Law Journal* 15 (2): 291–92.

Bradshaw, T. K. 2007. "Theories of Poverty and Anti-Poverty Programs in Community Development." *Journal Community Development Society* 38 (1): 7–25.

Collier, S. J. and A. Ong. 2005. "Global Assemblages, Anthropological Problems." In *Global Assemblages: Technology, Politics, and Ethics as Anthropological Problems,* edited by A. Ong and S. J. Collier, 3–21. Oxford: Blackwell.

Daminger, Allison, Jonathan Hayes, Anthony Barrows, Josh Wright. 2015. "Poverty Interrupted: Applying Behavioral Science to the Context of Chronic Scarcity." *Ideas42* website, May. Accessed November 14, 2016. http://www.ideas42.org/wp-content/uploads/2015/05/I42_PovertyWhitePaper_Digital_FINAL-1.pdf.

Deleuze, Gilles. 1979. Foreword to *The Policing of Families* by Jacques Donzelot, ix–xvii. New York: Patheon.

Egendorf, L. K., ed.1988. *Poverty: Opposing Viewpoints*. San Diego: Greenhaven Press.

Epstein, W. M. 1997. *Welfare in America: How Social Science Fails the Poor*. Madison: University of Wisconsin Press.

Foucault, Michel. 1978. *Discipline and Punish: The Birth of the Prison* translated by Alan Sheridan. New York: Vintage Books.

Foucault, Michel. 1988a. "Power and Sex" in *Michel Foucault: Politics, Philosophy, Culture*, edited by Lawrence D. Kritzman, 110–124. New York: Routledge.

Foucault, Michel. 1988b. "Practicing Criticism" in *Michel Foucault: Politics, Philosophy, Culture*, edited by Lawrence D. Kritzman, 153–156. New York: Routledge.

Galtung, Johan. 1969. "Violence, Peace, and Peace Research." *Journal of Peace Research* 6 (3): 167–191.

Gramsci, Antonio 1971 "Americanism and Fordism." In Selections from the Prison Notebooks, edited and translated by Quintin Hoare and Jeffrey Smith, 279–318. New York: International Publishers.

Goldstein, Donna M. 2001. "Microenterprise Training Programs, Neoliberal Common Sense, and the Discourses of Self-Esteem." In *The New Poverty Studies: The Ethnography of Power, Politics and Impoverished People in the United States*, edited by Judith Goode and Jeff Maskovsky, 236–272. New York: New York University Press.

Goode, Judith and Jeff Maskovsky (eds.). 2001. *The New Poverty Studies: The Ethnography of Power, Politics and Impoverished People in the United States.* New York: New York University Press.

Hale, Charles. 2006. "Activist Research v. Cultural Critique: Indigenous Land Rights and the Contradictions of Politically Engaged Anthropology." *Cultural Anthropology* 21 (1): 96–20.

Hall, P. D. 2010. "Historical perspectives on nonprofit organizations." In *The Jossey-Bass Handbook of Nonprofit Leadership and Management* 3rd *Edition* edited by David O. Renz, 3–41. San Francisco: Jossey Bass.

Hall, P. D. 2006. "A Historical Overview of Philanthropy, Voluntary Associations, and Nonprofit Organizations in the United States, 1600–2000." In *The nonprofit sector: A research handbook,* edited by Walter W. Powell and Richard Steinberg, 13–31. Yale University Press.

Hanks, Andrew S., David R. Just, Laura E. Smith, and Brian Wansink. 2012. "Healthy Convenience: Nudging Students Toward Healthier Choices in the Lunchroom." *Journal of Public Health* 34 (3): 370–376.

Harvey, David. 2005. *A Brief History of Neoliberalism.* New York, NY: Oxford University Press.

Hyatt, Susan Brin. 2001. "From Citizen to Volunteer: Neoliberal Governance and the Erasure of Poverty" In *The New Poverty Studies: The Ethnography of Power, Politics and Impoverished People in the United States,* edited by Judith Goode and Jeff Maskovsky, 201–235. New York: New York University Press.

Jones, Michael L. 2006. "The Growth of Nonprofits." *Bridgewater Review* 25 (1): 13–17.

Katz, Michael B. 1996. *In the Shadow of the Poorhouse: A Social History of Welfare in America.* New York: Basic Books Accessed March 10, 2017. http://ezproxy. memphis.edu/login?url=http://search.ebscohost.com/login.aspx?direct=true&db=n lebk&AN=583975&site=ehost-live&ebv=EB&ppid=pp_289.

Kerlin, Janelle A. and Tom H. Pollak. 2010. "Nonprofit Commercial Revenue: A Replacement for Declining Government Grants and Private Contributions?" *The American Review of Public Administration* 41 (6): 686–704.

Low, Setha M. and Sally Engle Merry. 2010. "Engaged Anthropology: Diversity and Dilemmas." *Current Anthropology* 51 (supplement 2):S203–S226.

Lyon-Callo, Vincent. 2001. "Homelessness, Employment, and Structural Violence: Exploring Constraints on Collective Mobilizations Against Systemic Inequality." In *The New Poverty Studies: The Ethnography of Power, Politics and Impoverished People in the United States,* edited by Judith Goode and Jeff Maskovsky, 293–318. New York, NY: New York University Press.

Morrill, R. L. and E. H. Wohlenberg. 1971. *The Geography of Poverty.* New York: McGraw Hill.

Mullainathan, Sendhil, and Richard Thaler. 2001. "Behavioral Economics." In *International Encyclopedia of Social Sciences,* edited by Neil J. Smelser and Paul B. Baltes, 1094–1100. Oxford: Pergamon Press.

Munsterberg, Emil. 1904. "The Problem of Poverty." *American Journal of Sociology* 10 (3): 335–353.

Naples, Nancy A. and Manisha Desai, eds. 2002. *Women's Activism and Globalization*. New York: Routledge.

Ropers, R. H. 1991. *Persistent Poverty: The American Dream Turned Nightmare*. New York: Plenum.

Thaler, Richard H., and Cass R. Sunstein. 2003. "Libertarian Paternalism." *The American Economic Review* 93 (2): 175–79.

Thaler, Richard H., and Cass R. Sunstein. 2009. *Nudge: Improving Decisions about Health, Wealth, and Happiness*. New York: Penguin Books.

Thatcher, Margaret. 1987. "Interview for Women's Own ("no such thing as society")." Margaret Thatcher Foundation website. http://www.margaretthatcher.org/document/106689 (accessed February 18, 2017).

Walden, Gwen I. 2006. "Who's Watching Us Now? The Nonprofit Sector and the New Government by Surveillance." *Nonprofit & Voluntary Sector Quarterly* 35 (4): 715–720.

Weber, Max [1930]2003. *The Protestant Ethic and the Spirit of Capitalism*. London: Allen and Unwin. Reprint, New York: Taylor and Francis Group. Citation refers to Taylor and Francis Group edition.

Weeks, Arland D. 1917. "A Conservative's View of Poverty." *American Journal of Sociology* 22 (6): 779–800.

Wies, Jennifer R. 2013. "Feminist Ethnography with Domestic Shelter Advocates: Negotiating the Neoliberal Era." In *Feminist Activist Ethnography: Counterpoints to Neoliberalism in North America*, edited by Christa Craven and Dána-Ain Davis, 53–68. Lanham, MD: Lexington Books.

Wright, Rachel. 2013. "When More Is Less: Contradictions of Nonprofit Work." *Anthropology of Work Review* 34 (2): 80–90.

World Bank. "Global INsights Initiative (#WB_GINI)." Worldbank.org website. http://www.worldbank.org/en/programs/gini (accessed November 14, 2016).

Whyte, W. F. 1991. *Participatory Action Research*. Newbury Park, CA: Sage.

Chapter 10

Organizational Change from the Inside

Negotiating the Dual Identity of Employee and Ethnographer

Shane Pahl, Angela Ramer, and Jo Aiken

Practicing anthropologists are uniquely positioned to raise awareness of and affect organizational-culture change in their places of employment.[1,2] They have been working for decades now with or inside businesses, non-profits, government agencies, and nongovernmental organizations (Jordan 2013a). Their numbers are expected to increase as anthropological practice and application take on a more prominent role, particularly among recent graduates (Ginsberg 2016; Fiske et al. 2010; Hepsø 2013; Rudd et al. 2008). When published, much of the work of these anthropologists focuses on particular projects in which they have been engaged (Caulkins and Jordan 2013a; Cefkin 2009; McCabe 2017). Less attention has been given to reflexive analyses of anthropological practice, with some notable exceptions (Nolan 2013).

This chapter has two goals. One is to use assemblage theory and provide a reflexive analysis of anthropological practice based on three case studies conducted in US-based organizations. The second is to examine the similarities and differences across the case studies. By comparing our work across three different organizations, we offer insights into organizational-culture change from the "inside" perspective. We also explain why greater emphasis on reflexivity in the anthropological literature on organizational change would be useful.

In a call for reflexive analysis, we explore our roles as insiders/outsiders (i.e., employees/anthropologists doing ethnography) in creating and sustaining change within our respective organizations. This insider/outsider role is different from traditional anthropological fieldwork (i.e., outsiders trying to learn the insider perspective) and different from many practicing anthropologists who are consultants who are also outsiders trying to learn the insider perspective. As employees/insiders, we are situated as internal change agents in the work practices of our respective organizations (Beers 2017). We analyze our insider/outsider role within assemblages of actors bringing about cultural change—as insiders, learning new skills and knowledge, and as outsiders, attempting unbiased observations about work practices despite our roles in trying to support business goals and technology design requirements (Cefkin 2014; Crain and Tashima 2013).

The remainder of the chapter is organized as follows; first, we discuss the theoretical foundation for our reflexive analysis of anthropological practice. We see this perspective emerging from a dialogue between work practice studies and organizational change. Second, we demonstrate how our insider perspective fits within assemblage theory, enabling us to explain organizational transitions through various change efforts. Then, we introduce our three case studies followed by a discussion about reflexive analysis of practice in which we compare and contrast our experiences within the framework of assemblage theory. Finally, we offer concluding thoughts on the strengths and weaknesses of assemblage theory and a put forth a call for a more reflexive approach to doing and writing about practice.

THEORETICAL ORIENTATION

Origins and History of Work Practice Studies

Current work practice studies within anthropology trace their roots to the Hawthorne studies of the 1920s that examined experimentation with labor and environment in organizational design (Cefkin 2009). These foundational work practice studies were predominately influenced by the disciplines of psychology and engineering which focused on the role of the individual (Cefkin 2014; Suchman 2011; Syzmanski and Whalen 2011). The next major shift in the epistemology of work practice came in the 1970s as sociologists and anthropologists entered the field of human factors engineering. Notable in this shift was the work of anthropologist Lucy Suchman at the Xerox, Palo Alto Research Center (PARC). Suchman famously captured on video the struggle of two computer scientists interacting with a supposed/presumed "user-friendly" copier. The video, "When User Hits Machine," serves as an important marker of a change in the way work practice was studied because it revealed the importance of the cultural context of work (Suchman 2011). In the video, two eminent computer scientists are shown attempting to make two-sided copies of a research paper. However, they experience extreme difficulty completing the task. Suchman explains: "the machine's illegibility was tied not to any esoteric technical characteristics, but to mundane difficulties of sense-making characteristic of any unfamiliar artifact" (Suchman

2011, 27). Pioneering observations such as these by Suchman added the anthropological dimension to the study of work practice; the anthropological dimension was one that called for a more holistic, *in situ* understanding of work.

The shift in work practice studies from analyzing work in a lab to analyzing it within workscapes, or the natural environment in which work is done, was brought about by developments in anthropology. Ethnomethodology, feminist research, and critical analysis all helped to rework the way in which work practice was conceptualized, asking not only what the worker's experience was but how the worker's experience was analyzed. Reworking how work is analyzed led to participatory design methods in which the workers' knowledge and experience were considered parallel inputs to those of the researchers. While certainly not an exhaustive list, other monumental contributors during this period included Eleanor Wynn, Jeanette Blomberg, Paul Luff, Jon Hindmarsh, Christian Heath, Julian Orr, Susan Newman, and Brigitte Jordan (Cefkin 2009; Cefkin 2014; Szymanski and Whalen 2011).

Melissa Cefkin defines work practice studies today as "the actions and practices of doing work, including the many social, material, and cultural factors and dynamics that produce and are reproduced in the doing of work" (2014, 286). The current form of work practice studies contains a clear methodological approach to conducting research. Cefkin provides four principles "required to deepen social and cultural insight" (2014, 288): say-do distinction, "emic" point of view, situated actor perspective, and systemic framework. The say-do distinction highlights how people talk about what they do compared to what they actually do. The "emic" point of view establishes a point of view constructed by insiders. The situated actor perspective shows that the capability of individuals is related to their relationships with other people, their environment, and artifacts such as technology or information. And finally, the systemic framework principle emphasizes the importance of *holism;* changing one part of the system can affect other parts.

The literature of corporate ethnography takes a critical position on the role of an ethnographer, including reflexive analysis of what anthropologists and ethnographers do within corporations, and the systemic impacts of their work (Cefkin 2013); Cefkin 2014; Jordan 2013b). One focus of corporate ethnography within work practice studies specifically explores organizational- culture change (Briody, Trotter and Meerwarth 2010; Cefkin 2014; Krause-Jensen 2010). These studies present ethnographic perspectives of organizations as they plan for and implement cultural change. Moving between this insider/ outsider role or hybrid emic-etic perspective allows us to look critically at changes our organizations adopt as a study of work practice. This type of work and perspective is best exemplified by Briody, Trotter, and Meerwarth (2010) in their work at General Motors. Their work outlines a process and a model for cultural transformation toward an organization's ideal culture. The transformation process involves identifying cultural obstacles to change and ways to mitigate them. More recently, work practice studies appear to have a pulse on opportunities for organizational innovation. As Cefkin (2014) notes, "work practice studies give rise to particular opportunities for innovation, development, design, and deployment, engaging others in the organization with a stake in those dynamics along the way" (2014, 294).

Organizational Change and Assemblage Theory

Assemblage theory provides an analytical lens through which to examine how ideas, industries, and people come together to enact change. To understand how organizations change, study of the relationships between the tiers of change-influencers or "scales of observation" as described by Desjeux (2016; 2014; 1987) is helpful. As the case studies in this chapter illustrate, our discourse on *how* change happens includes a description of the processes of change (see Briody, Trotter, and Meerwarth, 2010 for a thorough description of the processes of organizational change). In each of our cases, the process of change includes an analysis of the influence of "external factors" at the meso level that catalyze change, as well as the response of the organizations at the micro level (e.g., creation of multiple other projects, changes throughout each organization) to those changes (Suchman 2011). By examining organizational change through the lens of assemblage theory, we are also able to see the three levels of observation in our analysis: the macro level "metanarratives" help to understand the larger implications of innovations; cultural shifts or "external factors" at the meso level; our "actions" at the micro level as employees of the organizations we seek to change (see discussion of the levels of observation in McCabe's introduction to this book). To demonstrate these relationships, we explore the following questions:

- How might metanarratives (macro level) affect an assemblage during cultural change?
- What external (meso level) catalysts facilitate cultural change?
- What internal (micro level) momentum is used to maintain cultural change?

This Chapter's Assemblages as Case Studies

Various stakeholder responses to external catalysts, such as the development of new technologies, policies, and ideas about best practices, are a common feature across the three cases. We participate within each of our organizations as internal "actors," hired to help facilitate organizational change projects. Each of us uses reflexive analysis of *how* we do work to understand the impact of our work. Leveraging metanarratives also furnishes context in understanding the relationships across the various levels of observation. Our cases differ most in our specific roles within our organizations and in our relationship to the network that surrounds us. Comparing these variations is important to understanding conditions that may create effective organizational change.

BACKGROUND

HVAC/R INC

HVAC/R INC (a pseudonym), established in the mid-20th century, has been successful within the heating and cooling industry. Located in 20 sites across the United States, it has over 300 employees. Much of its success has been attributed to the company's devotion to providing the best customer service among its competitors. To maintain growth, senior leadership identified a need for investment in the development of operational management. Senior leadership decided to explore three topics: process management, safety culture, and employee onboarding, training, and development.

HKS

HKS (Harwood K. Smith), with 78 years of experience, is a global architectural firm consisting of architects, interior designers, graphic designers, marketing coordinators, project managers, researchers, accountants, executive leaders, legal and support service staff. Its system for design production includes over 1,400 employees across 26 offices operating within the critical, apprenticeship-oriented field of design. Governing bodies drive best practices of related industries (e.g., architecture, interior design, human resources, IT). An increasing inclination toward online/digital (vs. paper-based) workflows along with a retention of work practices has affected HKS' ability to adapt work processes. Employee interest in an engaging, internal feedback process, combined with leadership's decision to address issues of role clarity and conflict, set the stage for its change initiative.

NASA

The National Aeronautics and Space Administration (NASA) is a US agency rich in innovation, whose missions are driven by scientific curiosities, international politics, international collaborations, and advancements in technology design. Since the beginning of the American space program in 1958,

NASA has shifted from a technology-driven (or machine-centered) design to a human-centered (or user-centered) design. This organizational shift is an example of a fluid, dynamic cultural change due to four factors: politics, mission designs, international crew compositions, and design trends outside the agency. These elements converge and diverge to influence the space agency's operations as well as its organizational culture.

CASE 1: CREATING SAFETY CULTURE AT HVAC/R INC

HVAC/R INC's shift from a customer-centered organization toward an employee-centered organization is an example of cultural change. This shift was brought about as senior leaders within the organization examined industry best practices and expanded functions such as human resources, facilities maintenance, operations, and safety. This intentional development of work groups was a reaction to recent citations from US regulatory agencies, and the interest in preventing exposure to future citations. It was also proactive in that senior leadership's development of these work groups prepared the organization for an innovation shift currently occurring in US regulatory agencies (e.g., Department of Labor, Environmental Protection Agency). In recent years, these organizations began to pass legislation requiring digital reporting of incidents by organizations. This shift toward regulatory digitization was an effort to crack down on the falsification of reports and improve both the quality of reporting and response time by regulatory agencies.

Convergence: Regulatory Agencies

The HVAC/R industry must abide by regulations established to protect employees. Some of the major, federal regulatory agencies to which it must adhere include the Department of Labor (DOL), the Department of Transportation (DOT), the Environmental Protection Agency (EPA), and the Occupational Safety and Health Administration (OSHA). Recently, these agencies have adapted innovations in technologies allowing them to collect and analyze data pertaining to regulatory violations quickly. For example, the Federal Motor Carrier Safety Administration (FMCSA), a subsidiary of the DOT, passed legislation referred to as the "ELD rule" (i.e., Electronic Logging Device) in December 2015. This legislation requires that all commercial drivers, who are subject to logging the hours they drive a commercial vehicle (Hours of Service), must switch from paper logs to electronic logs by December 18, 2017. As stated by the FMCSA, "the ELD rule is intended to help create a safer work environment for drivers, and make it easier, faster to accurately track, manage, and share records of duty status (RODS) data" (FMCSA 2016). This legislation intends to improve compliance of commercial drivers taking necessary breaks from driving, only driving and working within their daily allowances, and getting enough rest.

Shift in Organizational Culture: Customer-Centered toward Operations-Centered

Over the past several years, HVAC/R INC has shifted from a customer-centered organization to an operations-centered organization. Senior leadership examined technological shifts and innovations in the industry (e.g., inventory management, warehouse management, employee recruitment/development). As a result, leaders created organizational functions such as human resources, facilities maintenance, operations, and safety.

Assembly: Creating a Team

Before I was hired as a full-time employee by HVAC/R INC in the summer of 2014, I conducted three months of research with them for my graduate thesis. My thesis focused on decision-making processes of new product purchases, and the subsequent onboarding and evaluation of those purchases. When I was hired as a full-time employee, HVAC/R was already familiar with my work and my training as an organizational anthropologist. My initial full-time role was to observe operations, recommend changes, and carry out operational improvement projects. At first, I worked exclusively at HVAC/R's distribution center. After approximately four months on that project, I learned about conversations among executives and HVAC/R's insurance brokers pertaining to "safety culture" improvement methods. An operations executive told me that my name came up because of the project at the distribution center and its parallels to "safety." He suggested to other senior leaders that I be included in these discussions. From that point on, I served as a program/project manager of the safety culture development project.

Safety Culture

Being responsible for "developing a safety culture" is a complex undertaking and begs several questions—most importantly, what is safety culture? Fortunately, there are a few anthropologists who have examined safety culture. For example, Jordan (2013a) states "'safety culture' includes attention to detail, carefully following procedures, open communication, and never trading safety for a chance to make more money" (2013a, 53). Haukelid (2007) indicates that safety culture is:

The shared and learned meanings, experiences and interpretations of work and safety—expressed partially symbolically—which guide people's actions towards risk, accidents and prevention. Safety culture is shaped by people in the structures and social relations within and outside the organization. (2007, 6)

From these definitions, concepts of procedures and risks emerge. Historically, the phrase "safety culture" came into colloquial use in the 1980s, as did the term "organizational culture" by management theorists as discussed by both Jordan and Haukelid. Indeed, safety culture is not actually separate from organizational culture. Haukelid explains: "I think it is important to stress that safety culture should not be something separate from—or in addition to—an organizational culture, but constitute an integrated part of this culture" (2007, 419). "Safety culture," understood anthropologically, encompasses procedures and ideas about risk within an organizational culture. Therefore the task of developing a safety culture entails establishing processes based on ideas about risks. Developing a safety culture becomes a form of organizational change.

Developing Expertise

The scope of industrial safety compliance ranges from federal, to state, to city regulations. "Safety" is commonly the general term used to describe all environmental, health, and safety regulations. Its stated purpose is to prevent humans from exposure to harm.

Senior leadership hired a Certified Safety Professional (CSP) to educate me on safety compliance, including structural and behavioral regulations. The first four months in this role was mostly comprised of my own education and training. For example, I completed a certificate program through the University of Alabama in Health and Safety Management; it included nine courses such as "Introduction to Workplace Safety" and "Introduction to Industrial Hygiene." These programs were not mandatory for someone functioning in my role. However, they helped me to learn and understand the regulations and develop programs to manage them. Additionally, I also hold certificates that are compulsory for my responsibilities including six certificates with the Fire Department of New York that certify my knowledge in handling, storage, and shipment of various hazardous substances, as well as a Hazardous Waste Operations and Emergency Response certificate (commonly referred to as "the HAZWOPER" or "the 40 hour") through Rutgers University.

The Case Study: Creating Safety Culture

With the objective of creating a safety culture, I planned to visit all 20 of the organizations' facilities beginning in February 2015. My intent was to introduce myself, explain my role, and obtain an overview of each site. At that time there were no organizational charts or facility maps. I acquired a list of branch manager names from a senior operations executive and contacted each of them via email to set up appointments with them and their staff. I explained that I wanted to learn about each facility: the type of employees working there and their knowledge of safety, and to identify any behavioral or structural safety hazards. The purpose of the visits and questions was to help to identify enablers and obstacles to cultural change (Briody et al. 2010).

Surveying the Cultural Landscape

Sometimes branch managers were available for a meeting. On other occasions, I had to return two or three times because the branch manager was either absent or busy providing service to customers. Branch manager availability became an important clue into competing priorities: sales versus safety. This dichotomy was an obstacle, reinforced in my informal interviews. Employees held varying degrees of safety regulation knowledge and in some cases could explain how certain safety practices were in conflict with customer service. I found that safety attitudes varied from enthusiastic to dismissive (e.g., another corporate initiative that will "never work"). Clarity surrounding the reporting structure also differed across facilities. Yet, clear channels and procedures for communication must exist for safety programs to be effective.

I toured each facility with branch managers to document all structural (physical) hazards (e.g., uncapped electrical wires, tripping hazards), explain safety equipment regulations (e.g., fire extinguishers that had not been inspected by their expiration dates), poor behaviors (e.g., not wearing a seatbelt while operating a forklift, running in the office). In my discussions with branch managers, it was apparent that safety culture was the purview of each branch manager. Given that the organizational relationships were blurred within the facilities, I also discovered that relationships extending to corporate headquarters were also not well defined. Branch managers neither knew to whom they reported nor how to report safety issues.

Analysis: Establishing Shared and Learned Meaning

After returning to headquarters with these findings, it was clear that senior management was not ready to make the reporting relationships between the branches and corporate headquarters transparent. Consequently, I focused on developing a process for addressing the structural hazards that existed within the facilities.

I wrote a technical manual describing ideal conditions. Each branch manager received a copy of the manual to retain at his or her facility. I scheduled appointments to revisit each facility. I met with each branch manager, toured each facility, and noted observations of existing or potential physical hazards. I then referred the branch manager to the appropriate page in the manual to explain ideal conditions. For example, an ideal condition might entail an unblocked path of egress at all emergency exits, an existing condition might be a blocked path, and a potential condition could be that a path of egress could be blocked.

Project Redesign

I returned to each facility a month later to find that virtually nothing had changed. Informally, I spoke with each branch manager and several employees at each location to learn why. I realized that by putting the onus of reporting and correcting hazards solely on the branch manager, I had put the responsibility on the person most affected by the competing sales vs. safety dichotomy. I also had not established any mechanisms of accountability. However, I found enablers to help address these issues. In our organization's union, warehouse employees were the greatest advocates of compliant facilities. I instituted two major changes. First, I put all warehouse employees through a training program called "Safety 101;" it was similar to the training I gave to branch managers to identify and understand safety compliance. Second, in addition to the technical manual, I created an excel spreadsheet-based inspection checklist for the branch managers. The checklist provided a simplified way for the branch managers to tour and inspect their facilities for compliance.

Next, I required branch managers to submit a checklist between the first and 10th of each month. Submitting after the 10th of the month would be deemed late while submitting after the 20th of the month would be considered a failure to report. To address measures of accountability, I created a monthly review of safety and a quarterly audit program. The monthly safety review included a review of metrics I established such as on-time reporting of checklists, accidents that had occurred and their root causes, up-coming or ongoing projects, and a topic of the month. This report would be submitted via email to all branch managers and executives of the operations management team within the first 10 days of the month, for the previous month. The public sharing of this information greatly increased the frequency and consistency of monthly submissions; it also created a routine of reporting issues from the branches to corporate headquarters. Lastly, I conducted quarterly audits of each facility. Audits would be checked against monthly inspection checklists submitted by branch managers for discrepancies to address any outstanding issues.

Reconnecting to Assemblages

These changes were effective in creating measureable change. Initially, the public dissemination of the safety reviews pressed branch managers to ask questions such as "Who should I report this to?" and "How do we solve this issue?" It also led senior leadership to develop a transparent reporting structure to address hazards. Frustrations emerged when immediate results were not evident during this initial period of discovery. To maintain momentum from the flow of branch information to corporate headquarters, special attention and effort were necessary to manage expectations regarding the pace of change. It was and continues to be a struggle to get full participation from the branches and headquarters each month. However, some branch managers became more active and vocal in using safety as a conduit for facility improvements. As one stated, "Before we had the checklist we had to figure out what to report about, but you came in and you streamlined it." More important than the checklist, in my opinion, was the formation of the processes to understand, communicate, and reduce risk at the branches. Gradually, employees have developed greater participation and confidence in the new system as they have seen improvement in their facilities.

CASE 2: ORGANIZATIONAL CHANGE IN AN ARCHITECTURE FIRM

Professional development is a large umbrella under which employee performance is often nested. Many US organizations rely on various forms of performance feedback. One of the most common is an annual performance review or appraisal. Its primary focus is to assess (and in the appropriate case, recognize) an employee's performance at regular intervals to ensure engagement, proper management, and long-term retention. Townley (1997), a vocal leader in management and creative studies, suggests,

> Performance appraisal is a powerful institutional myth, part of the rationale of what organizations need to be legitimate. Concerned with individual, and by extension organizational, effort, reward and effectiveness, performance appraisal comes recommended as a critically important managerial tool. (1997, 266–267)

Employees associate the value of the appraisal process with financial and career incentives: salary, raises, bonuses, and promotion. While this practice places a priority on measuring performance and can set standards of expectations, it also creates a climate of competition among employees, including those in creative industries.

Krause-Jensen's study (2010) of Bang & Olufsen culture highlights a major challenge for internal service groups such as Human Resource (HR) Management; designated the "soft" side of culture management, HR functions are often required to legitimize their existence and activities via "hard" business metrics (e.g., engagement and satisfaction via work output and turnover rates). Such potentially incongruent measures can create conflicting views of employees as either human capital (training focused holistically on the person and their employment experience) or as operational components (training for efficiency of the employee's job function). The Society for Human Resource Management (SHRM) published a telling article in 2015, citing firms like GE, Microsoft, Accenture, Adobe, Gap, and MedTronic indicating their departure from annual appraisals in favor of any combination of continuous, project/milestone/assignment-based feedback that is quick and open to managers and teammates (Wilkie 2015).

This shift away from previous programs and processes, and ratings and rankings, is prompting many organizations to identify alternatives for employee evaluation in the form of either industry-developed or proprietary software systems. However, these evaluation alternatives should be considered in the context of both the technology and human experience. In Rhea's (2003) discussion of "inside-out" (technology-focused) and "outside-in" (customer-focused) development approaches to the "fuzzy front end" of product development, we are reminded, "without technology, the product won't work. Without operational excellence, the product won't be profitable. Without design, the product won't evoke desire. And without customer relevance, the product won't sell" (2003, 146). Both "inside-out" and "outside-in" perspectives are required during the development of a successful product to ensure usability and adoption. Rhea's holistic assemblage perspective serves as a call to action for researchers "to articulate how their work can turn the 'fuzzy front end' into a predictable process for inventing the future of the organization, and advocate its value to senior management" (2003, 145). My case study sheds light onto the fuzzy front end of program development and highlights specifically how the fields of architecture and design are experiencing a paradigm shift from performance to professional development-oriented program design.

PROGRAM DESIGN

The fields of architecture and interior design are known for their apprentice-based internal training. Both represent industries with long-term employment practices. Employees progress or rotate through various levels and functions of employment in a firm via on-the-job experience as a kind of in-the-field education. However, this staged progression has resulted in an industry with employees that are assessment-oriented, promotion-focused, and acculturated to hierarchy.

In January 2016, HKS Architects launched ELEVATE, a professional development program meant to engage all staff, from new hires to C-suite executives, in structured processes of skills assessment, goal setting, and goal evaluation. ELEVATE is both a larger program with processes and procedures, as well as an online web portal that facilitates these processes through documentation. It took over 18 months of development to reach that January launch date. A small, interdisciplinary team with the support of senior leadership had direct instructions to provide a "simple and easy program to encourage firm-wide participation in professional development." While the program is still being finalized, it has been a successful step in formalizing feedback and goal setting, and in enhancing communication and clarity. My primary contribution to the core project team was to advocate on behalf of the end-user perspective. During the program's development, I was exposed to the fields of Professional Development and Information Technology. Specifically, my work on this project taught me new skills in web application design (e.g., developing workflow charts and rules for user interaction, thinking through scenarios of use and integrating with "sprint"-style project management).

My case study represents an assemblage of various job functions as it creates a professional development program consistent with the apprenticeship-oriented and exacting field of design. HKS employee interest in an engaging, internal feedback process, combined with leadership's desire to address issues of role clarity, brought together a collective of actors (our team) with interdependent agency to create cultural change within the organization. Externally, ELEVATE was influenced by the American Institute of Architecture and International Interior Design Association, and internally by the firm's recruitment and retention interests. ELEVATE was also responsive to an increasing use of online/digital (vs. paper-based) workflows, influence from previous professional development efforts, and diverse perspectives from Professional Development, Human Resources, and IT workgroups.

ELEVATE professional development program is a year-round process of interaction/engagement and a digital tool for documentation. It includes semiannual review discussions based on self-assessment and goal setting components. The ELEVATE program leverages an online tool to solicit and capture user input, which then prompts and facilitates informal conversations and reflection. Such discussions were ad hoc interactions with a completed participation rate of 70% in 2016. Consistent feedback on the program has been how it creates a structured pause in busy work lives to assess current status and plans for the coming year.

Process and Product Changes in Program

Chart Your Course served as HKS' firm-wide professional development program from approximately 2008 to 2012. This annual program consisted of a paper-based packet of instructional information with a progress reference scale and a single page self-assessment for review with one's supervisor. Initial program participation was strong. However, the program failed to endure as a process because it was paper-based, informal, and largely unendorsed by organizational leaders. Indeed, neither new hires nor new managers were consistently encouraged to use it. In a best-case scenario, forms were printed, handwritten, reviewed, and filed away in employee folders by Human Resources; this scenario exemplified minimally active engagement in employee evaluation. In a worst-case scenario, employees perceived the content and participation as a corporate mandate that was either not relevant for their position or ignored by their supervisor; this scenario reflected a total lack of engagement with Chart Your Course. The end result was mixed. The most engaged employees and middle management found ways to adapt the program to their own needs. For example, engaged supervisors assisting with reviews for bonuses or proactive junior employees seeking promotion might use it. Alternatively, employees abandoned the program.

In September 2014, the firm commissioned a third party "culture survey" as part of a larger effort to identify organizational development opportunities. Sixty-nine percent (N=556) of those full-time employees with at least one year of tenure at HKS completed the survey. Analysis was run by work group and office, and for the firm as a whole. Outcomes from this assessment highlighted opportunities for clarifying employee roles and responsibilities and as such, the effort to develop and implement an employee performance and professional development program began. Employees desired regular, formal feedback for professional development and compensation. Only a few work groups and managers still used aspects of Chart Your Course or created their own group-based review programs to address the lack of consistent employee evaluation. HKS hired a Director of Professional Development to present the culture survey findings to the firm and lead a taskforce to develop a new professional development program.

Starting in May 2015, the small taskforce began by auditing past professional development efforts at HKS and in the industry. The purpose was to understand key features of the Chart Your Course program as well as interim work group professional development efforts and enthusiasm to design and launch a new firm-wide program. The ultimate aim of the taskforce was to create a program with a process to facilitate and document meaningful professional development conversations throughout the year (emphasizing two required meetings for reviewers and reviewees). ELEVATE referenced materials and utilized lessons learned from previous efforts, including Chart Your Course, to prevent earlier errors and improve alignment with employee-stated interests.

Changes in Development

The ELEVATE program maintained a core team of professional development experts, an IT liaison, a marketing/branding graphic designer and me throughout its development. My role was to serve in data collection (via interviews and focus groups) and advocate on behalf of those representative end users during program development. Additionally, I was a connection between the HR, IT, and Professional Development groups to ensure that the technical execution was parallel to marketing/communication efforts. The core team was assigned to this project at varying levels of time allocation, with no one staffed full time. At various intervals, individuals from marketing, Human Resources, legal and senior leadership provided constructive feedback to ensure the appropriateness of the program, process, and interactive product for the organization's vision, taking into account legal considerations.

In the early phase of program development, the core team viewed recent product demos for performance and professional development management tools, focusing specifically on semi-customizable software platforms. These product demonstrations helped reveal some key content, interactivity, and visualization ideas to the team. However, their limited customization capabilities and high costs precluded their purchase. The assumption that HKS could produce its own tool at a lower cost, while not the eventual outcome, allowed the core team to include two developers. These developers were pivotal in building ELEVATE's online documentation tool—a web portal with an online assessment and goal setting form.

The development of this program's content and structure hinged upon the solicited participation of employees. The development process included 18 pre-program-development focus group participants (eight senior and 10 junior employees), 13 employee pilot participants of our initial online web application (eight senior and five junior staff), six senior leaders and over 1,000 employees who provided feedback at both the initial and revised product launches (January and August 2016, respectively). This collaborative approach positioned the ELEVATE team (as facilitators) *and* the employees as both cocreators and critics. Thus, the program was internally generated and promoted; we knew from past efforts that a top-down, mandatory program would result in employee skepticism and resistance. We invited employees to participate in our iterative development process to leverage user input and expectations for maximum acceptance. Our team was able to create a system of employee feedback and program changes based on that input. Typically, either technical functionality or required program participation milestones paused development cycles and served as catalysts for key decisions. However, by developing the program 100% in-house, we had significant flexibility to customize our ELEVATE online tool. Customization ensured that each component (and iteration) of the tool (e.g., the one-page, interactive self-assessment, text-entry goal-setting section) matched the branded look, language, and process of the larger ELEVATE program.

This effort to develop the program's process *and* product (i.e., initial program tool) simultaneously created an interdependent and effective progression of content and functionality. Tighter convergence within the assemblage resulted with several delays due to lack of clarity and direction on whether the program's process (e.g., structure, content) or the functional limitations of the digital user interface were in the lead. A bi-weekly sprint cycle for the developers, with check-in and demonstration meetings for the core team led by the IT liaison, proved the most effective means of maintaining development timing.

Changes in Structure

ELEVATE debuted as an "every-person's" professional development program. Adoption of and participation in the program required an interactive data entry and display tool, a technological shift away from the original Excel spreadsheet and paper-based products. The change to a digital workflow meant that work could be completed on one's own time and retained long-term. It signaled a well-designed professional development program sensitive to voiced concerns, experiences, and expectations of the end-user population. Indeed, ELEVATE was easy-to-use, online, intuitive, and integrated with other information systems.

We designed the semiannual conversations to facilitate discussion around the program's evaluation content known as "the form." Recommendations from HR and the latest professional development literature contributed to the form's development. The form has two parts. The first part is a 40-part self-assessment divided into five categories of skills, knowledge, and abilities relative to one's own career (e.g., professional practice, business acumen) with eight sub-measures (e.g., "Plans projects for efficient delivery of services"). The second part consists of a goal setting component that includes one required and two optional text-entry comment boxes to capture annual employee goals.

During its inaugural year (2016), ELEVATE used a five-point scale with both numeric and qualitative labels (e.g., 1= needs improvement to 5= excellence) for the self-assessment component. The self-assessment took on unexpected agency despite repeated communications about the assessment's general professional development purpose. The scale caused general confusion over the tool's interpretation. Moreover, assumptions about its implications for bonuses, raises, and promotions resulted in both distorted and inflated scores.

Based on employee feedback from those being reviewed and those doing the reviewing, the self-assessment scale was reexamined by the core ELEVATE team and HKS leadership. The scale was reenvisioned to assess goal setting rather than scoring current skills. Thus, the structure and function of the scale changed to include a three-point scale and the category not applicable: improvement needed, emerging, and strength response for the 40 measures. The self-assessment's functionally shifted from rating or ranking to opportunity identification. These updates to the digital platform reflect the intent and meaning behind the ELEVATE program as a framework and platform for facilitating the core professional development conversations.

Creating a Professional Development Platform

In general, performance-based employee appraisal continues to be an embedded practice (at varying levels of formality) within the architecture and interior design industries. However, recent shifts in actors and agency are occurring at the individual company level across these industry assemblages. For example, Gallup points out that the Millennial workforce desires feedback (Adkins and Rigoni 2016a) and professional development opportunities (Adkins and Rigoni 2016b). Such pressures have an effect across industries, potentially prompting companies to respond with programs to serve those interests.

ELEVATE is an example of a converged assemblage actively generating cultural change within an organization. Leadership and employees innovated within the context of industry best practices related to employee evaluation. ELEVATE was envisioned as a structured meeting process with documentation. It has evolved into a robust program with a responsive process and virtual platform to address employee expectations and desires for professional development. The ELEVATE program continues to evolve. It serves increasingly as a collaborative conduit for many of the firm's formerly disjointed and unsustainable programs (e.g., mentoring, 360 reviews, continuing education credits). ELEVATE, as a program and online tool, has already grown to include multiple reviewers (beyond the originally assigned reviewer) and has begun to integrate goal setting with HKS's new learning management software system. Goals link directly with training materials. It also includes more project-based feedback in the form of developing additional features such as project team and peer reviews. The future trajectory involves continuous development of the ELEVATE program and platform to serve the changing expectations of its users, and integrate those expectations formally into the changing organizational culture of HKS.

CASE 3: CHANGING PARADIGMS IN SPACECRAFT DESIGN

As humans travel farther from the Earth, the design of the spacecraft in which they voyage is of great concern. The development of habitable environments suitable for missions lasting longer than one year has become a priority for NASA in recent years. The Agency's objectives have turned from short-duration missions in near-Earth orbit (e.g., Space Shuttle) to long-duration missions on the International Space Station (ISS), and to Mars and beyond. Spacecraft designers have gravitated toward a more human-centered approach to design as longer missions away from Earth have become the priority. Human-centered design is user-centered, that is, the design meets the needs of the astronaut user. Previously, a technology-driven or machine-centered design had been the norm, in which the user served the operating requirements of the system. This shift among NASA designers is an example of an organizational-culture change within the Agency. I describe and discuss actors that have converged and diverged to prompt this change and offer a case study exemplifying this paradigm shift.

From Technology-Driven to Human-Centered Design

In 2003, experts in space and life sciences at NASA issued a technical memorandum on *Guidelines and Capabilities for Designing Human Missions* (2003). It called for an explicit shift in the design process from technology-driven to human-centered design. Technology-driven design, as defined in the memorandum, is concerned with developing new systems based on new technologies or capabilities with humans considered part of the integrated system (NASA 2003). By contrast, human-centered design revolves around "the human user's needs" (NASA 2003, 69). Although the safety of the human crew has always been a top concern for the Agency, placing astronauts' needs at the beginning of the design process reflects a change in NASA's design culture and in the status and power of the astronaut.

Astronauts, however, are only one component of the assemblage of actors on spacecraft design. Factors related to politics, mission designs, crewmember type, and design trends outside the Agency also converge and diverge to give rise to this shift in the organizational culture. Assemblage theory distributes agency among components of the assemblage (Allen 2011). These heterogeneous parts, ranging from spacefaring nation states to the practice trends of external designers, assemble and reassemble to explain a dynamic cultural change that was once technology-driven, is now human-centered, and may once again become technology-driven, at least in part.

Changes in Politics

Historically, the US space program has existed to serve the practical political goals of the federal government. Logsdon (2002) and Woods (2009) reaffirm that politics, whether through national or personal agendas, was the catalyst for every NASA program from Mercury (1959–1963) to the Space Shuttle (1972–2011) due to the effect of the Cold War on national security concerns. The design paradigm fueling the Apollo-era missions to the Moon was undoubtedly influenced by the need to "win" the "space race." During this time, budgetary resources were virtually unlimited and time, being "first" to reach the Moon, was of the utmost importance. To this day, the Executive Office of the President of the US and the US Congress remain the most prominent political influences on the design of American spacecraft. Every fiscal year, Congress influences the design of spacecraft by appropriating funds for NASA's budget. Once the source of competition, other spacefaring nations have become international partners as national agendas have changed and budgets for space travel have been reduced. Commercial partners also have increased since the end of the Shuttle-era and are expected to grow as NASA sets its sights on Mars.

NASA engineers have responded to years of diminishing resources by adopting a design model of reusability and repurposing. Budget cuts and ever-changing Congressional mandates have led to uncertainty about the space program's future. Consequently, spacecraft is expected to be "designed to the threshold of acceptability" which, in practice, places less importance on the user experience (Compton and Benson 2011, 136). Designing to the acceptable limits is a return to the technology-driven design approach, a reversal that is often at odds with the desire of contemporary human factors engineers and designers to adopt human-centered design. This change can be explained using assemblage theory; it represents an example of the fluidity and temporality of a dynamic organizational culture.

Changes in Mission Designs

Without the external driver of national competitive sprints into space, NASA has had time to focus its missions on scientific advancements. Since the establishment of the ISS, engineers and designers have had more time to give greater consideration to the human element of space missions. Life aboard the ISS means more time living and working in space. A human-centered-design approach reduces risks to human health and performance (NASA 2003). For example, it has become increasingly important for the design of a spacecraft to provide crewmembers with physical exercise, recreation, and privacy (Stuster 1996). Astronauts traveling to Mars expect to spend more than one year in space. New requirements for habitability and new unknowns in spaceflight will arise. Therefore, it is reasonable to predict that human-centered design will continue to play an important part in spacecraft design. However, if coupled with an unforeseen political agenda reducing the time to launch, or if a greater level of risk becomes acceptable to meet the demands of the mission, Mars' spaceship designs may revert back to the technology-driven design approach seen in the Apollo era.

Space travel is dangerous. The Agency has gone to great lengths over the years to create and sustain a culture of safety (Batteau 2003; Vaughan 1996). The Apollo-era design standards were not as robust as they are at present due to the cumulative lessons learned from NASA's history. Apollo-era astronauts operated under a higher level of risk due to the unknowns of exploring the Moon. Astronauts traveling to Mars will experience a new set of unknowns. Mission duration will be longer and the distance traveled by humans will be the farthest ever attempted by a space agency. In near-Earth orbit, risk to human health and performance is high, although it exists within a certain level of safety due to few communication delays and the possibility of a timely return to Earth in the event of an emergency. Predicting all potential risks in spaceflight beyond Earth's orbit is undoubtedly difficult for engineers, designers, physicians, and scientists.

Changes in Crewmember Types

According to historian and sociologist Matthew H. Hersch (2011), astronauts are most often viewed in popular culture as heroes, willing to do whatever it takes to accomplish the mission. The Mercury astronauts inspired the idea of "the right stuff" described by Tom Wolfe (1979) as military test pilots, the best-of-the-best, willing to accept the extraordinary dangers of spaceflight. This perception of heroic astronauts somewhat declined during the Shuttle-era as fewer "firsts" in space captured public attention and the news media focused more on incidents such as when an astronaut caught in a love-triangle drove cross-country allegedly wearing a space diaper (Newman and Hauser 2007). Yet, the 2015 film *The Martian*, based on Andy Weir's 2011 novel, portrayed a heroic astronaut doing the unimaginable to survive for over 500 days alone on Mars, reasserting the hero identity of astronauts within contemporary pop culture.

In astronaut selection today, NASA continues to place a premium on military applicants with "the right stuff." While military pilots are still in demand for spaceflight missions, scientists also have been highly sought as astronaut candidates, particularly since the Apollo era. Since missions to Mars most likely involve longer durations and distances, medical expertise is anticipated to be a highly desirable skill. In addition to physical well-being, the psychological well-being of crewmembers continues to be addressed by researchers interested in human performance and culture (Stuster 1996). Therefore, astronauts with amicable personalities and experience with international partners will be regarded as ideal candidates for a Mars mission since globally diverse crewmembers are certain to be involved. Indeed, it is likely that the diversity in professional and national cultures continues to inspire research and demand attention from spacecraft designers in the future.

Changes in Design Trends (Outside and Inside NASA)

Human factors research has focused historically on architectural, ergonomic, and psychological variables when designing work systems (Wasson 2000; Blomberg 1993; Blomberg and Burrell 2009). Wasson (2000) remarked on the change of design research from machine-centered to user-centered design in the 1980s. This same change also appeared in the work processes of human factors engineers at NASA; over the years, engineers have come to recognize the importance of contextualizing interactions between humans and work systems. Central to this paradigm shift among NASA engineers was the relatively recent introduction of user-centered design (Olson 2010) to the Agency. However, Olson (2010) noted that this paradigm shift at the NASA Johnson Space Center (JSC) was in its infancy as recently as this past decade as engineers began to favor a human-centered-design approach over a technology-centered design.

While NASA's approach to the design of a space habitat in which astronauts live and work can be considered "human-centered" since crew safety is its ultimate concern, crew safety continues to be viewed as part of an integrated system necessary for accomplishing the mission. A full adoption of human-centered design over technology-driven design may not be possible currently since designers do not have full access to their user group. ISS astronauts are a small population, and Mars astronauts have not yet been selected.

Design anthropology offers a solution to this problem through ethnographic research with an analogous population. It is common for ethnographers to conduct research on future-oriented questions to inform the design of products, systems, and communities through iterative and empirical analyses of a similar population. My case study illustrates the application of ethnography to solve a user problem in space. This example demonstrates the design paradigm shift at NASA given that a study was commissioned to investigate a crew's design concerns.

The Privacy Case Study: "Space in Space"[1]

I conducted research for NASA in 2013. My project explored perceptions of privacy and privacy needs among astronauts living and working in space as part of a long-distance, long-duration mission. The study addressed the complex privacy needs through ethnographic research of astronauts and astronaut-like populations (i.e., groups comparable to astronauts in terms of education, health, and age) living and working in isolated, confined, and extreme environments where there are challenges to basic human survival. The study resulted in 25 key findings about perceptions and behaviors relating to privacy in a space habitat environment. Findings included strong evidence that individual, permanent crew quarters are a necessity for long-duration spaceflights—a design requirement previously considered "nice-to-have" rather than a legitimate crew requirement. I also identified a shared meaning or emic understanding of privacy among astronauts that led to insights and recommendations encompassing the astronaut experience and had practical use in the design of space vehicles and habitats.

At the time of my case study, the human factors branch at JSC had adopted the term "user-centered" to describe its work. However, I observed that this change in paradigm was stronger in language than it was in practice. The ethnographic methods and anthropological approach I applied to the privacy study illustrated a holistic, user-centered approach to spacecraft design that was new to the JSC community. I encouraged the astronauts, and other space-industry participants, to play a central role in the research findings and design recommendations by adopting my participants' definitions of privacy. I offered empirical evidence supporting the privacy needs of astronauts as more than a "nice-to-have" design consideration. Due to the privacy study and others such as Jack Stuster's study of astronaut journals (Stuster 2016), the rights and personal needs of astronauts are becoming well-documented and addressed by NASA designers. As a result, spacecraft design is increasingly focused on the human users rather than being purely technology-driven.

The Changing Culture of NASA Design

An assemblage of politics, mission characteristics, crewmembers, and external design trends have agency in the shift from technology-driven to human-centered spacecraft design. Anthropologists, with an understanding of culture and context, can raise awareness of how such elements interact and affect changes in the culture of space exploration. The design culture at NASA is only one aspect of its larger organizational culture, and only one aspect of an even larger culture of space exploration. By utilizing assemblage theory, anthropologists have the ability to anticipate how actor components affect paradigms or practices of an organization, and how changes in the components of an assemblage, in turn, shape culture beyond a single organization. A Mars-era NASA is likely to adopt new norms in usability expectations as future Martians grow to maturity in a world filled with technology developed from a user-centered paradigm and otherworldly unknowns.

DISCUSSION

The work presented in this chapter continues a growing practice of applied anthropology within the broad genre of workplace studies. Building on earlier collective efforts at PARC (Szymanski and Whalen 2011) and Crain and Tashima (2013), our practices have largely occurred independently of other social scientists but within the context of other fields (e.g., management, architecture, engineering). While many of the earlier works were more consistently focused on establishing and exploring the connection of humans to machines/technology (Bloomberg and Burrell 2009; Syzmanski and Whalen 2011), our work emphasizes how technology and design mediate human-to-human interactions and relationships. In all three cases, technology and design are elements for facilitating better, safer, more meaningful interaction.

Additionally, co-creation or participatory design was a common component of those first studies using human-computer interaction and the human-centered paradigm (Syzmanski and Whalen 2011; Suchman 2011). Our work examines organizational structures and processes that are subject to regulation and affected by current industry standards. In the studies we conducted, policy, place, and people heavily influence our end users. Continuing the tradition of *in situ* study of human experience, we find ourselves deeply embedded in the work environment and culture. Our work differs from conventional workplace and organizational change studies since our focus targets understanding the constraints we experience and the agency we exercise as employees of the organizations we seek to change.

Assemblage Theory and Reflexive Analysis

At the beginning of this chapter, we asked the following questions:

- How might metanarratives (macro level) affect an assemblage during cultural change?
- What external (meso level) catalysts facilitate cultural change?
- What internal (micro level) momentum is used to maintain cultural change?

Responding to these questions, we first identify the commonalities across roles and projects. Next, we discuss the diversity of our skills, auxiliary topic knowledge, and methods contributing to our identities as professional anthropologists. Third, we highlight our influence on organizational change by combining reflexive analysis with assemblage theory in each of our organizations—a combination we believe to be unique. Fourth, we illustrate our combined assemblages and synthesize our discussion of assemblage theory's strengths and weaknesses. Finally, we offer some final thoughts on how and why we believe reflexive analysis should be an integral part of assemblage theory and the anthropological literature on organizational-culture change.

Commonalities across Roles and Projects

Each case comprised an organization-wide effort lasting between one and two years to set up and continues as an ongoing effort. The focus for cultural change was internal beliefs and behaviors related to organizational processes. Internal leadership was involved, though there was some variation in levels of support and review. The involvement of outsiders in the change effort included communication with external professionals and experts. The work processes we used were driven by ethnographic research methods and constrained by our project logistics (e.g., time, budget), role, and agency. More detail on commonalities is found on Table 10.1.

Diversity of Skills, Knowledge, and Methods

Despite commonalities across our roles and projects, the diversity of our skills, auxiliary topic knowledge, and methods are quite distinctive (see Table 10.1). Improvement goals highlight specific organizational objectives from environmental, health, and safety compliance, to professional development programs, and spacecraft design. Given the goal diversity, each of us needed to acquire specialized knowledge. Goal diversity also led to particular choices of anthropological methods. All three cases involved work at multiple sites, with the range from three to nearly 30 sites.

We have examined what we have learned, both individually and collectively, during these organizational-change efforts. Reflexive analysis has enabled us to understand attributes of our work better and simultaneously reinforced our professional identities. A striking pattern is the variation across key attributes of our case studies. For example, HVAC/R and HKS cases share an internal directive for intentional culture change while the NASA case focuses on documenting and supporting a cultural-change paradigm that originates outside the organization. The processes we used to influence cultural change differed, as did our roles (whether working as

Table 10.1 Case Study Assemblages: Scales of Observation for Organizational Culture Change

	Micro Level	Meso Level	Macro Level
Commonalities	Organization: Agency, organizational culture, research methods, applied anthropology	Industry: Technology, best practices	Global: Institutions seeking to improve treatment of employees/users and benefits to all
Differences			
• Case 1	Needs assessment, training	Adapting digital analytics and incident reporting	Federal government and regulatory agencies wanting employees safe in the work place
• Case 2	Program evaluation, communication planning	Adapting professional development software	Professional organizations wanting employees to be engaged in their organizations
• Case 3	Reflective observation, documentation	Adapting human factors / design research	Scientific organizations wanting users to be efficient and innovative in their space exploration efforts for the benefit of all humankind

independent professionals largely alone or as integrated team members), and the ways in which we supplemented our knowledge base to understand the project issues. The number, type, and breadth of our organizational relationships also varied ranging from hundreds to few, organizational leadership to members, and organization-wide to function-specific, respectively. We discovered that there was no common definition of anthropological project work or employment type among us.

Reflexivity and Communicating Ethnographic Work

Table 10.2 calls attention to what we can learn from using reflexive analysis as a theoretical framework overlaying assemblage theory to explain organizational change. Our discussion begins with an examination of reflexivity, and then expands to explore self-identity and the politics of the communication of ethnography to participants. Reflexivity is the continuous process of reflection on the research process by examining (1) ourselves as researchers—our concepts, assumptions, and preconceptions, how our views affect research decisions, particularly the selection and wording of questions and communication of insights, and (2) the research relationships—our relationship to the study participants and how the relationship dynamics affect interactions or responses to questions.

Table 10.2   Diverse Anthropologists; Diverse Project Conditions

Case Study	Case 1: HVAC/R INC	Case 2: HKS	Case 3: NASA
Improvement Goals	Environmental, health, and safety compliance	Professional development program within industry standards and software	Spacecraft design within governmental regulations
Auxiliary Topic Knowledge	Environmental, health, and safety regulations	Human-computer interaction design; web application development	Aerospace engineering
Anthropological Methods	Informal Interviews; work group sessions	Focus groups; Pilot testing; Demonstration sessions	In-depth interviews; Observations
Auxiliary Methods	Project and Program Manager; Audits/ reports; Employee training	"Sprint" style, interval development; Usability studies; Executive demonstration sessions/ reviews	Usability studies; Concept testing
Work Environment	20 facilities	26 offices	2 ground-based facilities; 1 space-bound lab

We must have a strong sense of self-identity to be aware of our effects on the research process. While Tables 10.1 and 10.2 pull several of elements of self-identity to the foreground, we highlight the aspect of agency within self-identity. First, we must understand society's effects on our self-identity. According to Beck, Giddens, and Lash's (1994) concept of reflexive modernization, society has become increasingly concerned with the process of modernization since the Industrial Revolution. The process of modernization means that people have become less concerned with problems of controlling fundamental aspects of nature, but turn instead to problems produced by the technological and economic developments they create.

Our cases represent some of the issues found in modern organizations. In Case 1, an HVAC/R company addresses the risks of not maintaining safety compliance; in Case 2, an architecture firm addresses the problem of effective employee engagement and development; and in Case 3, NASA explores the problem of privacy in spaceflight. All three of these problems are not naturally occurring (e.g., basic survival needs on the Earth) but products of modern developments in society. Beck, Giddens, and Lash (1994) refer to this ancillary concern with problems (real, perceived, or potential) as a "risk society" (1994, 2). People are reflexive in the sense that they are aware of potential risks and have the capacity to take action. Society is therefore comprised of individuals who are not only passively shaped by society, but who also actively shape themselves and, consequentially, society.

Giddens' (1991) mechanisms of self-identity bring to light awareness of our agency and potential for impact on our organizations and ourselves. The comparative analysis of our case studies enabled us to identify several key themes that aided our projects. Two of the most important themes were agency and key organizational relationships. In assessing our agency, we found that each of us experienced being both connected and constrained in our roles. Our positions inside our organizations connected us to other key employees—whether during the planning, data gathering, intervention, or reporting phase. We were able to share insights about cultural change as they unfolded because our coworkers and leadership were interested in our projects. This kind of organizational partnering is reminiscent of community-based participatory research (cf. Bolton, Greaves, and Zapata 2010), action research (cf. Tax 1958), and participatory action research (Whyte 1991), and contrasts sharply with the iconic image of the "lone anthropologist."

While we benefitted from our connectedness, working closely with others also acted as constraints on our projects to varying degrees. Constraints involved working against existing company culture, of which we have numerous examples: (1) being told someone had tried the same thing before and it did not work, (2) not having an established budget or schedule for a particular project because the projects we work on are typically at the frontier of a new idea for the company or are seen as secondary to serving our organizational clients, (3) not having to technical structure or processes to support projects, (4) not having full autonomy to enact the projects or aspects of the projects.

To overcome the constraints of our projects, we had to acknowledge the complexity of the communication of ethnographic work. The two most significant challenges of communication were dissemination of new ideas across multi-sited facilities and understanding concepts and terminology to communicate within the domains of our projects and project teams. Both challenges prompted each of us to seek out specialized knowledge. For multi-sited communication, each of us relied on a variety of modes, such as emails, fliers, one-on-ones, town hall announcements, and training sessions to aid in implementing our projects. Leveraging a shared understanding and vocabulary allowed us to communicate insights to colleagues and stakeholders during our projects and to gain feedback, generate buy-in, and iteratively refine our projects.

We find that organizational-culture change requires effective communication first during development and then during implementation. Organizational-culture change involves educating people in organizational settings, developing a common understanding, delivering insights using a shared vocabulary and keeping everyone aligned with the scope and objective of the project. Our positions within the organization were essential for understanding the full cycle of communication from the start of our projects implementation. We sought to identify and respond to challenges arising from discussion of project development and internal communication of organizational changes to end users (e.g., employees). Gaining access to and addressing immediate feedback also helped us to access key organizational relationships. Understanding key organizational relationships resulted from management support to scrutinize the effectiveness of project communication. The agency afforded us through management support facilitated scrutinization of communication both laterally across departments and vertically through the chain of command.

Analyzing the communication of ethnographic work is important because it builds on the relationship between power and knowledge production (Foucault 1980). As Clifford (1986) states, "Ethnographic work has indeed been enmeshed in a world of enduring and changing power inequalities, and it continues to be implicated. It enacts power relations" (1986, 9). Clifford further explains, "'culture' is always relational, an inscription of communicative processes that exist, historically, between subjects in relations of power" (1986, 15).

Analysis of our work calls attention to the inextricable relationship between culture and communication as well as power relations and knowledge production. This relationship is clearly seen in the challenges and inconsistencies between the two. For example, in Cases 1 and 2, insights were generated collaboratively whereas the findings from Case 3 were derived independently and then shared with various colleagues. In Case 1, a disconnect occurred between HR communications (based on applied anthropology insights) and managers accepting new information in an "it's always been done this way" mindset. It was a struggle in Case 2 to communicate changes to the ELE-VATE program for the year the program was active but also still under development. Both cases required clear and compelling internal communication first to (and with) the rest of the project collaborators prior to communicating to other internal entities for consistent messaging and, thus, a level of credibility. In Case 3, significant limitations to implementing a paradigm design shift are highlighted. Lack of access to the end-user population (largely because of small sample size) was an issue. This communication challenge was overcome by engaging analogous populations to gain understanding and then disseminate findings to the engineers and designers.

Assemblages and scales of observation

Returning to assemblage theory, we applied "scales of observation" as a methodological framework for analyzing ethnographic research and cultural change (Desjeux 2016; 2014; 1987). We used this framework to organize our assemblages of reflexive organizational-culture change. We found that focus should be placed on the communication and circulation of ideas, primarily at the micro level. Critical analysis of communication is the key to bring about an intended change. The discipline of anthropology contributed significantly to understanding existing cultural processes and designing interventions to be consistent with them (Orr 1996). Communicating the change process internally is an essential component of organizational change. For Case 1 and 2, communication involved numerous exchanges among organizational members in different job functions and levels, over time, often as part of a two-way exchange of giving and receiving information. Case 3, by comparison, was an individual project focused on communicating with primary stakeholders in the organization during the planning and reporting phases. While Case 3 follows the individual researcher model, it did not actively involve facilitating a formal organizational-change effort. Instead, the act of communicating the ethnographic method and research outcomes was one of the main contributions to cultural change.

Table 10.3 depicts the scales of observation for the assemblages in the three case studies. The three vertical columns represent the three segments of the scales of observation (i.e., micro, meso, and macro levels). Commonalities representing traits shared across cases are shown in the row across the top and the three rows below represent diversity across cases. At the macro level of our shared assemblage, we note the shared intention among institutions to improve treatment of employees. This intention is enacted at the meso level in

Table 10.3 Learning from an Organizational Change Experience Using Reflexive Analysis

Case study	Case 1: HVAC/R INC	Case 2: HKS	Case 3: NASA
Culture change	Assignment; Implementation	Assignment; Implementation	Research
Process used in cultural change	Audit; Needs assessment; Training	Existing state assessment; Program development; Communication planning	Reflective observation; Documentation
Role and Team Dynamic	Individual; Independent change agent	Team member; Internal support services collective	Independent investigator
Agency	Connected/Constrained; Instigator and implementer	Connected/Constrained; Cocreator under leadership guidance	Connected/Constrained; Passive observer; active participant
Involvement of End Users in Guiding Change	Partial: participants interviewed in ideation phases	Partial: focus groups, pilot groups, two cocreator groups (junior staff and managers)	Partial: crewmembers participated in usability studies and concept testing
Key Organizational Relationships	Reports to Chief Operating Officer; Independently responsible for all initiatives regarding EHS compliance for all employees	Integrated with multidisciplinary team	Individual

terms of industry concepts relating to best practices and technologies that can assist in achieving goals. Finally, across cases at the micro level, each organization demonstrated agency through efforts to understand organizational culture, use research methods, and apply anthropology to pursue its objectives. The scales of observation provide a framework with which to explain how actors at each level promote organizational change.

The video "When User Hits Machine" captured the struggle related to the "mundane difficulties of sense-making" of two computer scientists interacting with a user-friendly copier for the first time (Suchman 2011). Given the mundane difficulties of sense-making, we argue in favor of reflexivity as an important path (along with ethnographic skills) toward understanding the development, communication, and adoption of new ideas. We found that we had to assess regularly and often acquire new skills or knowledge outside of anthropology to aid our own understanding of the possibility of cultural change. Such information assisted with the communication of these new ideas to others in terms that were both meaningful and accessible. Others (Darrah and Dornadic 2014; Hepsø 2013) have spoken of the importance of this ongoing skill and knowledge building.

Strengths and Shortcomings of Assemblage Theory

Assemblage theory is an effective framework for identifying key stakeholders and entities of influence at varying levels of intensity, agency, and impact. It helps distinguish patterns emerging in the present that may be useful as organizations prepare for the future. Assemblage theory aids in identifying entities that influence the assemblage at all levels including those individuals and groups who would seek to bring about change. It depicts the relationship of human and nonhuman actors and their agency visually across the assemblage. However, assemblage theory alone may fail to identify those who are actively working in opposition to the assemblage. Reflexive analysis, in addition to assemblage theory, allows us to anticipate the poetics and politics of communicating ethnographic insights, the power we may challenge, and the constraints we may face.

Our cases reveal the complexity of negotiating stakeholder engagement, agency exercised within the assemblage, our professional identities, and our roles as change agents when situated within an organization. By defining these complex frames, we begin to understand how the communication of ideas from one level of the scale of observation to another may catalyze organizational change. An assemblage of stakeholders with agency was necessary for each of us to be part of the change process. However, stakeholders in the assemblage do not necessarily share the same goals, same degree of power and status, or same intent. The assemblage then is a way to visualize a structure, which includes whatever domains the researcher identifies as influential and necessary (e.g., ideas, perceptions, material items) for addressing an issue and all the stakeholders associated with it. But what is lacking from the structure is a clear depiction of how the agency of the anthropologist enables a project to overcome barriers to cultural change.

Conducting Anthropological Research as an Employee

A final, centrally compelling point in our understanding of how we work is the constant negotiation of our identities as insider, outsider, anthropologist, social scientist, ethnographer, change facilitator, and co-designer. Being an organizational "insider" has its advantages. For example, it is typically easier to gain extended access to your participants and collaborators. Additionally, most organizations have training programs so that form of job shadowing or on-the-job training is not uncommon for those being trained/exposed to internal processes (Hepsø 2013). However, it is also challenging to work as an insider employee and as an anthropologist, consistently negotiating dual identities with ourselves and with members of our organization. Hepsø describes these two identities as both "a disciplinary anthropological identity that comes from many years of training; [an employee identity tied to] … the company's work culture with its own expectations and goals" (2013, 158).

Often our employers do not fully understand our disciplinary training, and as a result our methods and perspectives are sometimes underestimated or miscommunicated. In some cases our formal, academic training is not wholly adequate to address a situation or engage with a group or in a project. Additionally, our identity within our projects often oscillates between insider and outsider depending on what information and/or recommendations need to be communicated, and to whom. Rethinking our approach to communication is consistently a top challenge in our work as we strive to serve as researchers and change-facilitators. In this role, we are positioned to varying extents as documenters, listeners, communicators, and implementers of innovations and cultural shifts.

This chapter highlights similarities and differences across our cases as applied anthropologists, working within dynamic organizations on efforts that facilitate cultural change. Each case varies in how directly each anthropologist participates in and facilitates these efforts. However, we each ask the question: What are the long-term effects of our work on our organizations? The literature on assemblage theory seems to converge around the question of what holds an assemblage together or creates disruption (Allen 2011). Work practice studies have evolved to focus on ethnography within corporations, where several practitioners have begun to call for a critical, reflexive analysis of how anthropologists do ethnography. We have learned the value of acquiring new tools, skills, and knowledge outside of anthropology to be most effective. Moreover, to assist in organizational transformation, we have found it necessary to transform ourselves. Thus, we suggest extending beyond assemblage theory as a strong tool for understanding change to consider continual, critical, reflexive analysis.

NOTES

1. This work was funded by the National Space Biomedical Research Institute via NASA Cooperative Agreement NCC 9–58.
2. We thank our organizations—HVAC/R, HKS, and NASA—for allowing us to share their insights and stories related to cultural change.

REFERENCES

Adkins, Amy and Brandon Rigoni. 2016a. "Manager: Millennial Want Feedback, But Won't Ask for It." June 2, 2016. http://www.gallup.com/businessjournal/192038/managers-millennials-feedback-won-ask.aspx.
———. 2016b. "Millennials Want Jobs to Be Development Opportunities." June 30, 2016. http://www.gallup.com/businessjournal/193274/millennials-jobs-development-opportunities.aspx.
Allen, John. "Powerful assemblages?" *Area* 43, no. 2 (2011): 154–157.
Batteau, Allen W. "A Perfect Report: Culture and NASA's Analysis of the Columbia Space Shuttle Tragedy." Paper presented at the American Anthropological Association Annual Meetings, 2003.
Beck, Ulrich, Anthony Giddens and Scott Lash, eds. "Living in a post-traditional society." In *Reflexive modernization: Politics, tradition and aesthetics in the modern social order,* 56–109. Cambridge, MA: Polity Press, 1994.
Beers, Robin. "Chapter 2: Humanizing organizations: Researchers as knowledge brokers and change agents." In *Collaborative Ethnography in Business Environments, 11–25.* Edited by Maryann McCabe. Routledge: New York, New York, 2017.
Blomberg, Jeanette, and Mark Burrell. "An ethnographic approach to design." In *Human-computer interaction: Development Process,* 71–94. Edited by Andrew Sears and Julie A. Jacko. CRC Press an impress of Taylor & Francis: Boca Raton, 2009.
Bolton, R., T. Greaves, and F. Zapata, eds. *Vicos and beyond: a half century of applying anthropology in Peru.* Lanham, MD: AltaMira Press, 2011.
Briody, Elizabeth, Robert T. Trotter II, and Tracy Meerwarth. *Transforming Culture: Creating and Sustaining Effective Organizations.* New York: Palgrave Macmillan, 2010.
Caulkins, D. Douglas and Ann T. Jordan, eds. *A Companion to Organizational Anthropology.* Malden, MA: Blackwell Publishing Ltd, 2013.

Cefkin, M., ed. *Ethnography and the Corporate Encounter: Reflections on Research in and of Corporations.* New York, NY: Berghahn Books, 2009.

Cefkin, Melissa. "Work Practice Studies as Anthropology." In *Handbook of Anthropology in Business,* 284–298. Edited by Rita Denny and Patricia Sunderland. California: Left Coast Press, 2014.

Cefkin, Melissa. "Limits to Speed Ethnography." In *Advancing Ethnography in Corporate Environments: Challenges and Emerging Opportunities,* 108–121. Edited by Brigitte Jordan. Walnut Creek CA: Left Coast Press, 2013.

———. Compton, W. David, and Charles D. Benson. *Living and working in space: A history of Skylab,* vol. 4208 (New York, NY: Dover Publications, 2011).

Clifford, James. "Introduction: Partial Truths," In Writing Culture: The Poetics and Politics of Ethnography, 1–26. Edited by James Clifford and George E. Marcus. Berkeley: University of California Press. 1986.

Crain, Cathleen and Niel Tashima. "An Anthropologically Based Consulting Firm," In *A Handbook of Practicing Anthropology,* 125–136. Edited by Riall W. Nolan. Malden, MA: Wiley-Blackwell, 2013.

Darrah, Charles N. and Alicia Dornadic. "Doing Anthropology, Doing Business." In *Handbook of Anthropology in Business,* 722–736. Edited by Rita Denny and Patricia Sunderland. Walnut Creek, California: Left Coast Press, 2014.

Desjeux, Dominique. "The itinerary approach of a business anthropologist: between mobility, diversity and networks." *Journal of Business Anthropology* 5, no. 1 (2016): 64–76.

———. "Professional anthropology and training in France." In *Handbook of Anthropology in Business,* 100–115. Edited by Rita Denny and Patricia Sunderland. Walnut Creek, CA: Left Coast Press, 2014.

———. *Scales of observation or the discovery of the discontinuity of observation between the macrosocial and the microsocial scales.* Unpublished manuscript. Translated from the French by D. Desjeux. 1987.

Federal Motor Carrier Safety Administration. "Electronic Logging Device." Last modified September 03, 2015. Accessed February 14, 2017. https://www.fmcsa.dot.gov/hours-service/elds/electronic-logging-devices.

Fiske, S.J., L.A. Bennett, P. Ensworth, T. Redding, and K. Brondo. "The changing face of anthropology: anthropology masters reflect on education, careers, and professional organizations." AAA/CoPAPIA 2009 Anthropology MA Career Survey. Arlington, VA: American Anthropological Association, 2010.

Foucault, Michel. *Power / knowledge: Selected interviews and Other Writings, 1972–1977.* Edited by Colin Tr. Gordon. New York: Harvester Wheatsheaf, 1980.

Giddens, Anthony. *Modernity and self-identity.* Stanford: Stanford University Press, 1991.

Ginsberg, D. "'AAA members outside the academy,' 2016 Membership Survey, Report #2," 1–15. Arlington, VA: American Anthropological Association, 2016.

Haukelid, K. "Theories of (safety) culture revisited—An anthropological approach." *Safety Science* 46, no. 3 (March 2008): 413–426.

Hepsø, Vidar. "Doing Corporate Ethnography as an Insider (Employee)." In *Advancing Ethnography in Corporate Environments: Challenges and Emerging*

Opportunities, 151–162. Edited by Brigitte Jordan. Walnut Creek, California: Left Coast Press, 2013.

Hersch, Matthew H. "Return of the Lost Spaceman: America's Astronauts in Popular Culture, 1959–2006." *The Journal of Popular Culture* 44, no. 1 (2011): 73–92.

Jordan, Ann T. *Business Anthropology.* Long Grove, IL: Waveland Press, 2013a.

Jordan, Brigitte. Introduction to *Advancing Ethnography in Corporate Environments: Challenges and Emerging Opportunities,* 7–22. Edited by Brigitte Jordan. Walnut Creek, California: Left Coast Press, 2013b.

Krause-Jensen, Jakob. *Flexible Firm: the Design of Culture at Bang & Olufsen.* New York: Berghahn, 2010.

Logsdon, John M. "The Development of International Space Cooperation." In *Exploring the Unknown: Selected Documents in the History of the US Civil Space Program,* 1–57. Edited by J.M. Logsdon. Vol. 1: The University of Chicago Press on behalf of The History of Science Society, 2002.

McCabe, M., ed. *Collaborative Ethnography in Business Environments.* London, UK: Taylor & Francis, 2017.

National Aeronautics and Space Administration (NASA). "Guidelines and Capabilities for Designing Human Missions." NASA/TM–2003–210785 (2013). Accessed February 10, 2017. http://spacecraft.ssl.umd.edu/design_lib/TM-2003-210785.pdf.

NASA Lyndon B. Johnson Space Center. "Behavioral Issues Associated With Long Duration Space Expeditions: Review and Analysis of Astronaut Journals Experiment 01–E104 Journals Phase 2 Final Report." Last modified August 2016. Accessed June 20, 2017. https://ston.jsc.nasa.gov/collections/TRS/_techrep/TM-2016-218603.pdf.

Newman, Maria and Christine Hauser. "Astronaut Charged With Attempted Murder." *New York Times,* February 6, 2007. Accessed June 20, 2017. http://www.nytimes.com/2007/02/06/us/06cnd-astronaut.html.

Nolan, R.W., ed. *A Handbook of Practicing Anthropology.* Malden, MA: Wiley-Blackwell, 2013.

Olson, Valerie A. "American extreme: An ethnography of astronautical visions and ecologies." PhD diss., Rice University, 2010.

Orr, Julian E. *Talking About Machines: An Ethnography of a Modern Job.* ILR Press an imprint of Cornell University Press: Ithaca and London, 1996.

Rhea, Darryl. "Bringing Clarity to the "Fuzzy Front End": A Predictable Process for Innovation". In *Design Research: Methods and Perspectives.* Edited by Brenda Laurel. 145–154. Cambridge: MIT Press, 2003.

Stuster, Jack W. *Bold Endeavors: Lessons from Polar and Space Exploration.* Annapolis, MD: Naval Institute Press, 1996.

Suchman, Lucy. "Work Practice and Technology: A Retrospective." In *Making Work Visible: Ethnographically Grounded Case Studies of Work Practice,* 21–33. Edited by M.H. Szymanski and J. Whalen. New York: Cambridge University Press, 2011.

Townley, Barbara. "The Institutional Logic of Performance Appraisal." *Organizational Studies* 18, no. 2 (1997): 261–285.

Tax, S. "The Fox Project." *Human Organization* 17, no. 1 (Spring, 1958): 17–19.

Vaughan, Diane. "Risk, Work Group Culture, and the Normalization of Deviance." In *The Challenger Launch Decision*, 77–118. Chicago: University of Chicago, 1996.

Wasson, Christina. "Ethnography in the Field of Design." Human Organization 59, no. 4 (2000): 377–388.

Whyte, W. F. *Participatory Action Research*. Newbury Park, CA: Sage, 1991.

Wilkie, Dana. "Is the Annual Performance Review Dead?" Last modified August 19, 2015. Accessed May 11, 2017. https://www.shrm.org/resourcesandtools/hr-topics/employee-relations/pages/performance-reviews-are-dead.aspx.

Wolfe, Tom. *The Right Stuff*. New York, NY: Farrar, Straus and Giroux, 1979.

Woods, Brian. "A political history of NASA's space shuttle: the development years, 1972–1982." In *Space Travel and Culture: From Apollo to Space Tourism*. Edited by M.P.a.D. Bell. West Sussex: Wiley-Blackwell, The Sociological Review, 2009.

Conclusion

Snapshots in Time: Assemblage Theory's Usefulness for Business Anthropology

Elizabeth K. Briody

Cultural change is an important topic of theoretical interest and one that is particularly relevant to organizational and consumer settings where people engage in the production, sale, and consumption of products and services. It is also an area that is ripe for new insights to enable improved understanding of the processes associated with issues of everyday life and work, that is, the shifts in beliefs, decisions, activities, material items, and the environment. In chapter 1, we presented our definition of *cultural change* as a cohesive pattern of change in an organizational culture or in a consumer community culture experiencing a shift in practices, identity and meaning of things. We also introduced our three goals for the book:

1. Theorize cultural changes we are witnessing as business anthropologists
2. Advance agency as a catalyst of change complementing other theoretical perspectives
3. Apply and develop assemblage theory further to explain cultural change.

Each of these questions is explored in this concluding chapter.

BUSINESS ANTHROPOLOGY ON CULTURAL CHANGE

Using a business anthropology perspective to document and explain cultural change presupposes the integration of several important characteristics of anthropology:

- Investigating the concept of culture in particular contexts; we define *culture* as "everything that people have, think, and do as members of their society" (Ferraro and Briody 2017, 10).
- Engaging in the comparison of cultural similarities and differences
- Framing the cultural issues holistically across time and space
- Combining emic (insider) and etic (outsider) understandings
- Applying ethnographic methodology, incorporating theory.

It also involves narrowing the focus of the investigation to emphasize the behavior in and surrounding organizations, including the behavior of those using the products and services of those organizations. The domain of business anthropology is a bit of a misnomer since it encompasses all types of organizations, not simply private sector organizations. This expansion in the domain is due to the commonalities shared across organizational types (e.g., government agency, nonprofit, family business) as *organizations,* compared with the vast majority of anthropological studies which are linked with communities. The ten articles in the book (comprising 12 cases) are tied to organizations in some way—some more strongly than others.

Capturing the Assemblage

All of the chapters employ assemblage theory as a point of departure. The authors specify some of the key features of assemblage theory, in light of their own case studies. For example, the authors emphasize the heterogeneity, contingency, complexity, and/or constant movement within the assemblages. In reading through the cases, it is clear that the various components are often unstable, temporary, fragile, and sometimes unpredictable. Such descriptors serve to prepare the reader for the ongoing disruption in particular components and alignments, as well as the overall evolution of a given assemblage over time.

The majority of the authors use a combination of two mechanisms to reveal cultural change: narratives and illustrations. The narratives are descriptive and explanatory, offering specifics about decision-making, timing, values, and pace of change, among a host of other details. Most authors create at least one illustration, and sometimes more, to depict their assemblage at a particular point in time. Illustrations are a visually powerful way of conveying cultural features and their interconnections. The illustrations vary both in form and in content, depending on the cultural features of the case and the graphical way in which the author(s) has opted to portray the assemblage.

For example, in terms of form, Newton (chapter 9) uses one-way arrows tied to the factors affecting the Lighthouse Partnership. In terms of content, Newton highlights the "Clients," "Mobile application," "Employees,"

"Funder expectations," "Guiding principles," and "Design process." As such, his assemblage incorporates people, objects, practices, discourses, and institutions (Arnould and Thompson 2015; Collier and Ong 2005; Latour 2005). Watts-Englert, Szymanski and Wall (chapter 5) offer a different visual in which "People" and "Technology" are connected by a double-sided arrow. "Technology" is linked with both "Software" and "Tools/Devices," while "People" is not connected to anything specifically. However, five factors (and multiple subfactors) are shown facilitating the adoption of smart devices, the subject of their chapter: "Discourses," "Practices," "Ideas," "Organizations," and "Trajectories." Watts-Englert and her colleagues describe the relationship between "People" and "Technology" in the text, referring to a "mutual identity … a new type of assemblage in which the person and the device have become intertwined in a co-evolving relationship." Thus, the illustrations used in the book are enhanced and further explained in the narratives.

While the illustrations stand out, the authors also use text to describe and explain the process of change and/or sequence of particular changes associated with their cases. In other words, they target *how* cultural change occurs. Especially effective are narratives accompanied by contrasting illustrations that document the cultural change over time. Desjeux and Ma (chapter 7), for example, compare the consumption of nonalcoholic beverages in the traditional system as well as currently. The authors discuss three primary domains identified with drink consumption: "Views," "People," and "Situations." In the illustration of the traditional system, each domain is linked to subdomains (e.g., "Situations" are tied to "Work" and "Home"), and further connected to other elements (e.g., "Home" is linked with "Drink-making items at home" and "Objects").

Desjeux and Ma's second illustration, depicting modern developments in the drink assemblage, is far more complex. It contains all of the elements of the traditional system, supplemented with the commercial production of beverages. "Consumption" and "Commercial Production" are connected by a double-sided arrow. "Commercial Production" is linked with the "Drinks company," which is linked with the "Anthropologists" conducting the study for the firm. It is also linked with "Machines and shops outside" where commercially produced beverages are sold. "Views" in the traditional system now includes the element of "Western influence" while "Situations" now include both "Restaurant" and "Transport" in addition to the earlier depictions of "Home" and "Work." These contrasting portrayals can be interpreted largely on their own, although the chapter provides much supporting detail. The comparison exposes the differences between the two (i.e., the gap) that relies on the narrative for elucidation. The availability of options open to consumers has increased significantly since the introduction of commercial drinks described in Desjeux and Ma's chapter. In response, "Confucianism and obedience," "Health concerns," and "Symbolic hot and cold" are all undergoing significant change.

The Change Trajectory

A trajectory is a path or route through time or space. It represents the direction, typically of an object, as it progresses or changes its course. In assemblage theory, a trajectory has to do with the likely path that a change might take. It is based on the current state, situated in historical context, and directed toward the future. Change trajectories are particularly relevant for changes in the marketplaces of global society.

Design anthropology, a subset of business anthropology, prides itself on its ability to shape both current and future states. Considered a transdisciplinary field, design anthropology involves collaborative work in an attempt to develop responsible designs. Miller (chapter 4) offers several examples of "future-making" in which social robots and "cobots" (collaborative robots) are central; robots with attributes of human faces work alongside workers in factories or interact with people in empathetic ways. Miller points out the change trajectory indicating, "*what is* might be transformed into *what might be.*" Hitch (chapter 1), also working in design, notes the DRIP irrigation program's strong acceptance among Cambodian farmers and its heightened sales. DRIP is a collaborative endeavor involving anthropologists, designers, farmers, and salespeople. She suggests that the "purchase of DRIP can set a trajectory of change toward the possible future" of secondary education since parents can afford to send their youth to high school. One other design case, written by NASA employee Aiken (chapter 10), raises issues regarding astronaut privacy on long-duration space flights of the future. She discovers that privacy is not simply "nice-to-have" but essential for the crew.

Rijsberman (chapter 2) shows that students of all ages are expressing interest in the EdTech field, in part because traditional higher education has neither dealt adequately with its costs, nor narrowed the gap between education and employment requirements. Indeed, the trajectory is toward EdTech with its online offerings, open access courses (e.g., MOOCs), and boot camp experiences, and away from the traditional forms of on-campus higher education. In their studies of smart devices, Watts-Englert, Szymanksi, and Wall identify three types of trajectories:

- Proximity trajectory in which keeping a device on oneself has evolved into smart watches
- Intimacy trajectory in which recommendations for personal change appear in areas of exercise and food consumption
- Interpersonal connection trajectory in which Facebook and multiplayer games may morph into real-time interaction among people located in different places.

The research by Watts-Englert and her colleagues highlights the multiple paths that a cultural change may inspire.

Emergence of Cultural Themes

The identification of key cultural themes is another characteristic of anthropology and business anthropology. These themes often appear at the interface of production and consumption. Onomake's study of brokerage since precolonial times in Nigeria (chapter 8) is a case in point in which the broker produces and the buyer of services consumes. She emphasizes relationship building and indispensability as salient in brokerage processes. She also points out that one of the two associations helpful in the formation of Nigerian-Chinese business connections seems to recognize the value of stressing cultural themes; it publicizes its "authenticity" based on its founder's early work as a diplomat in China. The multiple studies on which Delcore reports (chapter 3) underscore the value of equity among college students, irrespective of socioeconomic status. He also describes student engagement as an outcome of a changed pedagogy in which tablets feature prominently.

Giving voice to the study participants is another important theme that distinguishes the work of anthropologists from other disciplines in general. Discovering and conveying emic views using study participant words and behaviors as examples provide a genuine and rich source of evidence. All of the authors employ this anthropological feature. For example, Ramer's case (chapter 10) repeatedly draws on employee views to shape and refine the workings of the professional development program ELEVATE at her global architectural firm. The ELEVATE team is both producer and consumer (as employees) of the new program. Similarly, Pahl's case (also part of chapter 10) demonstrates the importance of learning from HVAC/R employees when putting a firm-wide safety-tracking program in place. Pahl, and his HVAC/R colleagues working closely with him, are both producers and consumers of the fruits of the safety initiative.

By contrast, Bhattacharyya and Belk's contribution (chapter 6) documents reactions to various types of technology—identified as "electricity, television, computers, fan, phone, cooking gas, kerosene, medicines"—related to low-income Indian residents in Kolkata and New Delhi. Several of their study participants interface with individuals, community organizations, and government agencies to gain access to or use particular technologies. In one dispirited instance, a study participant relays: "Yet we have to go to that office, day after day, smiling with our teeth out, talking gently, gently, trying to reason with them. Otherwise, if they wish, they can make things difficult and then there will be no cooking gas in the house for months." A powerful quotation like this has the virtue of conveying the frustration, strategy, and anticipated result should their planned visits to the government office fail. As a consumer, this study participant is largely at the mercy of the service provider, revealing the difficulties associated with daily survival for those with the lowest levels of income.

In summary, we note that cultural change is a process that happens in different ways, linked with diverse assemblage forms, and with variation in pace and effects. McCabe's (Introduction) rhizome metaphor is apt because of its "continuous and unpredictable movement" in its "roots and shoots." The cultural change process can

- Be prompted by a variety of conditions such as safety regulations (Pahl— chapter 10) or technological capabilities (Miller—chapter 4)
- Be planned, such as through a design process (Hitch—chapter 1), though unexpected circumstances may arise such as the inflated scores on the HKS employee self-assessment (Ramer—chapter 10)
- Be affected both by the past as in brokerage continuity over time (Onomake—chapter 8), and by the present such as a focus on the user in recent industry trends (Watts-Englert et al.—chapter 5; Aiken—chapter 10)
- Align with other change processes such as MOOCs and data science boot camps (Rijsberman—chapter 2) and in opposition to existing practices (e.g., degreed university programs)
- Change the way time is perceived including the fact that micro-moments matter (Watts-Englert et al.—chapter 5)
- Be evaluated for its merits along a continuum from negative (e.g., personal growth homework) to positive (e.g., focus in-school on ACT scores and scholarships) as in Newton's case (chapter 9)
- Lead to outcomes over varying time frames: in the nearer term, low-income women's rejection of certain technology (Bhattacharyya and Belk—chapter 6), and in the longer term, hybrids as the student device of choice for schoolwork (Delcore—chapter 3). And depending on the generation to which people belong, values and behaviors surrounding soda consumption have been and are in the process of being modified (Desjeux and Ma—chapter 7).

AGENCY AS A CATALYST OF CULTURAL CHANGE

Agency at Work

The contributions in this book demonstrate the salience of agency as a critical element in the process of cultural change. McCabe (Introduction) sees agency as a "theoretical provocateur in cultural change." Agency is the capability or capacity to perceive and act. It can stimulate, strengthen, maintain, weaken, or arrest the change process. Intentions and/or planned actions can have an impact—large or small—and affect the development, form, and function of the assemblage. Indeed, Ervin (2015, 6) points out that humans can "shape their circumstances" through various means.

Other writers such as Latour indicate that objects and ideas may have agency and contribute to the creation of meaning. A case in point is the emergence of the Internet of Things, fostered by Big Data and connected devices, as Miller describes (chapter 4). She states, "Objects acquire agency within social networks through M2M (machine-to-machine) communication" often decreasing the need for human workers. Cobots, or collaborative robots like Sawyer, have selected human features (e.g., eyes). Sawyer works alongside employees in the completion of manufacturing tasks. A carebot, or social robot that looks like a doll, represents another example of the Internet of Things. *Ik ben Alice* is designed to be a caring, interactive presence in an elder's residence. Similar kinds of innovative robots with "lifelike personalities" (Rose 2014, 37) are often viewed in positive ways by those interacting with them.

Tensions Unpacked

An assemblage may have a myriad of agentic forces colliding, aligning, and competing at any given point in time and over time. These forces influence the assemblage's general trajectory, as well as specific, localized changes to a particular component. Interconnections link certain components of the assemblage together—however briefly or tangentially, eagerly or resiliently. Often, however, tensions arise as shifts in the locus of power within the assemblage are affected. Pahl (chapter 10) describes his experience in trying to get branch managers to compare the safety manual (describing ideal conditions) with any safety hazards in their locations. Upon return to their facilities, Pahl finds that no branch manager took any action to address safety issues. After speaking with the branch managers, Pahl comes to realize that safety is in direct competition with sales, and that senior leaders have no appetite for creating unambiguous reporting relationships throughout the firm. These constraints lead Pahl to seize the opportunity and use his agency. He is able to develop and implement a plan and overcome both branch manager and senior leadership resistance.

Two reactions surfaced across the contributors' cases related to emerging tensions. First, the tensions continue unresolved. This response is evident in several cases, creating a certain level of ambiguity about both the present and the future. In the Rijsberman case (chapter 2), the gap between traditional higher education and EdTech remains wide. Matriculating students pursuing an on-campus degree is a known and recognized model in contrast to EdTech learning alternatives that are virtual, online, and not taught exclusively by academics. Students appreciate the career-oriented nature of EdTech as well as its affordability, though they find that there is no way currently to accumulate course credit and have that credit recognized by a traditional institution of higher education. The tensions are palpable especially for learners constrained by previous educational debt and/or family situations, and those eager to engage in a new field. Such students wonder what action they should take since they perceive they are "stuck" with no educational solution to address all of their concerns. Despite their agency, their future career path is shrouded in ambiguity.

Watts-Englert, Szymanski, and Wall (chapter 5) raise some interesting issues around the use of smart devices. The authors caution about the "potential over-reliance on and attachment to technology, the impacts on personal interactions, and implications for cultural change." The tensions here relate to the role of technology in one's life: the necessity of staying on top of new information, responding to that information quickly, and prioritizing it, to a certain extent, over face-to-face encounters. The resulting behaviors have been termed "addictive" with wide-ranging consequences for how people relate to each other, including changes in the cultural rules surrounding interactions. Difficulty arises particularly when the so-called addictive behavior is manifest in front of those not accustomed to the integration of smart device technology with the simple art of conversation. Texting while talking to someone can be perceived as both unusual and rude by one party, and normal by another. The perceptions and actions (i.e., agency) of both parties are at odds with each other.

A second response to a rise in tensions is accommodation. Desjeux and Ma (chapter 7) describe several accommodations made in Chinese culture to the introduction of commercial beverages. Many cultural rules are subject to revision due to the characteristics of these sweet, tasty, and cold drinks whose meanings are considered categorically different from drinks made at home and perceived to be "healthy, nutritious, and purifying for the body." The authors indicate that each member of the family "maneuvers around the rules, trying not to exceed the social limits so as to avoid sparking too many conflicts." For example, a person might choose a beverage that has a pleasant taste and is not considered damaging to one's health. Another adaptation involves allowing one's children pocket money to purchase a soda from time to time. A third accommodation entails the redefinition of situations in which one is permitted to consume a commercial drink (e.g., after sports, on the way home from work). Thus, we see that the variety of acceptable drinks, and the places in which they may be consumed, are widening in China due to the agency of both the commercial drink manufacturers and the specific types of individual consumers.

Phases in the Life Course of the Assemblage

An important characteristic of an assemblage according to Allen (2011) is that its components somehow manage to cohere without necessarily representing a coherent whole. The nature of an assemblage, particularly its fluidity and temporality, ensures it is changeable. The convergences and divergences can be a moving target, waxing and waning—sometimes unexpectedly and quickly, at other times predictably and gradually, and in still other instances, some variation of these attributes. What enables that process to occur: different or similar interests, complementary or opposing discourses, power disparities, shared beliefs and mutual benefits, or something else? Moreover, under what conditions do assemblage components shift and recede?

We know that agency plays a critical role in shaping the assemblage as it changes over time. It emerges at various points in an assemblage's evolution, associated with one or more human actors or with nonhuman actors. Notable about the assemblages in this collection is that they reveal instances of agency in the life course of an assemblage. Watts-Englert and her colleagues (chapter 5), for example, portray a changing assemblage in the evolution of smart devices. The agency of the ongoing feedback from users to developers contributes to the changes in the technology, technology that attempts to be responsive to user requests for change.

One might suspect that nothing stabilizes long enough for life course stages to be identified. However, we suggest that detectable "phases" may appear ranging from momentary to enduring, or may not exist at all, as indicated in the section labeled "Beyond the Realm of Possibility." The phases are useful in helping us to understand the evolution of assemblages as they form, change, and dissolve in both time and space.

Start-up

Agency is visible in what might be considered the start-up phase of an assemblage: the preparation and implementation of the DRIP irrigation system with the iDE anthropologists, designers, farmers, business analysts, and strategists working together. Indeed, Hitch (chapter 1) emphasizes that they, in conjunction with the farming practices and products "become embodiments and agents of hope." The Pahl case (chapter 10) is also indicative of the formation of an assemblage. Pahl seems to have been in the right place at the right time at HVAC/R. Safety becomes his purview, safety education his passion, and safety hazard investigation and resolution his focus.

Strengthening

Assemblages go through periods of strengthening. Technology has led to alternative choices to higher education for those seeking new knowledge and skills. Rijsberman (chapter 2) stresses the various options including the popular data science boot camps and online courses. Ramer (chapter 10) indicates "tighter convergence within the assemblage" when content and functionality efforts aligned during ELEVATE's development. An interdependency is created between these two domains and the HKS employees associated with them. Similarly, Onomake emphasizes the establishment of the NCBC in the early 2000s, which reinforces the new organizational brokerage pattern in place since NCFA's creation in 1994. Together these associations reflect the change from individual brokers to a mixed model.

Continuity

Periods of staying the course appear when a key component of an assemblage is retained. Emblematic of this pattern is the emphasis on tablets at the core of educational instruction and learning as Delcore (chapter 3) describes. Even when openly criticized, Fresno State's administrators are unwilling to acknowledge the evidence against tablets and in favor of alternative devices. It is likely they are not prepared to take a position against the tablet initiative headed by their boss, the university president. It takes a few years before policy flexibility prevails and any official list of approved devices disappears. Ironically, the DISCOVERe initiative continues, still referenced as the "tablet initiative." A different kind of continuity is suggested in Aiken's NASA case (chapter 10). User-centered approach to design is likely to carry forward given the anticipated duration of future space travel. Aiken's research demonstrates the importance of privacy in the design of future spacecraft so that astronaut living conditions will not detract from their effectiveness and productivity.

Weakening

Assemblages, and the components within them, can falter. A case in point is Newton's (chapter 9). The partnership between Lighthouse and the CPC weakens when student agency largely rejected the Needle application because of its "personal development" content rather than content specifically targeting improvement in ACT scores and scholarship acquisition. Fortunately, CPC responds quickly and prepares more appealing content for Needle's student users. However, we do not know if the new Needle content is ever tested again with a new cohort of high school students. We are left to wonder if this modification in the assemblage leads to greater student success or if Needle is abandoned completely. The case presented by Desjeux and Ma (chapter 7) also indicates weakening in the traditional drink assemblage. No longer are drinks only prepared at home for consumption during the day. Today, both traditional and commercial beverages are in place; greater choice in beverage consumption is available and accessible—at least to some age groups in China.

Disappearance

Miller (chapter 4) documents changes in the Internet assemblage over time. She writes of three waves: the first involving a fixed Internet, the second involving a mobile Internet, and the third involving an Internet of Things. For all practical purposes, the fixed Internet has vanished, an artifact of history. It has since been superseded by the second wave and the emerging third wave.

Beyond the Realm of Possibility

An assemblage can ignore, or at best, fail to appeal to certain segments of the population as occurred in Bhattacharyya and Belk's case (chapter 6). The authors show the effects of technology on low-income individuals and households. Particularly revealing are the differences in gender use of computer technology in Indian society. Women point out how busy their daily lives are, given the combination of their household and paid work responsibilities. As one woman expresses: "If people like us (women) sit around with things like those (laptops), how will things [life] work, tell me?" Technology, in this case, has bypassed a significant part of the population that has neither the time nor the resources to access it. For them, using the technology is both inconceivable and unattainable. As a result, they do not even attempt to access it.

Agency Complementarity with Other Theoretical Perspectives

The cases in this book demonstrate that assemblage theory, with agency as its hallmark, align well with other theoretical perspectives. McCabe (Introduction) suggests that agency has the potential to add "explanatory power to theories of cultural change." Note the range of theoretical literature used in conjunction with agency in our contributors' chapters. This book offers numerous examples from Bourdieu's (1977a; 1977b) practice theory to Foucault's (1978) emphasis on power, and from work practice and technology studies (Orr 1996; Suchman 2011; Cefkin 2014) to studies of hope and morality (e.g., Crapanzano 2003; Miyazaki, 2004).

Perhaps one reason for agency's complementarity with other theoretical orientations is its ability to give voice to particular human and nonhuman actors in a way that adds insight at the micro level of ethnographic analysis. Agency is able to make visible existing patterns of actor behavior without contradicting or being dismissive of cornerstone concepts associated with work practice studies, for example. Another possibility is that 11 of the 16 authors have been actively engaged in the research and implementation of recommendations or interventions. Given that situation, agency becomes particularly salient as the researchers-turned-implementers seek to deliver solutions to address preexisting issues.

ASSEMBLAGE THEORY'S FUTURE POTENTIAL FOR CULTURAL CHANGE

Learning for the Future

Learning from research results and from past experiences is critical for advancing a field of study, for posing new questions to explore, and for improving researcher capabilities. Those using assemblage theory have concentrated largely on identifying attributes of the assemblage—an ever-changing form, embedded with disparate components, all of which exercise agency. The cases in this book attest to the heterogeneity, instability, and flows connected to assemblages. The components represent varied interests, situations, beliefs, and perceptions with actors converging and diverging over time, negotiating and adapting, existing in harmony and in tension, and being coherent and incoherent. The cases illustrate how people and organizations interact with things and give meaning to them. Collectively, they document the value of applying assemblage theory to the process of cultural change. They offer insightful descriptions, revealing visualizations, compelling explanations, and in 10 of the 12 cases, targeted direction in planning for cultural change in global organizations and marketplaces.

Yet, how are we learning for the future? The cases offer three important mechanisms for learning from the results. First, visual media is a powerful way of learning. The drawings represented in this book, along with other visuals, leave their mark. They represent one type of output from the cases—one that helps us grasp the key features of an assemblage in picture form, preserving it as part of the documentary record. For example, the visual assemblage by Watts-Englert and her colleagues (chapter 5) highlights the two-way connection between people and technology, in which each component influences the other. Some of the chapters (Miller—chapter 4, Onomake—chapter 8, and Newton—chapter 9) incorporate multiple drawings illustrating the changes that transpired over time, while others make comparisons with alternate assemblages at the same point in time (Hitch—chapter 1, Bhattacharyya and Belk—chapter 6, and Desjeux and Ma—chapter 7) or capture changes over time in one assemblage (Delcore—chapter 3).

A second mechanism for learning is mentioned in two of the chapters. Both the Ramer (chapter 10) and Aiken (chapter 10) cases build on previous "lessons learned" associated with their respective organizations. Taking the time to create a set of lessons from a work project or program is fairly typical in organizational settings. It is a useful practice for documenting goals, decisions, sequences, and evaluations of a project's effectiveness. With such lessons in hand, it is possible to move relatively quickly and smoothly into a new initiative and conceivably reduce or avoid mistakes from the past. Such lessons can become "guides" for new endeavors, paving the way for new assemblages that are lower in complexity and higher in successful outcomes.

A related mechanism associated with "lessons learned" entails developing and testing hypotheses. Assemblage theory has the potential to move beyond exploration, confirmation, and validation to hypothesis testing. Although not posed as hypotheses per se, statements made by some of the authors could be proposed for testing with other samples:

- "a "trial-like" purchase experience [can] help farmers build trust in the product, overcome aversion to risk, develop an investment mindset, and overcome capital barriers" (Hitch—chapter 1)
- "As a result of ... contending agencies in a structure where power was more diffuse than hierarchical, the program shifted over time" (Delcore—chapter 3)
- "power disparity can have [a considerable role] in decelerating or stopping the adoption of technological change by the poor" (Bhattacharyya and Belk—chapter 6)
- "Poverty can change as a whole when both systemic change is made and individuals are empowered" (Newton—chapter 9)

By developing and testing hypotheses, assemblage theory becomes an even more valuable resource for researchers, and for the organizations and communities with whom they work.

Methods for the Future

Let's begin this section by taking stock of what methods were put to work in this collection. Ethnography, consisting of a combination of research techniques, is used by the majority of the authors. For example, the contributors combine participant observation with interviews and/or surveys and/or focus groups and/or diaries. Some of them rely largely on participant observation (Pahl—chapter 10; Ramer—chapter 10), while others used interviews as a primary data collection technique (Rijsberman—chapter 2; Bhattacharyya and Belk—chapter 6), and still others stress the integration of at least two distinct bodies of knowledge (e.g., methodology, discipline): ethnography and design (Hitch—chapter 1), history and design anthropology (Miller—chapter 5), ethnography and history (Onomake—chapter 8; Newton—chapter 9).

The authors also employ a variety of analytic techniques in their chapters. First, content analysis figures prominently throughout the book. Second, statistical analysis is applied to survey data (Delcore—chapter 3). Third, metaphors serve to explain the concept, situation, or reaction at hand. They are applied in three of the chapters:

- Cultural change as a rhizome (Introduction)
- Career adjusters as reflective of folktale attributes (e.g., "magic wands" or university degrees; "blockers and antagonists" or student loan debt) (Rijsberman—chapter 2)
- Indian poor's relationship with technology (e.g., as a toy, albatross, mystery) (Bhattacharyya and Belk—chapter 6).

Fourth, scales of observation are employed in two of the chapters to sort and compare data falling into micro, meso, and macro categories (Desjeux and Ma—chapter 7; Pahl et al.—chapter 10). Fifth, networks figure prominently in two of the chapters (Delcore—chapter 3; Onomake—chapter 8). Finally, contrasting types are used as heuristic devices:

- Current and future, and early and late adopters (Hitch—chapter 1)
- Types of EdTech students: Nondegree holders, new career seekers, career adjusters, career advancers, and hobbyists (Rijsberman—chapter 2)
- First-generation and continuing-generation (Delcore—chapter 3)
- First wave, second wave, and third wave (Miller—chapter 4)
- Ideal and actual (Bhattacharyya and Belk—chapter 6)
- Traditional and modern, and generation of scarcity, generation of economic reform and the single child family, and generation of abundance (Desjeux and Ma—chapter 7)
- Precolonial, colonial, and contemporary (Onomake—chapter 8)
- Insider and outsider (Pahl et al.—chapter 10)
- Inside-out and outside in (Ramer—chapter 10)
- Machine-centered design and human-centered design (Aiken—chapter 10)

How might assemblage theory change from a methodological standpoint? There are potential answers to this question in some of the chapters in this collection. Several chapters combine at least two distinct bodies of knowledge—typically, ethnography/anthropology with design or history. The blending of disciplinary and methodological knowledge and approaches is likely to strengthen assemblage theory and extend it in new directions. For example, Onomake's (chapter 8) discussion of precolonial and colonial brokerage places contemporary brokerage in Nigeria in its historical context. While the two Nigeria-China business associations represent a new form of networking and brokerage, the foundation of their work—networking and brokerage—are centuries old. Thus, the associations symbolize both continuity and change. Similarly, Hitch's (chapter 1) merging of ethnography and design approaches emphasizes a holistic and collaborative effort to bring an irrigation system to Cambodian farmers. The IDEO design process that the team employs has the benefit of on-site anthropologists, always on the lookout for cultural commonalities, differences, inconsistencies, and contradictions. When completed, the project appears to meet the expectations of designers and anthropologists, as well as the various groups of local leaders, salespersons, and farmers. A follow-up evaluative study would confirm this expectation.

Interdisciplinary and transdisciplinary work continue to gain traction within the broader research community. No single method, perspective, discipline, or approach is equipped to address all thorny research questions. Moreover, the era of the "lone anthropologist" is declining. Collaborative, cross-disciplinary and transdisciplinary projects are increasingly the norm. We believe that the assemblage theory of the future would benefit from the contributions of different types of researchers pooling their questions, data collection techniques, analysis methods, and explanatory frameworks together.

Problem Solving for the Future

Ten of the 12 cases in this book represent examples of application or anthropological practice. Indeed, six of the cases are written by those employed by a particular firm (Rijsberman—chapter 2, Watts-Englert et al.—chapter 5, Newton—chapter 9, Pahl—chapter 10, Ramer—chapter 10, and Aiken—chapter 10), while two others are associated with consulting (Hitch—chapter 1 and Desjeux and Ma—chapter 7). Two additional cases are prepared by university-based researchers engaged in applied anthropology (Delcore—chapter 3 and Bhattacharyya and Belk—chapter 6).

The research framework for these ten projects is largely problem oriented, attempting to address a particular organizational or community issue. Their outcomes typically involve the development and implementation of a particular intervention (Hitch—chapter 1, Newton—chapter 9, Pahl—chapter 10, and Ramer chapter 10) or the generation of recommendations or policy (Rijsberman—chapter 2, Delcore—Chapter 3, Watts-Englert et al.—chapter 5, Bhattacharyya and Belk—chapter 6, Desjeux and Ma—chapter 7, and Aiken—chapter 10). As such, these researchers (possibly except Bhattacharyya and Belk) are directly involved as actors in the process of cultural change. The roles they perform are varied and include explorer, listener, facilitator, thought leader, team member, analyst, debater, cheerleader, evaluator, and problem solver, among many others. They exhibit agency in the performance of their many roles.

The authors of these 10 cases are part and parcel of their respective assemblages, often influencing the course of the assemblage. They typically have gathered significant knowledge about the cultural context and of the issues of concern to their clients and other constituents. They work collaboratively as a rule, whether with other researchers, with their project sponsors, with their employee colleagues, and with their study participants. They try to influence outcomes through their work as a way to improve working and living conditions. They find meaning in the work they do, hoping through their work that they will have made a difference in the work and everyday lives of people affected by change.

We believe that assemblage theory of the future should continue this trend of embracing application and practice. The global and local organizations and marketplaces have much to gain from a problem-oriented focus. Cultural change researchers have the knowledge and skills sets necessary to ferret out the issues and work with organizational and community members on potential solutions. They are also accustomed to work relatively quickly yet effectively.

Snapshots Now in Planning for the Future

We will continue to observe shifts in identities and meanings as organizations develop new work practices and processes, and as consumers adopt or reject products and services. A longitudinal approach has the potential of exposing changes, as well as a life course, as an assemblage matures and transitions. Agency influences what those changes and transitions are. When identity and meaning are altered, cultural change occurs.

Planning for the future is not always simple and straightforward. It requires a holistic understanding of assemblages, agency, and trajectories from the past. It also necessitates a careful observation of the current state to lay bare the agentic actors playing a critical role. Finally, it entails consideration of what an ideal future state might be for an organization or community, and a process or set of steps for getting as close to that ideal as possible. Snapshots of assemblages, much like the ones our contributors have produced for their chapters, are helpful in placing the past and present in context, while imagining a distinctive future based on the cultural changes that have transpired.

REFERENCES

Alexander M. Ervin. 2015. *Cultural transformations and globalization: Theory, development, and social change.* Boulder, CO: Paradigm Publishers.

Bruno Latour. 2005. *Reassembling the social: An introduction to actor-network-theory*, Oxford, UK: Oxford University Press.

David Rose. 2014. *Enchanted objects: Design, human desire, and the Internet of things*. New York, NY: Scribner.

Eric J. Arnould and Craig J. Thompson. 2015. "Introduction: Consumer culture theory: Ten tears gone (and beyond)." In *Research in consumer behavior,* Volume 17, edited by Anastasia Thyroff, Jeff B. Murray and Russell W. Belk, 1–21. Bingley, UK: Emerald Group Publishing.

———. 1977b. "Cultural reproduction and social reproduction." In *Power and ideology in education*, edited by Jerome Karabel and A.H. Halsey, 487–511. New York, NY: Oxford University Press.

Gary P. Ferraro and Elizabeth K. Briody. 2017. *The cultural dimension of global business*. London, UK: Taylor & Francis.

Hirokazu Miyazaki. 2004. *The method of hope: Anthropology, philosophy, and Fijian knowledge*. Stanford, CA: Stanford University Press.

John Allen. 2011. "Powerful assemblages?" *Area* 3(2):154–157, June.

Julian E. Orr. 1996. *Talking about machines: An ethnography of a modern job*. Ithaca, NY: Cornell University Press.

Lucy Suchman 2011. "Work practice and technology: A retrospective." In *Making work visible: Ethnographically grounded case studies of work practice*, edited by Margaret H. Szymanski and Jack Whalen, 21–33. New York, NY: Cambridge University Press.

Melissa Cefkin. 2014. "Work practice studies as anthropology." In *Handbook of anthropology in business,* edited by Rita Denny and Patricia Sunderland, 284–298. Walnut Creek, CA: Left Coast Press.

Michel Foucault. 1978. *Discipline and punish: The birth of the prison*. Translated by Alan Sheridan. New York, NY: Vintage Books.

Pierre Bourdieu. 1977a. *Outline of a theory of practice*. Cambridge, UK: Cambridge University Press.

Stephen J. Collier and Aihwa Ong. 2005. "Global assemblages, anthropological problems." In *Global assemblages: Technology, politics, and ethics as anthropological problems,* edited by Aihwa Ong and Stephen J. Collier, 3–21. Malden, MA: Blackwell Publishing.

Vincent Crapanzano. 2003. "Reflections on hope as a category of social and psychological analysis," *Cultural Anthropology* 18(1): 3–32.

Index

Abdelwahed, Omar, 105
Accenture, 95
accommodations, 13, 21, 191, 206, 278
acculturation, 2, 3, 10, 11
actor-network theory (ANT), 3, 100–1
actuals (Schechner), 110
advertising, 12–13
Africa, 191–95.
   See also Nigeria
agency:
   in assemblage theory, 3, 5–8, 138,
      165, 279;
   and cultural change, 5–8, 21,
      276–82;
   and design, 19;
   of farmers, 32;
   limits of, 29;
   at the micro-level, 11;
   in the Nigerian brokerage
      assemblage, 187, 206;
   within nonprofits, 223;
   of objects, 113;
   and possible futures, 44;
   of students, 49–50, 52, 67, 83;
   and technology adoption and
      use, 144
agency complementarity, 281–82
agentive practice, 70
"Alice" (social robot), 105–6, 277

Allen, John, 7, 279
ambient devices, 95, 107
American Institute of Architecture, 247
Anastassakis, Zoy, 108–9
ANT (actor-network theory), 3, 100–1
anthropological practice, 109, 111,
   235–36, 285
anthropological research, 266
anthropological studies, 194
anthropology, 2–3, 237;
   applied, 21, 235, 257;
   characteristics of, 271–72.
   See also design anthropology
Apple iPhone, 125.
   See also smart devices; smartphones
app economy, 119
apps, 126–27
architecture, 246–47
Arnould, Eric J., 7, 70
artificial intelligence (AI), 49, 105
assemblages:
   agency in, 277, 279;
   consumption, 145;
   continuity phase, 280;
   cultural change in, 17;
   disappearance phase, 281;
   formation of, 70;
   innovation and, 165;
   instability of, 230–31;

About the Contributors

Jo Aiken (Presidential Management Fellow, NASA Johnson Space Center; PhD Candidate in Anthropology, University College London) is focusing her research on material culture and organizational anthropology. She received her MA in Applied Anthropology from the University of North Texas in 2014. She works full time in Organizational Development at the NASA Johnson Space Center while conducting research for her thesis on human-robotic interaction and astronaut culture with NASA's Human Research Program.

Russell W. Belk (PhD, University of Minnesota) is York University Distinguished research professor and Kraft Foods Canada Chair in Marketing, Schulich School of Business, York University. He is past president of the International Association of Marketing and Development, and is a fellow, past president, and Film Festival cofounder in the Association for Consumer Research. He also co-initiated the Consumer Behavior Odyssey and the Consumer Culture Theory Conference. He has received the Paul D. Converse Award, two Fulbright Fellowships, and the Sheth Foundation/*Journal of Consumer Research* Award for Long-Term Contribution to Consumer Research and has approximately 600 publications. He recently published *Consumer Culture Theory: Research in Consumer Behavior* (Emerald 2017), *Qualitative Consumer and Marketing Research* (Sage 2013), *The Routledge Companion to Identity and Consumption* (Routledge 2013), and *The Routledge Companion to the Digital Consumer* (Routledge 2013). In 2014, a ten-volume set of his work was published by Sage entitled *Russell Belk, Sage Legends in Consumer Behavior*. He is currently coediting *Romantic Gift Giving* (Routledge) and *Handbook on the Sharing Economy* (Edward Elgar). His research tends to be qualitative, visual, and cultural. It involves the extended self, meanings of possessions, collecting, gift giving, sharing, digital consumption, and materialism.

Arundhati Bhattacharyya is an assistant professor at the Indian Institute of Management-Udaipur, India. Her research interests include consumer trust and loyalty under ambiguous/liminal conditions, advertising and promotions, branding, consumer culture, subsistence markets, critical theory, and qualitative research methods. She has published on topics in the areas of consumers' sense making of technological assemblages, consumption of cyborgs, and consumers' socialization toward radical new technologies. She holds a PhD in Marketing from Schulich School of Business, York University, Canada.

Elizabeth K. Briody founded Cultural Keys LLC in 2009 (culturalkeys.us), a consultancy that helps organizations transform their culture, reach their potential, and attract and retain new customers. She has had a long-standing interest in organizational culture and change, both in the United States and globally. Her projects have spanned many industries including automotive, health care, research institutions, aerospace, and consumer products, among others. Recent books include *The Cultural Dimension of Global Business* (2017) and the award-winning *Transforming Culture* (2014). Briody holds an MA and a PhD in Anthropology from The University of Texas at Austin.

Henry D. Delcore is a professor of Anthropology at California State University, Fresno. His research explores the nature of work and its relationship to political economy, modernity, technology, and the natural and built environments. Dr. Delcore has a MA and PhD in Anthropology from the University of Wisconsin-Madison and a BS in Foreign Service, Asian Studies, from Georgetown University.

Dominique Desjeux is an anthropologist, professor emeritus at the Sorbonne, Université Paris Descartes, Sorbonne Paris Cité. He worked with Michel Crozier on the industrial politics of France for two years from 1969 to 1971. Then he worked for eight years in sub-Saharan Africa on kinship, witchcraft, and land tenure and then for seven years in a French College of Agriculture in Angers. He has been carrying out qualitative field studies with consumers since 1987. For 40 years, he has worked at the interface of academia and business about innovation, consumption, and the decision-making process in companies and families. Recently he has managed several studies on body care and makeup up in France, Brazil, China, and the United States mainly for L'Oréal, Danone, Pernod Ricard, and Chanel. At the Sorbonne, he directed the Professional Doctoral Program in social sciences from 2007 to 2014.

Emilie Hitch works with Human-Centered Design labs, agencies, and strategy groups dedicated to cultural and social change. She has led ethnographic, innovation, and strategic planning projects for many industry clients such as Nike, Bauer, and Land O'Lakes, as well as NGOs such as The University of Minnesota, The Quetico Superior Foundation, and growers' associations across the world. From designing a new way to engage with the public for the Minnesota Department of Transportation to cocreating a new model of philanthropy with Eat for Equity, her work is always rooted in anthropology, strategy, and the Common Good. A graduate of Yale and the London School of Economics with degrees in anthropology, Emilie also holds a Master's degree in governance and policy from the Humphrey School of Public Affairs, University of Minnesota.

Ma Jingjing is a PhD candidate in Anthropology and Sociology at Paris Descartes, Sorbonne Paris Cité University, under the direction of Professor Dominique Desjeux. She has been conducting ethnographic research for four years on water management in China and daily life in the home and the surrounding urban area.

Maryann McCabe is the founder of Cultural Connections LLC, a consumer research consultancy that works with organizations on branding and positioning strategies. She is a "research associate," University of Rochester, Department of Anthropology, where she has been teaching courses on market research, entrepreneurship, and sustainability. Her research interests are creativity, agency, materiality, advertising, and gender. Her publications include *Collaborative Ethnography in Business Environments* and numerous articles on consumer behavior in peer-reviewed journals. She holds an MA and a PhD in Anthropology from New York University.

Christine Miller (Associate Clinical Professor of Innovation, Stuart School of Business, Illinois Institute of Technology) completed an interdisciplinary PhD in Anthropology and Management at Wayne State University where she conducted an ethnographic study of process formalization and the relationship between innovation and formalization at a Tier One automotive supplier. Her research interests include sociotechnical systems (STS) and the ways in which sociality and culture influence the design of new products, processes, and technologies. She studies the emergence of co-located and technology-enabled collaborative innovation networks (COINs). Chris participates in project-oriented learning programs and studies technology-mediated communication, knowledge flows within pluridisciplinary groups and teams. As a Co-PI on an NSF study of the ethical culture of STEM research groups, she is exploring how to increase the efficacy of ethics education in STEM by creating opportunities for lab members to cocreate context-specific ethical guidelines for their labs and research groups.

Kevin M. Newton works as the experience researcher at ServiceMaster. He also teaches psychology and anthropology courses as the University of Memphis. He holds a Master of Arts in Applied Anthropology and a Master of Science in Experimental Psychology. During his day job, he researches consumer behavior in relation to technological products, including how products and services fit into the daily lives of those who use them. His academic research interests center on the effects of neoliberalism on community building, nonprofit organizations, and private businesses.

Shane Pahl (Environmental, Health, and Safety Manager) is interested in organizational culture and change management. He received an MS in Applied Anthropology from the University of North Texas in 2014. His thesis research focused on how competing values affect decision-making within organizations. His current research continues to explore decision-making within organizations as they pertain to "safety culture" and safety compliance.

U. Ejiro O. Onomake is a consultant and lecturer. Having worked in both the private and public sectors, her areas of expertise and interests include international business, international development, corporate social responsibility, transnationalism, intersectionality, and pop culture (television dramas and social media). Onomake holds a PhD in Social-Cultural Anthropology from the University of Sussex as well as an MBA in International Business and an MA in International Policy Studies, both from the Monterey Institute of International Studies. She is multilingual (English, Japanese, Mandarin Chinese) and has lived in Asia, Africa, Europe, and North America.

Angela Ramer is a design anthropologist at HKS, a global architecture firm based in Dallas, Texas. She holds a MS from the University of North Texas' Applied Anthropology program and a BA in anthropology from Elon University. Her studies and interests in business, technology and design are well positioned within the field of architecture. Her user-centered, ethnographic perspective highlights for design team and clients alike the need to understand the breadth of human experience that occurs within and around built environments. Angela's work transcends industry sectors to include current work in corporate/office design, workplace strategy, educational environments, campus planning, sports and entertainment and urban planning. In addition to external-facing client work, she also collaborates with internal clients on firm-wide projects related to Information Technology, Human Resources, and Research and Professional Development.

Marijke Rijsberman is Product Research Manager at Coursera. She has a long-standing research interest in cultural, conceptual, behavioral, and linguistic change and in the dissemination of behaviors, values, and linguistic imagery. She holds a PhD in Comparative Literature from Yale University.

Margaret H. Szymanski is a member of the re*THINK Enterprise Group at IBM Almaden Research Lab in San Jose, California. Peggy's work practice and conversation analytic research includes topics in service encounters, learning activity, social interactions amidst technology, and voice and text-based analytics. In 2011, her coedited volume *Making Work Visible: Ethnographically grounded case studies of work practice* represents the corporate ethnographic research legacy pioneered at Xerox Palo Alto Research Center. Peggy earned her PhD from the University of California, Santa Barbara with an interdisciplinary emphasis on Language, Interaction, and Social Organization.

Patricia Wall is a member of the Adjunct staff in the Saunders College of Business at the Rochester Institute of Technology where she coaches student teams in the Applied Entrepreneurship program. Prior to this, Patricia was the manager of the Work Practice & Technology area in the Xerox Research Center Webster where she conducted sociotechnical studies of customer work in order to inform the design of new technologies, practices, and services. Patricia earned her Master's degree in Psychology and Human Factors from North Carolina State University. She has design and technical patents and several publications focused on the application of ethnographic methods to inform technology and service design.

Jennifer Watts-Englert is a member of the User Experience Research and Analytics team at Paychex in Webster, NY, and is an adjunct professor at the Rochester Institute of Technology. She has led user experience research and interface design projects for over 20 years, focusing on small business work processes, healthcare, privacy, customer care, data analytics, production printing, consumer imaging, and the future of work. She is the coauthor of 18 patents, and is author or coauthor of over 40 book chapters and papers. She has worked as a visiting scholar and lecturer at The Ohio State University, and was a user interface designer and user experience researcher at Microsoft, Apple, NASA, Kodak, Xerox, PARC, and Conduent Labs. Jennifer earned her PhD in Cognitive Engineering from The Ohio State University.

Lightning Source UK Ltd.
Milton Keynes UK
UKOW06n1610101117
312536UK00002B/93/P

9 781498 544511